Reading Experimental Writing

for Yves

Reading Experimental Writing

Edited by
Georgina Colby

EDINBURGH
University Press

Edinburgh University Press is one of the leading university presses in the UK. We publish academic books and journals in our selected subject areas across the humanities and social sciences, combining cutting-edge scholarship with high editorial and production values to produce academic works of lasting importance. For more information visit our website: edinburghuniversitypress.com

© editorial matter and organisation Georgina Colby, 2020, 2021
© the chapters their several authors, 2020, 2021

Edinburgh University Press Ltd
The Tun – Holyrood Road
12(2f) Jackson's Entry
Edinburgh EH8 8PJ

First published in hardback by Edinburgh University Press 2020

Typeset in 11/13 Adobe Sabon by
IDSUK (DataConnection) Ltd

A CIP record for this book is available from the British Library

ISBN 978 1 4744 4038 7 (hardback)
ISBN 978 1 4744 4039 4 (paperback)
ISBN 978 1 4744 4040 0 (webready PDF)
ISBN 978 1 4744 4041 7 (epub)

The right of Georgina Colby to be identified as the Editor of this work has been asserted in accordance with the Copyright, Designs and Patents Act 1988, and the Copyright and Related Rights Regulations 2003 (SI No. 2498).

Contents

List of Illustrations	vii
Acknowledgements	ix
Preface	x
Charles Bernstein	
Introduction: Reading Experimental Writing	1
Georgina Colby	
1. 'Fog is My Land': A Citizenship of Mutual Estrangement in the Painted Books of Etel Adnan	15
Jennifer Scappettone	
2. Reading Happily with John Cage, Lyn Hejinian and Others	51
Alex Houen	
3. Experiment, Inscription and the Archive: Kathy Acker's Manuscript Practice	74
Georgina Colby	
4. Rereading Race and Commodity Form in Erica Hunt's *Piece Logic*	99
Chris Chen	
5. Contemporary Experimental Translations and Translingual Poetics	123
Sophie Seita	
6. On Joan Retallack's *Memnoir*: Investigating 'the Experience of Experiencing'	145
erica kaufman	
7. A Queer Response to Caroline Bergvall's Hyphenated Practice: Towards an Interdependent Model of Reading	163
Susan Rudy	

8. Reading Language Art in Digital Media: Reconfigurations of Experimental Practices 185
John Cayley

9. Charles Bernstein's Walter Benjamin, Among Other Things 205
Peter Jaeger

Notes on Contributors 227
Bibliography 231
Index 251

List of Illustrations

1.1 Etel Adnan, *Rihla ila Jabal Tamalpais (Journey to Mount Tamalpais)*, 2008. Watercolour and Indian ink on Japanese book, 30 x 10.5cm x 54 pages : 30 x 567cm. Private Collection. Copyright Etel Adnan. Courtesy of Galerie Claude Lemand, Paris. Donation Claude and France Lemand, Musée, Institut du monde arabe, Paris.   16
1.2 Etel Adnan, *Al-Sayyab, Mother and Lost Daughter*, 1970. Ink and watercolour on a Japanese notebook. Signed, dated and titled by the artist. Closed, 33 x 25.2cm x 24 pages. Open, 33 x 612cm. Private Collection. Copyright Etel Adnan. Courtesy of Galerie Claude Lemand, Paris. Donation Claude and France Lemand, Musée, Institut du monde arabe, Paris.   28
1.3 Mohammed Melehi, covers of the quarterly review *Souffles* 4 (1966), 5, 6, (1967), 10–11, 12 (1968), 13–14 (1969).   30
1.4 Etel Adnan, opening of Poem I of *The Arab Apocalypse* (Sausalito, CA: Post-Apollo Press, 2006), p. 7.   35
1.5 Etel Adnan, from Poem XII of *The Arab Apocalypse* (Sausalito, CA: Post-Apollo Press, 2006), p. 30.   37
1.6 Etel Adnan, from Poem XXIV of *The Arab Apocalypse* (Sausalito, CA: Post-Apollo Press, 2006), p. 43.   39
3.1 Kathy Acker, page from the original artwork for *Blood and Guts in High School*. Box 29, Folder 1. Kathy Acker Papers, David M. Rubenstein Rare Book & Manuscript Library, Duke University.   86
3.2 Kathy Acker, page from 'The World', original artwork for *Blood and Guts in High School*. Box 29, Folder 1. Kathy Acker Papers, David M. Rubenstein Rare Book & Manuscript Library, Duke University.   88
3.3 Kathy Acker, page from 'The World', original artwork for *Blood and Guts in High School*. Box 29, Folder 1. Kathy Acker Papers, David M. Rubenstein Rare Book & Manuscript Library, Duke University.   90

3.4	Kathy Acker, page from 'The World', original artwork for *Blood and Guts in High School*. Box 29, Folder 1. Kathy Acker Papers, David M. Rubenstein Rare Book & Manuscript Library, Duke University.	91
3.5	Kathy Acker, page from 'The World', original artwork for *Blood and Guts in High School*. Box 29, Folder 1. Kathy Acker Papers, David M. Rubenstein Rare Book & Manuscript Library, Duke University.	93
3.6	Kathy Acker, page from 'The Journey', original artwork for *Blood and Guts in High School*. Box 29, Folder 1. Kathy Acker Papers, David M. Rubenstein Rare Book & Manuscript Library, Duke University.	94
5.1	Uljana Wolf, 'Annalogue on Oranges', in *Subsisters: Selected Poems*, trans. by Sophie Seita. Belladonna, 2017.	128
5.2	Uljana Wolf, 'Tatting', in *Subsisters: Selected Poems*, trans. by Sophie Seita, Belladonna, 2017.	129
5.3	Uljana Wolf, 'Tatting', in *Subsisters: Selected Poems*, trans. by Sophie Seita, Belladonna, 2017.	130
7.1	Caroline Bergvall, *Ragadawn* at the Estuary Festival, Southend, September 2016. Photo credit: Benedict Johnson, 2016.	177
7.2	View of Caroline Bergvall, 'Alpabet' [sic] and 'For Walls' at the Arnolfini Gallery 3, Bristol. Photo by Jamie Woodley.	179
9.1	*Veil* (detail). Bernstein 1987: n.p.	217

Acknowledgements

This book is indebted to the contributors, Charles Bernstein, John Cayley, Chris Chen, Alex Houen, Peter Jaeger, erica kaufman, Susan Rudy, Jennifer Scappettone and Sophi Seita, who have generously given their time and commitment to produce the chapters that comprise this collection. It has been an honour to work with scholars whose critical approaches open the field and offer new forms of criticism that complement the avant-garde works they are addressing. I would like to thank Caroline Bergvall, not simply for the cover image from the remarkable work *Drift* that points to new literary forms in the contemporary period, but for posing to me critical questions regarding the nature of the term 'experimental'. 'Experimental' sits uncomfortably and intentionally paradoxically with the word 'reading'. The unease yielded by the title is an affectual mark of a tension this book seeks to explore. The two readers' reports for this collection were indispensable. Both readers pointed to the significance of the collection in terms of its socio-political reach, and encouraged the approach to editing that highlighted the relation between the contemporary condition and new ways of reading. Michelle Houston at Edinburgh University Press has been especially patient and generous, offering exceptional editorial guidance. As always I'd like to thank Robert Hampson for his friendship and support. I am grateful to my partner, whose support has been inexhaustible – without it, this book would not have been finished in a timely fashion. Over the course of editing the work, two people became three. This book is dedicated to our child.

Preface
Charles Bernstein

Firewood/Foreword

Give me a place to sit and I can *mysthink* the world.

That is to say, every attempt to instrumentalize poetry diminishes its power. In other words, two steps behind, three steps over.

Or to translate: depth is just another kind of surface and surface is either the stutter of inconsequence or a concretization of the sublime.

Let's put it this way: don't mind the store, mine words.

Or then again – if you bought it, you have to live with it, and life ain't worth the paper it's printed on if you lose heart.

A reign of dullness is not the fate of poetry but a bad weather condition.

Wind alert: Efforts to avert the conventional are met with every possible defamation and denunciation.

Ice storm: Poetry of ethical, aesthetic, and moral challenge is dismissed as morally deranged, aesthetically inadequate and politically wrong-headed.

The history of poetry is pockmarked by innovation and invention, by the struggle for the new *not as novelty but as necessity*. And this aesthetic struggle has often, though not always, been led by those previously denied a place in literary history. Over the past two centuries, this *pataquerical* imperative has become Western poetry's activist center. The macadamized verse of conventional poetry (MVCP) proliferates like lawn ornaments in a museum of suburban life. In such works, coherence and expression metamorphose into a Coke and Pepsi *mélange*, concocted for sipping on a smoky, hot day. MVCP abhors aesthetic pleasure and semantic license, supposing it can save meaning by suffocating it.

William Carlos Williams, *Paterson*:

> Without invention nothing is well spaced,
> unless the mind change, unless

> the stars are new measured, according
> to their relative positions, the
> line will not change, the necessity
> will not matriculate: unless there is
> a new mind there cannot be a new
> line, the old will go on
> repeating itself with recurring
> deadliness: without invention
> nothing lies under the witch-hazel
> bush, the alder does not grow from among
> the hummocks margining the all
> but spent channel of the old swale,
> the small foot-prints
> of the mice under the overhanging
> tufts of the bunch-grass will not
> appear: without invention the line
> will never again take on its ancient
> divisions when the word, a supple word,
> lived in it, crumbled now to chalk.[1]

'unless there is/a new mind there cannot be a new/line' is the motto of an Emersonian poetics, echoing a Romanticism that resists lyric containment, even if it elides the material and social barriers to such transformation. Even so, this remains a motto for a poetics of democratic social space, whether we call it avant-garde, experimental, exploratory, innovative – or, and here's the rub, *rootless cosmopolitism.*

Ezra Pound's attack on Jews as rootless cosmopolitans echoes in today's culture debates. The ahistorical/revanchist quest for a deep or authentic identity as the sole propriety of a single group, which has fueled the rise of the global right, is toxic for the kind of poetry I want.

In contrast, identity remains a volatile issue for the poetics of invention: the identity of the poet as well as the poem, the identity of language as well as the social world, the identity of politics as well as emotion. The kind of poetry I want reveals in every line that meaning is as plural as human consciousness. In this light, avant-garde aggrievement is the malaise of a poetry that is under siege from those who reject its calling as epistemological enquiry, as secular, as resisting closure, as anti-authoritarian. Aggrievement negates the sublimity of the formalist imaginary, turning what can be an exhilarating agonism into self-destructive resentment.

---

[1] William Carlos Williams, *Paterson: Revised Edition*, ed. Christopher MacGowan (New York: New Directions, 1992), p. 50. Thanks to Richard Cureton for citing this passage.

In large measure, the poetry canon is a history of heterodoxy. That is why it's worth noting that the 2018 sixth edition of the *Norton Anthology of English Poetry* has turned against the values of the tradition it proposes to profess. While this always problematic flagship anthology includes a fair number of the poets who comprise a radical tradition of invention in English-language poetry over hundreds of years, among the several dozen living poets, there is a total shut-out of US and UK poets recognized as, or championing, the necessity of aesthetic invention in poetry (as reflected by inclusions in the major British, US, international, African American, Asian American and women's anthologies and annuals recognizing such work, not to mention the poets discussed in this collection). People talk about the crisis of the humanities: this is no small part of it. The publisher and editors necrotize their own authority by turning away from poetry as a living art. To exclude mavericks and pioneers also trivializes the work of many worthy poets who are included and deserve to have more robust company.

The lesson is not new: official verse culture is pernicious not so much for formally radical poetries, which have developed alternate means of production and reproduction, but for the history of poetry and the centrality of poetry within contemporary culture. The Norton peddles its wares as a valuable introduction while proclaiming poetry's death.

But *it's alive*! This collection continues the necessary work of both celebration and reflection on poetry as a living art.

Provincetown, Massachusetts
16 August 2018

Introduction: Reading Experimental Writing
Georgina Colby

This book is about reading experimental writing. Specifically, it explores the way in which experimental writing changes reading practices in the contemporary period. The question of how to read is the issue that is in dispute in many works of contemporary experimental writing. In bringing together expert scholars whose works employ theoretical approaches from literary and linguistic, sociological, political, psychoanalytic and economic fields, the book recognises the heterogeneous forms of reading that experimental writing precipitates. Experimental writing today is bound to a politics of reading. The contributors gathered here examine the experimental works' resistance to interpretation, the issue of 'reading' in contemporary culture, and timely questions surrounding the capacity of the works under scrutiny to generate new forms of meaning and voicing. My aim in editing this volume is to harness and present a prevalent view among critics of contemporary avant-garde literature: that it is precisely through the changed nature of reading that experimental writing can intervene in current socio-political discourses.

The twenty-first century has seen a proliferation of studies that take up literary experiment.[1] Before attending to the current circumstances of the field of experimental writing, the question of what constitutes 'experimental' in the context of this book needs addressing. Semantic, formal and syntactic difficulties abound in the works taken up in this volume. So, too, do thematic perplexities that resonate with the difficult times in which we live. The term 'difficult' has been taken up in a number of recent studies, notably Charles Bernstein's *Attack of the Difficult Poems: Essays and Interventions* (2011); Thomas Fink and Judith Halden-Sullivan's *Reading the Difficulties* (2014);

and, most recently, Charles Altieri and Nicholas D. Nace's collection of writings and essays, *The Fate of Difficulty in the Poetry of Our Time* (2018). For Fink and Halden-Sullivan: 'What is perhaps most difficult about difficult innovative poetry is its relation to language – its commitment to experiences with languages that valorise the unexpected, not the accessible.'[2] Altieri and Nace's study takes up what the authors call 'comparative difficulty studies'[3] as an approach to contemporary poetry. As these titles suggest, 'difficult' is a term often chosen in place of 'experimental'. It avoids the possible complexities of 'experimental' and the implicit gesturing to a non-experimental mainstream writing from which 'experimental' is often understood as diverging, and by which it is marginalised. In the introduction to their volume, Altieri and Nace observe a shift they encountered in the process of editing their collection of essays. At first they conceived of 'difficulty' in a formal sense, as 'a matter of how poets organized languages of poetry', expecting 'to engage with poems that ennoble modes of complexity, density, indeterminacy, opacity, and abstraction'; an expectation they acknowledge sharing with 'self-consciously "innovative" poetry'.[4] Such an assumption proved to be problematic, principally due to the editors' presumptions that authorship in poetry is 'a kind of mastery, bringing the intensity of personal engagements with situations into a kind of order that would provide structure for passion and intensity for the work of mind'.[5]

Many of the essays submitted to the editors highlighted the limits of this concept of mastery and challenged some of the assumptions that it concealed. This revelation that Altieri and Nace confronted during the editorial process is indicative of a widespread shift that has taken place in the field of contemporary avant-garde studies, although it has been part of avant-garde practice since at least the 1970s. The editors observe that the authors of the twenty-six essays in their collection 'emphasize a level of authorship that does not offer confessional sincerity as a badge of authenticity but instead makes visible a sense of struggle that precludes any stable identity position'.[6] In place of this outmoded idea of mastery, Altieri and Nace detected that 'these writers seek from the audience an intimacy with their own confusions and tensions about the position of a writer'. Significantly, the authors discern a desire on the part of contemporary poets to 'share a condition' over an inclination to 'instruct and delight'; indeed, they note, it is often the case that 'this sharing is not based on an inner life so much as on painful encounters with structures that organise social reality'.[7] This refusal of mastery impacts on the relation of the reader or audience to the author and the text:

we had to recognize that many of our poets do not either assume or construct an audience but assume a position of need that invites the audience to participate creatively in the space marked out by the poem. The divided author needs to have not only the presence of a sympathetic audience but also hope that the writing can help form communities capable of modifying the social conditions that generate the desire in the first place.[8]

Informed by such critical insights that point to the capacity of difficult writing to harbour resistance to current social conditions through the creation of sympathetic communities, *Reading Experimental Writing* starts out from a position that recognises the avant-garde writer's resistance to the mastery of authorship and the relation of this resilience to yielding works that are capable of socio-political intervention.

Reading Experimental Writing maintains the term 'experimental' in part precisely because of its disruptive relation to conventional forms of reading, and in part due to its proximity to newness. The writers discussed in this study are consciously experimental and avant-garde. In the 1983 study of Gertrude Stein, *A Different Language: Gertrude Stein's Experimental Writing*, Marianne DeKoven defines literary experiment as 'that writing that violates grammatical convention, thereby preventing normal reading'.[9] This impediment to 'normal' reading can be extended to specifically incorporate the demand experimental writing makes for new forms of reading practices. 'Experimental writing' as it is conceived in this volume refers to new forms of writing that require new forms of reading. These new forms of reading, in turn, generate new modes of perception and reception of socio-political conditions. Elizabeth Robinson discusses the practice of rereading that difficult texts demand. 'Returning to a text,' she states, 'rereading it, demonstrates to the reader how perception and apprehension (indeed content itself) are themselves variable.'[10] The act of rereading, Robinson argues, increases attention: 'As a reader reconsiders a poem multiple times, but each time with varying insights and valuations, her investment in the process is likely to increase.' However, 'This does not ensure that meaning becomes more stable.' Instead, as Robinson contends, 'what emerges is that there is no final reading for, or of, any given text'.[11] In the difficult text this heightening of the act of attention and the incremental relation of this attention to interest and value is related to the text's perceived indeterminacy. The indeterminacy of reading precipitated by literary experiment has an important socio-political resonance. This account of the reading process of experimental writing offers a model of a new association between text and reader in which disruption is productive of a non-authoritative relationality. As Robinson puts it: 'Reading as a complex adaptive system redistributes the authority of meaning-making back and forth between reader and text so as to create a dynamic and productive disequilibrium.'[12] This 'productive disequilibrium', and the capacity of the experimental text to demand reading practices that give rise to 'non-authoritative relationality', is central to the politics of reading experimental writing.

Importantly, then, 'experimental' in this volume also gestures to the outwardness that Joan Retallack conceives of in 2007 when she states: 'experiment is a reaching out to experience things that cannot be grasped merely by examining the state of our own minds'.[13] In this sense 'experimental' as apprehended in this volume shares the 'avant-garde' commitment that in Gerald Prince's 1985 conception of the term involves 'a compulsion to seek a radically different future, the desire to modify the very foundation of personal and cultural economy, the belief in the social significance of the literary act'.[14] For Retallack, making specific reference to climate change and ecology, it is the contemporary social and political order that is a catalyst for formal experimentation. 'Working on related poetic projects in an atmosphere of socio-political concerns, thinking of poetics in the context of collectivities', she states, 'has stimulated formal experimentation that in some way recapitulates the scientific turn to empiricism on the threshold of humanist modernism.' Retallack argues: 'In poetics something analogous has been happening in the turn toward alterity via a new foregrounding of the material realities of languages as forms of life.'[15] The relation between formal experimentation and the social and political concerns in the works of the writers gathered in this book emerges as evidence of a continuation of the legacies of humanist modernism in late twentieth and early twenty-first century experimental writing.

As argued above, the political import of experimental writing is intimately bound to the new forms of reading it produces. However, an engagement with capital and its operations is also relevant here. Altieri and Nace express their surprise at the extent to which the poets studied in their volume are preoccupied with 'the visible consequences of the world produced by late capitalism'.[16] Christopher Nealon's *The Matter of Capital: Poetry and Crisis in the American Century* (2011) specifically attends to capitalism's bearings on poetry. Focusing on twentieth-century American poetry through the work of Ezra Pound, W. H. Auden, John Ashbery, Jack Spicer and Lyn Hejinian, Nealon argues that 'poets respond to the social changes wrought by capitalism by making recourse to different ideas of poetry as textual and rhetorical "matter" – a source of varying subject matter, of topics, even of arguments'.[17] The poets Nealon focuses on share 'a link [. . .] between poetry as a textual art and the resources of that textuality for preserving poetry in the face of disaster'.[18] Recent scholarship on textual culture, such as Martin Irvine's *The Making of Textual Culture* (2006), Nealon claims, 'makes clear the link between textual culture and civilizational crisis'.[19] In this context, Nealon's principle objective concerns new reading practices. 'My wish for all of us', he writes, 'is to work out a reading practice for poetry of the last century adequate to greet the new one, because the best poetry the new century has produced, so far, clearly demands it.'[20] More recently, Ben Hickman has taken up the issue of poetry and crisis specifically in relation to the US avant-garde. Hickman's study is alert to the way in which 'moments of crisis can sharpen our sense of the historical force of poetry, and how American poems have sought to intervene in specific political upheavals'. Hickman argues that the concept of 'crisis', as it is manifested in its urgent sense in and by contemporary conditions, has the ability to 'illuminate poetry's capacity for simultaneous response and intervention in a way occluded by both the speculative preoccupation with poetry's relation to the commodity and historicism's immoveable "context"'.[21] Hickman's timely analysis of the works of Louis Zukofsky, Muriel Rukeyser, Charles Olson, Amiri Baraka and the Language Poets is emblematic of the groundswell in recent scholarship to discern the political significance of avant-garde writing in the twentieth and twenty-first centuries.

The present volume can be situated in the current critical terrain as a work that builds on studies such as Altieri and Nace's, Nealon's and Hickman's in its recognition of the socio-political value of experimental writing and the alliance between textual art and resistance. Through the volume's focus on 'reading', its contributors spotlight the varied dimensions of reading practices yielded by new forms of writing. Each of the chapters in this volume engages specifically with the question of form. The works addressed in this book by writers such as John Cage, Kathy Acker, Charles Bernstein, Erica Hunt, Therese Hak Kyung Cha, Rosmarie Waldrop, M. NourbeSe Philip, Caroline Bergvall, Erín Moure, Uljana Wolf, Samantha Gorman, Danny Cannizzaro and Dave Jhave Johnston, among others, are all new forms of writing. In its methodologies the present volume differs from Altieri and Nace's collection. Rather than providing very close readings of a single poem, the contributors in this collection were invited to respond to the wider question: 'What does it mean to "read" experimental writing in the contemporary climate?' Emphasis was also placed on the desire to yield a heterogeneous collection. In response to the works under discussion, the contributors explore experimental forms of reading; read works through ideas of modularity, intertextuality, disjunction and direct appropriation; examine the radical formal means of experimental poetry used to address issues of racism, misogyny, xenophobia and authoritarianism; analyse sonic innovations alongside experimental writing; scrutinise the power of experimental writing to highlight the importance of language; investigate manuscript practice and new forms of meaning; consider experimental translations and multilingual poetics; bring to light interdependent models of reading; theorise the idea of 'xenoglossic' texts; and interrogate reconfigurations of experimental practices in digital media. Through these key chapters, the book offers the reader a variety of new ways of reading experimental writing.

The chapters engage directly with global political events since the 1950s as well as recent socio-political changes such as Brexit; the inauguration of Trump; and issues surrounding migration, border closures, globalisation and racial justice resulting from such developments. Jennifer Scappettone examines Etel Adnan's xenoglossic poetics in *L'apocalypse arabe* (1989) (*The Arab Apocalypse*) through the prism of the dream of Arab unity that emerged during the Algerian war of independence. erica kaufman's concern in her study of Joan Retallack's *Memnoir* (2004) is to expose the way in which experimental writing reminds readers of the importance of language in a climate of 'post-truth' in the USA, a political landscape in which emotional appeal overrules facts. Sophie Seita explores the relation between the 'transnational turn' in literary studies in the twenty-first century and contemporary multilingual poetry, with a particular focus on Uljana Wolf's politically engaged poetry. In Wolf's writing, Seita reveals how experimental tactics such as neologisms, multilingualism and unusual syntaxes and prefixes work to critique borders and fixed ideas of nationality. The capacity of multilingual poetries and experimental translations for new political critiques is an issue pertinent to Scappettone's chapter on 'xenoglossic texts', and also to Rudy's chapter that analyses Bergvall's multi-media, multilingual and interdisciplinary works *Drift* (2014) and *Ragadawn* (2016). Meanwhile John Cayley explores the ways in which the digitalisation of cultural practices in the twenty-first century poses a challenge to conventional forms of reading. Cayley's chapter specifically offers an understanding of new forms of reading that are emerging in digital cultures today.

As a consequence, the volume offers a diverse range of approaches as well as both historicist and comparative critical methods of approaching experimental writing. Gaps, however, are inevitable in collections, and the limitations of the present volume need to be addressed here. A number of the writers discussed in the volume, such as Kathy Acker, have connections to, or are a part of, the New Narrative movement. The New Narrative writers are a group established in the 1970s in San Francisco by Bruce Boone and Robert Glück. They understood the central role avant-garde writing played in the Gay Liberation movement and sought to continue this. Recently New Narrative has experienced a revival with the anthology edited by US experimental writers Dodie Bellamy and Kevin Killian, *Writers Who Love Too Much: New Narrative Writing 1977–1997* (Nightboat Books, 2017). New Narrative has also flourished in new iterations in the UK, most notably in the work of Isabel Waidner, who collects writing from contemporary writers such as Jay Bernard, Steven J Fowler, Nisha Ramayya, Roz Kaveney and many others in the volume *Liberating the Canon: An Anthology of Innovative Literature* (Dostoyevsky Wannabe, 2018). Waidner's anthology is concerned to bring together intersectional identity and literary innovation, featuring predominantly working-class queer writers. These are important new works in the field of avant-garde writing, and symptomatic of a new resurgence of writing that sees avant-garde aesthetics as offering a new radical progressive literary politics in the current sociopolitical climates in the US and the UK. There is much critical work to be done on these emerging new writers' works that is, for reasons of publication timing, beyond the scope of the present volume.

Attentive to the critique of the majority of genealogies of avant-garde or experimental writing in English by scholars such as Anthony Reed, who observes that such modes of categorisation 'tend to neglect black writing, often owing to the granular attention to particular networks, coteries and traditions of writers and writing',[22] *Reading Experimental Writing* is intentionally not structured around groupings of writers or writers, and resists imposing a genealogy on experimental writing, or suggesting a historicisation of experimental writing, although the chapters are loosely structured chronologically. There is a seeming emphasis on US-based experimental writing in the volume, and on poetry, leanings that arose unintentionally. However, whilst many of the writers addressed in the volume reside in the States, they are originally from outside the States. This fact marks a key theme of the collection: experimental writing is a form of literature that is able to represent the contemporary *zeitgeist* in which human movement, exile and diaspora are central. This experience is also central to the politics of new forms of writing in the contemporary. In the UK, recent works of the multimedia artist Caroline Bergvall and the poet and writer David Herd have engaged explicitly with the politics of human movement and the way in which the arts and humanities can intervene politically through voicing the voices of those who are politically disenfranchised within the contemporary socio-political climate. And it is precisely the new forms of their works that enable such interventions. Caroline Bergvall's multi-media works *Drift* (2013), *Ragadawn* (2016), *Oh My Oh My* (2017) and her recent work *Conference (After Attar)* (2018) engage with migratory politics through a multiplicity of platforms: installation, performance, film and ambisonic conversation-performance. The multimodal nature of Bergvall's compositions yields new forms of writing and reception. *Drift*'s moving sea of words, which draws the receiver into a 'meditation on migrancy, exiles and sea travel',[23] requires of the reader a process of journeying rather than a conventional act of reading (which it defies). Bergvall's work 'both allows and transforms the reading experience into a fluid and perceptually subtle mode of connection between live voice and textual material'.[24] The multisensory site-specific performances of *Ragadawn* draw upon sunrise traditions and address 'the linguistic territories of the UK and the EU' to engage with migration and its contemporary politics.[25] In her description of her 'Dawn Chorus of Languages' Bergvall states: 'At the heart of *Ragadawn* is the process of revitalising connections between poetic forms as well as minority or migratory languages active in Europe. Anciently rooted languages, as well as those present through more recent settlements.'[26] The multi-dimensional nature of Bergvall's new literature, of which writing is just one component, promotes the formation of a new perceptual apparatus with which to apprehend the contemporary. To receive and to 'read' Bergvall's work is to respond to the demand to develop new forms of listening and visual and verbal cognition that are, in their movement away from conventional concepts of reading, listening and comprehension, tools of perceptual transformation. David Herd's poetic work *Through* (2016), and his project *The Refugee Tales* (2016), like *Drift* address language as a border and a public space. In the Preface to *Through* Herd understands the decisions that are taken at the AIC in Islington – the Asylum and Immigration Centre on Rosebury Avenue, London – to be, in effect, decisions about who leaves the language.

Through is a critique of, and counter to, Theresa May's 2013 call to create a 'hostile environment' for immigrants seeking asylum in the UK. In his collection Herd also shares with Bergvall the pursuit of new forms and uses of language, which, embracing multiplicity, can become languages of transition, inclusion and intimacy to counteract the political and social forms of exclusion that people seeking asylum encounter in institutional procedures and public discourse.

Related to such activist works, the twenty-first century has seen a groundswell of writerly and scholarly interest in the politics of translation. Sophie Collins's anthology *Currently and Emotion* (2016) collects contemporary poetry translations by writers such as Lisa Roberston, Chantal Wright, Zoë Skoulding, Anne Carson, Vahni Capildeo and Sonja Kravanja, among many others. New forms of translation and scholarly work are by necessity bound to the politics of reading. In Erín Mouré's words: 'There is a sense in which every reading of a text by an individual is a translation, because ink and paper, or pixelated light and darkness, are "read" through a body, an individual apparatus impossible to replicate in terms of its cells and experiences and the ways in which that experience has affected its neural maps and capacities.' Mouré implores: 'We must respect the work of the other. We must give our own linguistic borders a porosity that lets the work of others in other cultures into our own'[27] – a statement Sophie Seita explores further in Chapter 5. Such porosity demands new forms of reading. A number of the contributors here – Jennifer Scappettone, Sophie Seita and Susan Rudy – offer chapters that engage with multilingual works, issues of translation and the importance of multilingualism to the new horizons of experimental writing.

The volume opens with Jennifer Scappettone's chapter '"Fog is My Land": A Citizenship of Mutual Estrangement in the Painted Books of Etel Adnan'. In a 1989 essay entitled 'To Write in a Foreign Language', Etel Adnan described the trajectory of her relationship to Arabic, a language associated with shame and sin in the context of her French education in Beirut, but which her Syrian father had her copy by rote from an Arabic-Turkish grammar as a desperate means of recuperation. Her family's common languages were Turkish and French; of the Arabic letters whose knowledge Adnan acquired through a channel more somatic than semantic, she writes, 'I did not try to have them translated to me, I was satisfied with the strange understanding of them: . . . it was like seeing through a veil, looking at an extraordinary scenery through a screen.' During the Algerian war of independence, when a dream of Arab unity emerged, Adnan's attitude to the languages of her inheritance changed: 'I didn't need to write in French anymore, I was going to paint in Arabic.' Scappettone asks: 'How does this dream, itself transitory, constitute itself in Adnan's works?' And how, Scappettone asks, are readers to read across the sometimes unintelligible sign systems that result? Scappettone's chapter explores the geopolitical implications of Adnan's 'xenoglossic' poetics, which sporadically merges the media of writing and painting, to contemplate how her practices of transcription and supralinguistic gesture enable us to revise reigning discursive categories of cultural nativity and solidarity, citizenship and statelessness.

Alex Houen considers the idea of happiness in the present sociopolitical climate through the recent work of Sara Ahmed and Claire Colebrook. Through this theoretical engagement Houen explores what it is 'to open up to wider possibilities in the form of the happenstance and the precarious' and what this might look like in practice. For Houen, experimental writing is 'effective in opening up the intimacies between possibility and the happenstance'. As a consequence, experimental writing has 'presented new forms of happiness as a practice'. To demonstrate this claim, Houen reads Lyn Hejinian's sequence *Happily* (2000), bringing to light the way in which her work, as a form of 'literary potentialism', 'explores textual possibilities to develop powers of personhood'. By then looking at reparative modes of reading identified by Eve Kosofsky Sedgwick, John Cage's 'chance determinations', which were also reading experiments, emerge as a tool to 'make the happenstance happen'. Houen considers Cage's alignment of experimental praxis with Buckminster Fuller's humanitarian, utopic thinking, reading this as a complement to Cage's desire for his work to open people's minds to 'their chances of improving world environment'. Through thinking socially with people, Houen contends, Cage offers an experimental reading of writers' works.

Georgina Colby explores the significance of the archive to a reading of experimental writing, taking the work of Kathy Acker as a case study. Utilising a framework of genetic criticism, the chapter explores the relation between the avant-texte and an avant-garde politics of materiality. Addressing Acker's original artwork for *Blood and Guts in High School* (1978) housed in the Kathy Acker Papers at Duke University, Colby contends that the avant-textes reveal a feminist politics of materiality at work in Acker's compositions. Acker's original materials are often very different in their material forms to the final published works. Through the lens of Johanna Drucker's work on diagrammatic writing and performative materiality, Colby argues for the avant-texte as a site of socio-political material resistance. The diagrammatic in Acker's work demands new reading practices commensurate with this resistance.

Christopher Chen's chapter, 'Rereading Race and Commodity Form in Erica Hunt's *Piece Logic*', reads Erica Hunt's writings as interrogating 'the conditions of social legibility that regulate differential incorporation into a postwar political, economic and social order organised around what the poet describes as rigid and mass-produced social roles'. For Chen, Hunt's is an 'investigatory poetics' that has the capacity to complicate 'the normative boundaries of such roles'. *Piece Logic*, in Chen's analysis, 'reimagines an oppositional poetics and politics by synthesising historically segregated antiracist and anticapitalist political imaginaries'. *Piece Logic* is read as an allegory of 'broken' things which 'reveals how the "brokenness" of the postwar economy has been consistently displaced onto specific "broken" populations'. Furthermore, *Piece Logic* 'stages a simultaneously antiracist and antcapitalist critique of the mirror or commodity form itself as evidence or "proof" of the pathological character of a social order organised around a single measure of abstract value'. Hunt, Chen argues, 'represents radically devalued persons and objects as stamped with the spectral imprint of an entire society-wide process of abstract value production that is both racially organised and organising'. Exploring the necessity of problematic 'historical forgetting of origins' to the process of 'establishing national unity', Hunt's poem emerges in the chapter as making visible the way in which 'such acts of forgetting are repeated in the lives of national subjects as the basis for an associated freedom that paradoxically constitutes a formative principle of what political theorist Benedict Anderson has famously called the "imagined communities" of modern nations'. Chen's chapter adopts a Marxist approach to posit Hunt's work as a critique of racial and gender inclusion within the contemporary US, a 'House of Broken Things' which, for Chen, 'inevitably produces brokenness itself as a kind of mass-produced object'.

The nuances and difficulties encountered in reading and translating contemporary multilingual and translingual poetry, in particular the work of the German poet and translator Uljana Wolf, is the focus of Sophie Seita's chapter. Engaging with the politics of translation, Seita highlights the need for diversity in translation if the present '(the past the future will read)' is to be inclusive. A critique of the 'imperialist trappings' of translation, Seita contends, is able to change our habits of reading. Seita understands Uljana Wolf's works as 'a migratory poetry and poetics that engages with social issues', a praxis that 'demonstrates how contemporary hyphenated identities can be expressed in poetry'. Thematically, and through experiment in language, Seita's analysis reveals Wolf's critique of borders, nationality and 'mother tongues'. Seita's work draws on her own practice of translation of Wolf's work as a form of comment on Wolf's work, recognising that translation should not be seamlessly congruent but a praxis that acknowledges misunderstandings and ambiguities, yielding 'a new articulacy'. Seita locates a 'translational thinking' in the work of Wolf, Cha and Waldrop and from this approaches M. NourbeSe Philip's *Zong!* and Wolf's translation of *Zong!* Multilingual translation, Seita understands, is 'a work of transformed and transformative failure, a confrontation with impossibility, a giving up of mastery, and a political rejection of monolingualism'.

erica kaufman reads Joan Retallack's *Memnoir* (2004) as an antidote to the limitations associated with generic memoir. Formal features such as the sparse use of the 'I' and Retallack's use of the page as a unit yields kaufman's comparison between Retallack and Dewey's observation that 'experience is omnipresent and ever important'. The poetic form offers a new form of memoir for Retallack, one that calls into question the project of recollecting one's past. Reconceiving the idea of the memoir as 'mindful' rather than 'memory', kaufman's close analysis blended with critical experiment reveals new forms of attention to the experimental work. kaufman's chapter is indicative of the current move in experimental writing away from authorial mastery discussed at the outset of this Introduction. Reconceiving memoir apart from the confessional form of Sylvia Plath or Anne Sexton, kaufman argues that '[t]o tell one's own story is to tell a story always in motion, always affected or in conversation with what Joan Retallack describes as "the mess of the contemporary".' kaufman explores Retallack's essay 'What is Experimental Writing & Why Do We Need It?', addressing Retallack's '"angle of enquiry" that emphasizes "complex interrelationships" instead of first-person tunnel vision'. kaufman's scrutiny of the way in which Retallack's work 'complicates the first-person persona that normatively connotes some kind of hypothetical "truth"' is significant in its intervention into the way in which new forms of memoir demand a panoply of forms of attention from the reader.

Caroline Bergvall's hyphenated practice is the subject of Susan Rudy's chapter. Rudy explores the hyphenated relation between writer and reader. Drawing on Jessica Benjamin, who argues that in the mother-child bond we find an alternative theory of the production of meaning, Rudy argues that the mother-child relation also offers an affective theory of the reception of experimental work, since such work offers spaces where readers can also become 'different, new'. Rudy contends that Bergvall's 'hyphenated practice' calls for and models a new understanding of the relation between writer and reader. In what Bergvall describes as 'the event of reading', the author is called back into the work as reader. Rudy approaches the queer texts in this 'expanded field' as a queer literary critic. Drawing on the work of Lisa Ruddick and practices of intersubjectivity, the chapter addresses Bergvall's multilingual practices. Rudy explores the idea that through such practices Bergvall's writing has become a 'public project' into which we are invited to enter.

Through the prism of Johanna Drucker's recent work, combined with a Derridean exploration of what he theorises as 'grammalepsy', John Cayley examines recent digital language art ('an emergent aspect of experimental writing'), probing Drucker's concluding statement to *The General Theory of Social Relativity* (2018), 'The time of tongues is past.' For Cayley, such sentences 'are new quanta and constituents of experimental writing'. Reading is renegotiated in Cayley's chapter 'as a word for what we do, both when we hear-and-understand and when we scan-and-"hear"-and-understand'. Cayley argues that today, 'we need an understanding of reading that is not overdetermined by formal tokenisation, grammatisation and computational models of creativity in an arbitrary and abstracted support materiality'. This conception of reading, which Cayley conceives of as 'grammaleptic', is explored in the chapter in relation to reading experimental digital language art. Offering shrewd analyses of contemporary works such as Samantha Gorman and Danny Cannizzaro's *Pry* (2014) and Dave Jhave Johnston's *ReRites* (2017), the chapter yields an understanding of the importance of this conception of reading to encountering such works, and to inhabiting a landscape of emerging digital language art.

Peter Jaeger's 'Charles Bernstein's Walter Benjamin, Among Other Things' concludes the volume. Jaeger's coda offers both a reading of Charles Bernstein's work and a piece of experimental writing to be read. Jaeger's chapter takes up citational methodology as a formal approach to critical writing, through reading Charles Bernstein's work via Walter Benjamin. Employing poetic tactics such as modality, intertextuality, disjunction and direct appropriation, Jaeger offers a new mode of experimental criticism in practice. In ending on Jaeger's reading of Bernstein, the collection provocatively invites reflection on the very form of criticism in the field of experimental writing, as well as actively ushering the reader into new reading practices.

Notes

1. See Bray et al., *The Routledge Companion to Experimental Literature*. The view of literary experimentalism taken in the volume is in line with Alex Houen's 2014 study *Powers of Possibility: Experimental American Writing Since the 1960s*. Other recent studies that have also focused on more specific lines of enquiry include Ellen E. Berry's *Women's Experimental Writing: Negative Aesthetics and Feminist Critique*; Anthony Reed's rigorous *Freedom Time: The Poetics and Politics of Black Experimental Writing*; and Alison Gibbons, *Multimodality, Cognition and Experimental Literature*.
2. Fink and Halden-Sullivan, *Reading the Difficulties*, p. 3.
3. Altieri and Nace, *The Fate of Difficulty*, p. 2.
4. Ibid. p. 1.
5. Ibid. p. 2.
6. Ibid.
7. Ibid.
8. Ibid. p. 3.
9. DeKoven, *A Different Language*, p. xv.
10. Elizabeth Robinson, 'Reading and Reading', in Fink and Halden-Sullivan, *Reading the Difficulties*, pp. 18–28; p. 19.
11. Ibid. pp. 19–20.
12. Ibid. p. 20.
13. Retallack, 'What is Experimental Poetry and Why Do We Need It?'
14. Prince, 'Recipes', p. 209.
15. Retallack, 'What is Experimental Poetry and Why Do We Need It?' I would have liked in this collection to have engaged more with significant new forms of writing emerging from the Cambridge School that engage with critical ecological questions, such as Drew Milne's ongoing work on lichens and the biotariat. See the collection 'Lichens for Marxists' in *In Darkest Capital: The Collected Poems of Drew Milne* (Manchester: Carcanet, 2017), pp. 372–422.
16. Altieri and Nace, *The Fate of Difficulty*, p. 3.
17. Nealon, *The Matter of Capital*, p. 1.
18. Ibid.
19. Ibid. p. 2.
20. Ibid. p. 35.
21. Hickman, *Crisis and the US Avant-Garde*, p. 3.
22. Reed, *Freedom Time*, p. 3.
23. Bergvall, *Drift*.
24. Ibid.
25. Bergvall, *Ragadawn*.
26. Ibid.
27. Mouré, 'But do we need a second language to translate?', p. 29.

Chapter 1

'Fog is My Land': A Citizenship of Mutual Estrangement in the Painted Books of Etel Adnan
Jennifer Scappettone

In her 1989 essay titled 'To Write in a Foreign Language', the poet, essayist, and visual artist Etel Adnan (b. 1925) describes the trajectory of her relationship to Arabic: a language equated in childhood with shame, backwardness, and sin through her French convent schooling in Beirut during the French Mandate for Syria and Lebanon (1923–46), and evolving in its political affiliations in tandem with a series of intercultural wars that directly impacted her family – World Wars I and II, the Algerian War of Independence, and the Lebanese Civil War. Arabic was the language of her father, Assaf Kadri, a Sunni Muslim from Damascus born to an Albanian mother – and a high-ranking officer of the Ottoman Empire, who taught her the alphabet when she was a child.[1] Determined to overcome what he regarded as the propaganda of the French, he had the only child of his second marriage copy pages upon pages from an Arabic-Turkish grammar hailing from his days as a cadet, which she would use to decline verbs, but ultimately lacked the discipline to study for comprehension. The child would have needed discipline dearly in a context where she lacked a patient teacher – and where for the students referred to by the nuns as *les indigenes*, speaking Arabic in school was forbidden.[2] Those caught doing so would be forced to bear stones in their pockets – a performative form of punishment that transforms heritage into a burden in this colonial context.[3]

'To be a refugee is not to go away, it's not to be able to come back,' Adnan told me in a 2017 interview; hers was a family of refugees.[4] Greek was the language of her mother, an Orthodox Christian who grew up in the Smyrna of the Ottoman Empire – a city burned to the ground during its definitive Turkish occupation in 1922. Though Adnan's father – equally defeated by the fall of the Ottomans, though

Figure 1.1 Etel Adnan, *Rihla ila Jabal Tamalpais (Journey to Mount Tamalpais)*, 2008. Watercolour and Indian ink on Japanese book, 30 x 10.5cm x 54 pages : 30 x 567cm. Private collection. Copyright Etel Adnan. Courtesy of Galerie Claude Lemand, Paris. Donation Claude and France Lemand, Musée, Institut du monde arabe, Paris.

from a more privileged socio-economic position – saved his second wife's family from poverty and starvation, the fact that he was Muslim led some close relations violently to reject the union; indeed, their marriage would be impossible in the Lebanon of today, where civil unions remain prohibited, in spite of activist campaigns to the contrary. They spoke Turkish together, and while on the battlefront, he sent his wife romantic, almost novelistic letters in the language of her primary convent schooling, French, lucidly inscribed in pen and ink. Adnan's parents moved to Beirut at the end of World War I, where her father could continue to operate in an Arab context – though under French occupation, Arabs were effectively demoted to the status of aliens in their own land. The family's common languages were spoken Ottoman Turkish, which held within it a great deal of Arabic and Persian filtered through Qur'anic study; spoken Greek; and increasingly, the French of educational systems occupying the Levant.[5]

The Arabic script itself must have harboured a particular melancholic charge for Adnan's father, given that upon the founding of the Turkish Republic, Mustafa Kemal Atatürk (his former classmate) launched a series of linguistic reforms: in 1928, as part of a modernising, Westernising, secular and nationalist agenda, Atatürk replaced the Perso-Arabic script that had been used to convey Ottoman Turkish for a thousand years with the Latin alphabet, while campaigning for the replacement of Arabic and Persian loan words with Turkish equivalents. Abandonment of the Arabic writing system would coincide with an immediate boost in literacy rates in a territory where knowledge of the *abjad*, a consonantal alphabet now deemed ill-suited to conveying Turkish vowels and other phonemes, had been limited to a privileged elite – so that for the vast majority of Turkish speakers in the fallen Ottoman Empire, this script would have been as mysterious as it was for the vanquished officer's five-year-old daughter.

The notion of linguistic nativity is thus braided with contradiction for Etel Adnan. Of the Arabic letters she absorbed through a childhood channel more somatic than semantic, and to which she would return later in life, she writes, 'I did not try to have them translated to me, I was satisfied with the strange understanding of them: bits here and there, sentences where I understood but one key word; it was like seeing through a veil, looking at an extraordinary scenery through a screen.'[6] Adnan's lifelong process of upholding this distressed relationship with her father's tongue, for which the streets of Beirut served as her other incomplete teacher, drafts a maquette of cultural belonging that obliges engaged readers to revise still-prevalent assumptions of immediate authentic claims on cultural heritage – beginning with the essentialist biological trope of the mother tongue, whose naturalisation of language acquisition is undermined by ever-shifting geopolitical realities.[7] With the onset of World War II, the English of Anglophone armies occupying Beirut would become more and more prevalent in Lebanese intellectual and commercial life, rivalling or even eclipsing French in an emerging triangulation of cultural forces – and when she moved to California in 1955, US English would become a vital crucible for Adnan, offering a liberation of expression akin to a 'rebirth', in her own terms.[8] The disjunctive map of linguistic attachment borne out by Adnan's eventual (but not exclusive) predilection for English, and her experimentation with Arabic and other non-Latin writing systems, reflects affective landscapes of dislocation and continuity that have evolved over the last century of global conflicts more accurately than any narrative resorting to reigning discursive categories of cultural nativity, or political binaries of citizenship and statelessness – while urging us to revise attitudes towards diglossia as well.[9]

For Adnan, the screen, the veil, through which she perceives Arabic does not signal blockage alone, but instead intensifies the power of the occluded text, whose mystery can be traced but not comprehended in the lettered sense. Placing herself behind a veil metaphorically also locates her inside the Arab world, but from the discursively compromised standpoint of a woman – in a paradoxical self-Orientalising move for an outspoken writer who played her part in a social revolution as one of the first generation of Arab girls who went to work.[10] What can these depicted genres of exclusion mean for a poet? Might the mediation of the screen function beyond the obvious foreclosure from standard definitions of nationally or ethnically conscripted identity, to open up the possibility of a more plastic relationship to cultural heritage and geopolitical futurity?

Lacking a dominant native tongue, Adnan's work constitutes a rebuke to both nationalism and acritical ethnocentrism generated by what I will call 'xenoglossic' poetry, adapting a term for the intelligible use of a natural language one has not learned formally or does not 'know'.[11] Hailing from the Greek for language foreign or opaque to use, *xénoglossie* was coined in 1905 by a French physiologist to describe the mysterious facility in Greek achieved by one Madame X – a medium who, though lacking a classical education, was able to write long passages from Plato and the New Testament hailing from the Franco-Greek Dictionary of Byzantios while in a trance; the concept secularises a phenomenon mythologised in the New Testament narrative of Pentecost.[12] Lacking the perceived birthright or proper education, authors of xenoglossic poetry occupy languages in discomfiting ways. Through manipulation by an artist of Adnan's alternately trans- and subnational sensibility, the never-quite-mother languages of the father and of the state – and even the seemingly dictatorial instruction of transcription – become instruments of buoyancy and resistance. Forging textscapes capable of accommodating multiple linguistic systems, this poet working in an embattled linguistic contact zone of global modernity manifests the wide-ranging implications of the 'wireless imagination' theorised by Futurists in 1913. Their manifesto 'Destruction of Syntax – Wireless Imagination – Words-in-Freedom' sought to transgress provincial consciousness and claim immediate relations to contemporaries around the globe by means of poetic innovation that was conceptual, formal and grammatical. Yet authors of minor poetries like Adnan flout the nationalist and supranationalist imperialist politics driving the futurist forebears of the global avant-garde.[13]

In the wake of the world wars and the period of widespread decolonisation, tactics of painterly abstraction offered literary artists across the globe one route to such transnational, translinguistic communion. Beyond the dream of universal communicability pervading the postwar fervour of internationalism, alphabets subject to the gesticulations of action painting appeared to offer the promise of subversive occupation: of ideological dislodging. The scrawled passages on canvas by Adnan's contemporary Cy Twombly became theorised by Italian poet-philologist and artist Emilio Villa, for instance, as refutations of authoritarianism: as 'whistles/in the fasces of uniform graphemes', and the very formation of 'an ideal nationality'.[14] Mohammed Melehi, modernist Moroccan artist, professor at the École des Beaux-Arts of Casablanca and editor of the transregional arts journal *Intégral*, to which Adnan contributed (1971–8), witnessed such fermentation of painterly abstraction in postwar Rome when he moved there to study in 1957, enjoying what he identified as 'la démocratie qui régnait entre les artistes à Rome', unique within Europe.[15] Melehi suggests that in countries where populations are divided by language (such as Morocco's French, Arabic and varieties of Berber), painting has a specific suturing capacity, enjoying a more immediate and universal impact than text – though *Intégral* as a journal of 'plastic and literary creation' as well as Melehi's works themselves dissolve any binary opposition between language and visual art, devoting space to sites of their imbrication such as calligraphy and political posters. In a 1967 questionnaire, Melehi characterised Arab art in utopian key as '*permanent, présent et accessible à tout individu indépendamment de sa formation ou de sa culture*', contrasting it with a Western figurative genealogy that relies on the cultivation of bourgeois taste. He moreover dissolved the line between reading and visual scanning that is blurred in calligraphy with the statement: '*La lecture est la pure identification visuelle d'un message et l'écriture est la pure transmission d'un message visuellement conçu*' (emphasis in original).[16]

Admitting to being haunted by such desires for immediate communicability, Adnan asks what she calls an unanswerable question: 'What can I say of the fact that I do not use my native tongue and do not have the most important feeling that as a writer I should have, the feeling of direct communication with one's audience?'[17] (It is difficult to pin down what Adnan means by 'native tongue', but we can presume that she is referring here to Arabic.) Her visual art offers a nondiscursive answer to the unanswerable, being intimately tied to her shuttling across languages both under duress and by choice.

Although critics mark a topical and tonal dichotomy between her writing (characterised as politicised and dark) and her visual art (depicted as cognitive/metaphysical, sensuous and bright), studying the interweaving of these practices in her oeuvre draws us away from the facility of such dyads into a more ambiguous sociolyric space. More than a 'bridge' between writing and artmaking, which is the metaphor that Adnan's recent biographer uses, Adnan's painting in accordion books underscores that – as she puts it in another piece – 'Writing is drawing, drawing is writing, writing is drawing . . .', especially if not exclusively in Eastern contexts: that drawing itself is a kind of language.[18] The uncertain signs of her drawn and painted texts complicate presumptions of literate accessibility that attend adherence to national and native languages, and by extension, prevailing concepts of citizenship and diaspora. Adnan's painted texts problematise even more rigorously than her printed texts do a centuries-old imposition of the monolingual paradigm traceable to the French Revolution, while registering its lasting personal and political impacts.[19] This writing/drawing forges a version of solidarity with poets, refugees and other marginalised subjects across and beyond linguistic affiliation and nation. The resultant linguistic climates propose refuge in mutual unmastery, and can even be seen to perform decolonisation on an intimate scale.

For beyond her teeming corpus of lucid and freely styled works of verse and prose, Adnan has developed a body of writing whose relationship to its adopted languages is more distressed. Adnan herself singles out this aspect of her oeuvre as special, both for its unusual methods and for its historic significance, yet it has received cursory critical treatment thus far. In this essay, I will explore the geopolitical implications of this body of work, which veers into the painterly: of poetic texts that toe the line between writing and drawing, xenoglossia and glossolalia. On the one hand, Adnan experiments with a spontaneous, seemingly purely gestural idiom, as in her masterwork *L'apocalypse arabe*; on the other, in painting on accordion books, this queer poet assumes the transcription of that father tongue over which she has never assumed perfect control – one that was occluded, that under colonisation and new forms of nationalism she was not supposed to know. Adnan finds a positive valence in this occlusion: 'I think that I loved the act of writing things I did not understand, and I pretended that I was learning a language . . . just by writing it down. There must have been something hypnotizing about these exercises because much later, and for different reasons, I ended up doing practically the same thing.'[20]

Transcription of Arabic texts becomes a method for dwelling in a tongue that is destined by the undertow of Western influence to remain 'foreign', withheld, and yet known on some translinguistic, translettered level. The opacity of Arabic appears to have opened up alternative landscapes of belonging over the course of Adnan's career. Regarded as a generative withdrawal from political ontologies imposed by an occidental worldview, opacity becomes a form of resistance to demands for colonised peoples' transparency voiced in 1969 by Édouard Glissant, in a groundbreaking statement at the National Autonomous University of Mexico: '*Nous réclamons le droit à l'opacité*' ('We demand the right to opacity').[21]

Adnan presents English, Arabic and painting as discovered idioms that offered alternatives to the imperial language of her education. She had fallen in love with poetry while studying under the diplomat and literary critic Gabriel Bounoure, the brilliant and charismatic founder of an experimental school in Beirut, the École des Lettres – devouring such French modernists as Baudelaire and Rimbaud. Detecting her genius, Bounoure encouraged Adnan to apply for the scholarship to study in Paris that eventually led her to leave Lebanon for the first time, breaking violently from her now widowed mother's staunchly traditional expectations. She studied aesthetic philosophy at the Sorbonne from 1949 onwards with Gaston Bachelard and Étienne Souriau in a context scored by World War II; but living among Americans in the international house, Adnan became drawn to the unknown territory of the US, which held out the promise of surpassing mere affirmation of her early formation. She would move to the Bay Area in 1955 on a scholarship for graduate studies in philosophy at Berkeley. After two and a half years of classes at Berkeley and Harvard with teachers such as Stanley Cavell, and a semester's break in Mexico between the two, she abandoned her doctoral programme: her grasp of English had hardly prepared her for the Anglo-Saxon philosophical schools' intense focus on linguistics and symbolic logic, and in the academic context of analytic philosophy at the time, thinkers she treasured such as Nietzsche were considered to be poets, thereby being disqualified from value as philosophers. She became enthralled by the wonder and adventure of the American language, however, and it would lead her more squarely in the direction of poetics.

It was at UC Berkeley that Adnan first met Arabs who were not Lebanese or Syrian, and became involved with the desire for Arab solidarity in concert with the Algerian War of Independence (1954–62). As a secular dream of pan-Arab unity emerged, Adnan began to resent her colonial education, having to express herself in

French, and to reject a notion of *francophonie* reserved exclusively for the subjects of colonised nations: through a transformative relationship with an artist from Mill Valley she would eventually decide: 'I didn't need to write in French anymore, I was going to paint in Arabic.'[22] As with the polyglot refugee poet Amelia Rosselli, the choice to write in the tongue of the father harbours particularly urgent political possibilities. Yet the result is neither strictly patrilinear nor monolithic, for Adnan simultaneously rejects any form of tribalism or sectarianism tied to what she calls 'relative identities', stressing active acceptance over the naturalisation of kinship.[23] A discussion of the word 'son' in an interview with Lynne Tillman, for instance, reveals that Adnan regards this term through its vernacular usage in Semitic languages, which goes back millennia to the Aramaic of the New Testament: 'When Jesus said, "I am the Son, Father," he meant "I am accepted, and what I say is agreeable to the Father . . ."'[24] In this conception, acceptance and agreement herald affiliation, not blood. Adnan's painted language furthers this possibility of denaturalised kinship: merging traditions normally rarefied from one another, her calligraphic transcriptions carry Arab culture into global contexts where it may be received unmediated by exogenous myths of the East.

How exactly does this dream of painting in Arabic constitute itself in Adnan's written works? And how are readers to travel across the competing sign systems in which it takes root? Towards the end of 'To Write in a Foreign Language', Adnan characterises Frantz Fanon's indictment of the French colonial system and the psychological effects of its linguistic policies as 'beautifu[l]', while declining to 'accus[e] the old colonial system' herself, claiming full responsibility for her language use as an Arab writer, stressing the difference between the Arab condition and that of Black Africans whose native tongues were eradicated under colonisation. Adnan and Fanon were exact contemporaries, and her reading of his work was clearly formative; yet Adnan forces the languages that circumstance imposed on her into plastic conditions, demonstrating through poetry and what was strategically described in a transcontinental Arab milieu as '*arts plastiques*' that 'international' linguistic systems can be altered or broken from within – producing politically and aesthetically expansive, even explosive results.[25] By alternating between and merging the mediums of writing and painting, her poetry eludes the antinomies characterising her contemporaries' critiques of linguistic ideology to propose a paradox, or both/and proposal: 'Poets are deeply rooted in language and they transcend language.'[26]

Adnan's relationship with drawing and painting, a 'language beyond words',[27] was spurred by a sudden encounter, in concert with learning English, in the period when her alienation from France led her to feel that she was lacking a means of self-expression. Upon finding the analytic philosophy taught in the US incommensurate with her interests in aesthetics, and herself in need of money, Adnan took on a job teaching aesthetics at Dominican College in San Rafael. (Significantly, she declined to teach French, choosing instead to teach philosophy in English.) Ann O'Hanlon, a progressive product of the WPA and Buddhist founder of the college's art department, provoked Adnan into practice in 1959 by suggesting that one couldn't teach Philosophy of Art without direct experience of the subject. She offered Adnan pastels and narrow scraps of paper left over from her classes, and the results of Adnan's observations of landscape were immediately compelling. The narrow proportions of the paper scraps (about 3 x 10 inches) would have invited an analogy to writing, and they prefigured the 'leporello' format that Adnan would eventually deploy with great success. In the 1960s, Adnan started using discarded scraps of canvas that O'Hanlon provided on which to paint with a palette knife. 'Abstract art was the equivalent of poetic expression; I didn't need to use words ... I didn't need to belong to a language-oriented culture but to an open form of expression,' she recalls of this discovery; 'I understood ... that I moved not on single planes but within a spherical mental world, and that what we consider to be problems can also be tensions, working in more mysterious ways than we understand.'[28] Abstraction here offers the possibility of remapping one's relation to language and culture altogether.

Though she had published a book of poetry in Beirut at the age of twenty (*Le livre de la mer*), Adnan affirms that it was untranslatable because its founding eroticism between the sea (gendered feminine in French) and sun (masculine in French) is inverted in Arabic. She consistently describes her emergence as a poet as coinciding with her first publication in English, a language which (though she has not commented upon it) would have offered a route out of these gender binaries. Adnan, who has been openly queer for decades, had been mocked as a '*garçon manqué*' (literally, 'failed boy') as a child, making being a boy 'both appealing as a fact and shameful as a desire', and she recalls being happy to have her hair cut '*à la garçon*' and to be dressed in boys' clothes: 'it must have reinforced my identity of being neither just a girl, nor a boy, but a special being with the magical attributes of both'.[29] To write poetry in the

California of the 1960s brought into being a different condition of solidarity, transgressing gendered discursive constraints, religious doctrine, even species: 'That was a time when poetry became . . . the only religion which has no gods and dogmas, no punishments, no threats, no hidden motivations, no commercial use, no police and no Vatican. It was an open brotherhood open to women, men, trees and mountains.'[30]

At the École des Lettres Adnan had developed a sense of poetry itself as 'a counter-profession', 'an expression of personal and mental freedom' and a 'perpetual rebellion' that eventually led her to 'cut all ties with home and country'.[31] She entered this utopian fraternity out of shared desperation over war atrocities – publishing her first English-language poems, 'The Ballad of The Lonely Knight in Present-Day America' and 'The Enemy's Testament', in the *S-B Gazette*, a free pamphlet series opposing the Vietnam War printed covertly by Leon Spiro on the presses of San Francisco City Hall. A torn scrap of paper communicated in 1961 that her writing was 'muchly accepted', and 'The Enemy's Testament', narrated from the point of view of a murdered Viet Cong soldier, became the second poem in the seminal anthology *Where is Vietnam?* Says Adnan, 'I became an American poet that way.'[32] This strong claim for a citizenship other than one justified by *jus sanguinis* or *jus soli* – a nationality constructed through writing – is remarkable on multiple accounts.

> They got me out of my lair
> for I was infesting my own land,
> and they, the foreigners, came to liberate me,
>   liberate me of my share.[33]

Not only does Adnan claim US affiliation through poetry composed in an American idiom rather than through the rule of law. She asserts solidarity with a republic of thought more ideal than that which would pledge allegiance to the flag leading troops into atrocity: ventriloquising the hypocritical rhetoric of the very nation-becoming-empire to which it asserts belonging through its ironic opposition, through the mouth of the dead which enflesh its logical repercussions. Identification with a Viet Cong soldier signalled solidarity with Asians who were previously subject to French colonialism, but was a means of connecting with her past as well: Adnan's family had taken in an orphaned boy named Pierrot, the son of a French mother and a father from French Indochina, during school holidays.[34]

The fact that Adnan sent her anti-war poetry to Robert Kennedy (and that he responded to it) shows how much optimism Adnan still harboured about the direction of the United States at that time.[35] Adnan's self-identification has never ended at 'American', however, and as she herself confesses of this period of poetic rebirth, 'The old ghosts had not disappeared.'[36] Notwithstanding the fact that she cannot compose in Arabic, but only speaks the language of the street, Adnan holds to her identity as an Arab writer; when pressed for categorisation, she agrees that the term 'Arab American' applies best, but such hyphenation is deceptively crude: for 'an identity is not always a geographic territory. My identity was in not wanting to be rejected by Arab poets.' She describes herself as being integrated into Arabic poetry in the mid-1960s by Yusuf al-Khal, the first gallerist of modern painting in Beirut, editor of the crucial little magazine *Shi'r* ('Poetry', 1957–70), and translator of such works as *The Waste Land*.[37] Al-Khal supported and published her work in translation by the expatriated Iraqi poet Sargon Boulus, and even translated Adnan's work himself; Adnan's biographer Wilson-Goldie writes that al-Khal's blessing allowed her to join the so-called Arab republic of letters.[38] Adnan in turn had a part in enabling a transnational 'brotherhood' of Arab poetry by connecting the Beirut scene with Abdellatif Laâbi, the Rabat-based editor of the radical tricontinental magazine of *'decolonisation culturelle' Souffles-Anfas* in 1966 – recognising him as a fellow student of Bounoure.[39] (Adnan was to be the only woman poet published in *Souffles*.) Regardless of these relationships, as Lisa Suhair Majaj and Amal Amireh pointed out in their 2002 anthology devoted to Adnan's work, its literary reception continues to fall through the cracks of nationally and linguistically siloed traditions that it superimposes; and the fact that she does not compose in Arabic has led her to remain undercanonised in the Arab literary sphere, particularly outside of Lebanon.

When in 1972, after fourteen years in California, Adnan returned to a culturally vibrant Beirut and became the incisive cultural editor of *Al Safa*, a newly founded French-language newspaper, she piqued interest in her provocative editorials by way of their signature alone; for her name registers mixed origins. Etel was an ancient Greek name in disuse; Adnan, strictly Muslim, and usually a male first name, was only adopted as a family surname by her father upon the 1932 census, when French authorities required all families to register their names as citizens of the Republic.[40] It was a name that resonated with the rise in Arab national feeling, since according to a tradition revived in late nineteenth-century Turkey as part of an Ottoman nationalism,

'Adnān was an ancestor of the Northern Arabs, and therefore the equivalent of a Romulus or Remus.⁴¹ *Adnan* in Turkish and Arabic (عدنان) embeds within it the paradoxical meaning of 'settler; pioneer', or 'the person who has existence in two parallel worlds'. It seems as though Adnan took the performative force of her name to heart; her art harmonises ever-multiplying sets of parallel worlds, in aesthetic, gendered and geopolitical terms – at times at great personal risk. Those risks – and the death threats that accompanied the Arabic publication of her novel *Sitt Marie-Rose* in the midst of the Lebanese Civil War – ultimately led her and her partner Fattal to return to the Bay Area in 1977. Adnan's construction of identity inheres in dynamic re-occupation, re-circulation rather than being tethered to bounded forms that would isolate certain subjects as extraterritorial – she writes of maps that they 'are not about shapes, but about energies flowing in and out of places', yet adds to this a qualification of the cosmopolitan freedom of movement: 'They are about directions and obstacles.'⁴² Her politics unfolds through the battle to assume solidarities, freed from while never turning a blind eye to the violent day-to-day walls and blockades of nation and empire. She speculates that the embattled state of the Arab world is the very foundation of her identification as such: 'If the Arab world weren't forever at war, and so much under attack, maybe I wouldn't have been Arab,' she says to Hans Ulrich Obrist in an interview. 'But the daily politics of it keep me from getting complacent.' Later, she returns to the question of writing itself: 'I would have had another life if I had written in Arabic.'⁴³

What difference does it make, then, that Adnan has not written, but instead painted in Arabic? Experiencing Arabic as a 'lost paradise', Adnan forged another way to write into this part of her heritage in the immediate aftermath of the Algerian War. Having discovered accordion books – Japanese *orihon*/折本 or in Italian, *leporelli* – in the early 1960s through Rick Barton, an artist living on the margins of San Francisco, she became enthralled by the way that these long folding scrolls invited reading in time – and found in them a channel for connecting with Arab writers. She began a practice of copying and illuminating Arabic texts into leporellos found in Japanese shops that endures to this day, a collaborative practice that Simone Fattal has identified as building a politicised 'anthology' of contemporary poets Adnan knew and loved. Rather than emulating the 'codification' of classical calligraphy, she deployed her 'extremely imperfect' handwriting to manipulate the inherently plastic Arabic alphabet – gesturing simultaneously towards East Asian calligraphic traditions through the matrix of the *orihon* itself and through her fluid, energetic strokes.[44] And she took on the most radical authors in doing so, beginning pointedly with the work of Iraqi poet Badr Shakir al-Sayyab (1926–64), who had just passed away young and penniless – once an avowed communist who was exiled and imprisoned for his political beliefs, and who introduced modernity into Arabic poetics through impassioned and highly personal experiments in free verse.[45]

Amid the furore of her rise to the status of a global art-world sensation following her 2012 participation in Documenta 13, which has led to much focus on her abstract landscapes on canvas, Adnan has begun to emphasise the revolutionary significance of these hybrid works on paper – stressing that she was the first Arab painter besides Shaker Hassan al Saïd to use personal, non-traditional handwriting in calligraphic art.[46] Critics have taken note. In a pioneering taxonomy of the globally disseminated 'Calligraphic School of Art' (traditionally known as Hurufiyya), Wijdan Ali presents Adnan and Shaker Hassan as pioneers of the 'calligraffiti' style, in which personal handwriting by artists not necessarily trained in classical calligraphy becomes a channel of expressive freedom.[47] As a creative practice evolved from her father's dictated exercises in copying from a Turkish-Arabic grammar, Adnan's transcriptions herald, in gestural form, the grammatical detournements of French and English language lessons in Theresa Hak Kyung Cha's *Dictee*.[48]

Al-Sayyab, Mother and Lost Daughter (1970; Fig. 1.2) is one of few early leporellos in homage to Arabic work that circulates, because Adnan normally gave these artist's books as gifts to the Arab poets transcribed. The piece incorporates the dispersed signifiers of al-Sayyab's revolutionary verses against a luminous blue, orange and yellow ground sporadically becoming salience – becoming line, umbilicus, language, dissolving the threshold between gesture, scribble and alphabet. The work obliges a uniquely estranging reading process: a reader who does not know Arabic (the author of this essay) may be reeled in until total opacity becomes intolerable, spurring an effort to discover both the foreign alphabet and an author still obscured by lack of translation and occidental provincialism; yet native speakers experience defamiliarisation as well, struck by the initial impression that there is no language here, yet recovering more and more of the alphabet upon closer study. In a 1973 essay, Abdelkebir Khatibi analysed such a 'split' and disfiguration of the linguistic sign in calligraphy: 'it offers us a text and its usual meaning, then takes it away little by little, disfigures it, recovers it, mirrors it'. In 'transport[ing] language into another code, another realm of the imaginary', thereby slowing the production of meaning, Khatibi

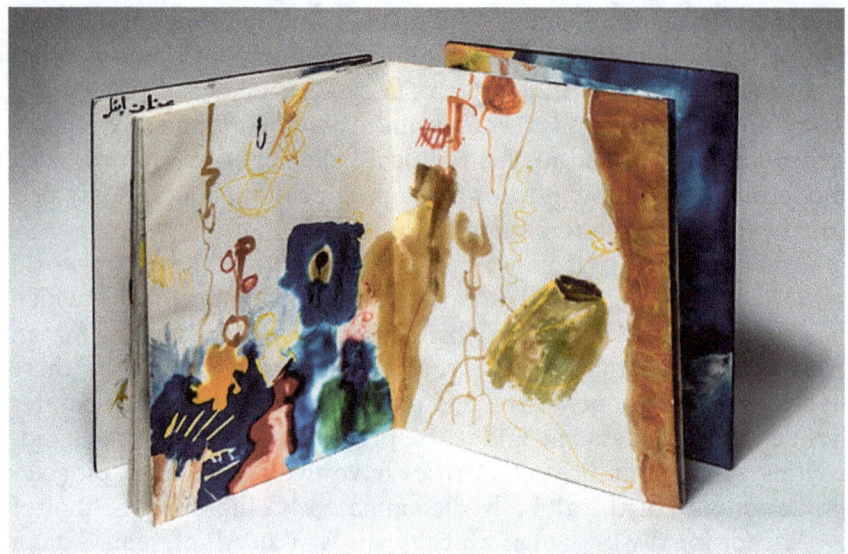

Figure 1.2 Etel Adnan, *Al-Sayyab, Mother and Lost Daughter*, 1970. Ink and watercolour on a Japanese notebook. Signed, dated and titled by the artist. Closed, 33 x 25.2cm x 24 pages. Open, 33 x 612cm. Private collection. Courtesy of Galerie Claude Lemand, Paris. Donation Claude and France Lemand, Musée, Institut du monde arabe, Paris.

argues, calligraphy is akin to poetry.[49] The humility, or approachability, of Adnan's calligraphy jumpstarts a process of exiled reading and – under hospitable conditions – of transcultural understanding that we do not normally associate with untranslated and untranslatable poetry.[50] It makes the process of translation aggressively visible without 'giving us' or eclipsing the original in any way.[51]

Adnan's writing poses an oblique supra- or subdiscursive dialogue with al-Sayyab's 1961 poem of supplication, which calls on a thirsty child compared with the sun (shams, شمس, which can also be a girl's name) to drink the speaker's blood as water. The single page spread to which we have access contains no obvious words, though seeking divulges gestures towards depiction of an explosive alphabet.[52] The first line of al-Sayyab's poem bids the sun to stop and refrain from setting – as night brings death, and those missing cannot return to family if darkness falls. Though al-Sayyab was invested in breaking the monorhyme of classical Arabic poetry, structure arises in his verse through repetition: the lam, ل ('L') recurs throughout the beginning of the poem. On Adnan's left page, a hook form recalling the ل appears prominently in orange at the top of the right page, and its mirror image appears in black on the left, superimposed over what appears to be an abstract evil eye. Meanwhile, two explosive devices – a thick yellow form resembling a cannon and an outlined phallus on the right (possibly wrought of mīms ('M', م – the abbreviation for male)), and an orange mass shooting out orange rays in the bottom left corner – appear to be expelling the letter ن (nūn; 'N') in various orientations and species of perspective (in gold on the right page, and in a cluster of red on the left). As nūn ن is the abbreviation used for the feminine, the visual drama of this page spread may bespeak the way that masculine warrior tactics have imploded the (feminine) sun, dispersing the daughter. Ultimately, these signs hover between lettered and unlettered experience: they appear to have been painted with both the curiosity and the pleasure of one who approaches a language from the outside, who is unalphabeted in the strict sense.

Such painting/writing must be read for its contribution to the transcontinental discourse surrounding radical experimental Arab arts at the time. The sun and explosive marks resonate with the trademark cover of *Souffles-Anfas* (1966–72; Fig. 1.3), designed by Mohammed Melehi, which was dominated by an explosive sun in shifting colours heralding the formation of Arab *arts plastiques* – with the *plastiquer* of this phrase being a militant reference to the revolutionary fervour of that moment of Third-Worldism: to dynamite, bomb attacks.[53] These explosive suns would return as the central icon of Adnan's *Arab Apocalypse*, discussed below.

Not all of Adnan's transcriptions display the radical transmogrification of the alphabet at work in this early leporello. A more recent work pays homage to the Sudanese writer al-Tayyeb Salih, transcribing the first paragraph of his 1971 novel *Bandarshah* into legible Arabic script, and naming itself after the author and his subtitle, *Daw al-Bayt* ('The Light of the House'; Fig. 3). *Bandarshah* tracks the transformation and redemption of the agricultural village of Wad Hamid on the Nile in Northern Sudan in the 1960s, which is being devastated by urbanisation. The passage Adnan has chosen to transcribe alongside her watercolour and ink paintings depicts a wizened character addressing his grandson, the book's protagonist, who returns to the village after years of exile. The excerpt Adnan illuminates ends with these words:

> He said, aiming his words at the sand at the bottom of his cane, 'You have long been absent from home [*balad* ("our country; homeland; village, town")].'
> I began to think. What would I say in these circumstances? 'Yes, years.'[54]

Figure 1.3 Mohammed Melehi, covers of the quarterly review *Souffles* 4 (1966), 5, 6, (1967), 10–11, 12 (1968), 13–14 (1969).

That the words are aimed as much at the sand as at the grandson bespeaks a double displacement: not only that of a younger generation fled to the Global North, as in Salih's celebrated *Season of Migration to the North*, but that of the matrix of this home: the sand itself. We can presume that the elder character's address to the sand would have had powerful resonance for Adnan, who has charged the European notion of 'homeland' imposed upon Arab territory with contradiction. In an interview, she asserts (controversially, perhaps fancifully) that the idea of 'the land' or *la terre* doesn't exist in the nomadic Arab world: that 'Arab poetry is interested in the surface of the planet' because there the desert hosts not agriculture, but drought, sandstorms, cosmic events.⁵⁵ Constantly shifting, redistributed, sand challenges the conceptual basis not only of 'land' but of the very term *deterritorialisation*, doing away with oppositions between territory and statelessness based on the assumption of rooted earth.⁵⁶ The sand as evocation of landscape would have dual resonance for Adnan, who in recent years has been unable to travel to the coastal places where she feels most at home (her native Beirut or the California where she was 'reborn'), residing instead and as if accidentally in the inland metropolis of Paris (where the consummate signifier of 1960s utopianism was the beach to expose below the paving stones). Adnan inscribes the name and date of Salih's original work on her page, and concludes by inscribing the leporello with her own signature, the year and site of transcription/displacement: Paris, forty years later.

The paintings Adnan paired with these lines from *Bandarshah* exist in a rather oblique relationship to their content; they are not illustrations but simultaneities, perhaps images of the home in which she was reading the novel.⁵⁷ True to the word 'illuminations', the pages we can access depict homely objects in the tradition of the still life, shot through by a searing Mediterranean 'light of the house'. Understood by Adnan as 'the ultimate material for art', the medium of Muslim mystics and opalescent Syrian glass as well as of the Space Age, with its neon sculptures and 'light shows', the envelope of light here assumes a performative force that, one imagines, itself embodies the house, home, homeland.⁵⁸ Adnan's illumination depicts through infusion the binding force of the sun, which puns on the kinship-through-acceptance of the 'son' in Arabic or Aramaic terms.

Adnan's process of transcription can be viewed as a devotional practice, one reaching back to the scribes and persisting through conceptual and other contemporary poetries. She describes the ritual preparations with which she would begin each leporello as entry into a sacral rite analogous to that of the painters of icons her Greek mother cherished, upholding a centuries-old tradition while 'still carrying on to new shores the inherent possibilities of Arabic writing'.⁵⁹ For Trithemius (1462–1516), writing at the dawn of moveable type in Europe that would displace the scribe, 'Nothing will draw the monk more closely to active perfection' than the basic channelling of the Word; the framing of his *De laude scriptorum* thematises the humility of being without language, as well as the promise of its assumption through a physical, nearly amorous act that the progress of printing will eclipse: 'my whole being is filled with the desire for, and the love of, writing'.⁶⁰ Associated in modern life with the mechanical motions of Bartleby, whose preference not to obey the commands of a Wall Street lawyer leads to the paradoxical freedom of mere being before a prison wall, copying emerged as both a negation of subjective authorship and a trending topic during the recent surge of self-conscious conceptualism in poetry. In the work of Caroline Bergvall with English translations of the first tercet of Dante's *Inferno* in 'Via: 48 Dante variations', or more recently in Aaron Kunin's paraphrase of George Herbert's 'Love [III]', we see an admission of humility accompanied by a longing for a connection with the actual *writing* of one's predecessors, its literal incorporation.[61] Bergvall describes her labours as scrivener of Dante's translators in the British Library: 'My task was mostly and rather simply, or so it seemed at first, to copy each first tercet as it appeared in each published version of the *Inferno*. To copy it accurately ... To reproduce each translative gesture. To add my voice to this chorus, to this recitation, only by way of this task. Making copy explicit as an act of copy.'[62] In contradistinction to the aloof and slapstick procedures of Kenneth Goldsmith's 'uncreative writing', which end up reifying notions of originality and creativity by way of negation, Bergvall emphasises a forging of historical relations that the somatic act of copying enables. By working with translations of Dante, Bergvall's piece admits to the mediated quality of her experience of the *Commedia*, and heeds its collective production and metamorphosis over time. Yet the humbling manual labour involved in copying and the work's eventual articulation as voiced performance also makes the material one's (s)kin in a way that transcends (or subtends) discursivity. 'There are ways of acknowledging influence and models, by ingestion, by assimilation, by one's total absorption in the material. To come to an understanding of it by standing it in it, by becoming it. Very gradually, this transforms a shoe into a foot, extends copyism into writing, and perhaps writing into being.'[63] The shoe assumed as externality metamorphoses into a foot which can move one, in accordance with the poem's own scansion.

Adnan's practice, predating these phenomena by several decades yet overlooked by Goldsmith's accounts of the life and reputed death of cross-media poetry, opens up a series of related but more complex questions of cultural belonging.[64] What does it mean to assume somatically a language from which one has been shut out in the lettered sense? Adnan's transcription practice exposes cultural belonging as an active passion. She has remarked that the continuum between drawing and painting, and emphasis on the word, unites all of Asian culture, claiming that 'Writing is seen as the most magical of arts, and the most important of religious arts, because it brings you closer to the Quran, and therefore to the direct word of God . . . The prestige of the written word unites all of Asia.'[65] Her leporellos extend an Arabic literary tradition and revolution at once, marrying it with the matrix and gestural energy of an East Asian tradition, and translating it consciously into foreign cultural contexts. Appreciating 'the flow, the apparent lack of boundaries, the river image of these long unfolding papers' used in Chinese and Japanese literary traditions,[66] Adnan describes the leporello as a musical score on which the mind never rests as it scans, and as a visual translation that transports, as the original Greek term suggests. The modular form of the accordion book makes for flexible readings whose permutations are infinite due to the variety of juxtapositions enabled by folds. Moreover, modulating lines of letters or images allow each reader to translate the writing into their own 'inner language, or languages, into that which we call the understanding'.[67] This inner language seems to be a way of indexing consciousness, a site into which, as Adnan has elsewhere described it, inner and outer world, subject and object 'melt'.[68] This language courses below the workings of 'national' languages to transform what we mean by understanding itself. In translating the comprehension of written texts through affinity into figurative and abstract signs, Adnan hopes to present 'a vision of reality as a permanently transformed score meant to remain obscure as such but "heard" or "seen" through the translatorial powers of our minds'.[69] This neologism – translatorial – provides a useful inroad into understanding the transfiguration of the illuminated image as it moves across varieties of sensory experience.

How are we to understand the aesthetic and political work done by these elusive artefacts? In her 2017 study of *Art & Language*, Christiane Treichl characterises the artists of the Hurufiyya movement of modernising Islamic calligraphy as enacting an evacuation of meaning: 'The characters become pure signs, and temporarily emptied of their referential meaning, they become available for new meanings.'[70] These formal operations understood in post-structuralist key must be read in concert with Iftikhar Dadi's politically saturated analysis of the 'heroic' phase of 'calligraphic modernism', which developed in the decades following decolonisation in Asia and Africa (1955–75). Dadi points out that artists of former colonies were under intense national pressure 'to produce nothing less than the development of a new cultural language that would exploit the opening provided by decolonization'.[71] While acknowledging the importance of national uplift to the development of these styles, Dadi stresses above all how these works exceed the nation-building project as diasporic artists exposed to canonical and contemporary Western artworks launched new international affiliations and constellating identities. Dadi also traces, of necessity, the emptying out of the promise of decolonisation as freedom in the face of a neocolonial globalisation process. Yet he sees in works of calligraphic modernism a resistance to the media spectacle that determines contemporary occidental imaginations of Islamic culture, invoking Dipesh Chakrabarty in an assertion that they help us conceive 'a global Muslim ethics and community that is predicated upon the persistence of a textuality that is not fully translatable within western enlightenment ideals', offering up 'a theoretical model with the potential to extend the critical goal of "provincializing Europe"'. Works of calligraphic modernism testify, in Dadi's analysis, to the fact that *a threat of opacity* to the western-universal norm exists, aesthetically and ethically'.[72]

In Adnan's literal handling, opacity makes for a durational experience of understanding that surpasses blunt blockage or threat; for it can also be a beckoning. In this visual ecology the image is exposed as an entity encompassing 'thickness' – consisting in fact of transit between layers, so that we can read the veil or the screen as enrichment and draw. As Adnan clarifies in conversation with Lisa Robertson, 'Images . . . are moving things. They come, they go, they disappear, they approach, they recede, and they are not even visual – ultimately they are pure feeling. They're like something that calls you through a fog or a cloud.'[73] A leporello of highly defamiliarising script like Adnan's *Al-Sayyab, Mother and Lost Daughter*, then, exists not only as a private conversation between Arab poets across the chasm of linguistic difference, but as a first translation of this exiled Iraqi poet – in the more literal, Poundian mode of 'traduction'. It is more appealing, in the sense of address, than a so-called 'literal' translation naively claiming to convey the immanent and instantaneous authority of the original text – while being truer to the distressed conditions that attend any such cross-cultural transmission.[74]

Adnan ultimately saw fit to transmute the fugitive gestures of her 'calligraffiti' into poetry appearing under the sign of the French and English languages as well. She began her masterwork *L'apocalypse arabe* (1980; Fig. 1.4) in Beirut, two months before the Lebanese Civil War, as 'an abstract poem on the sun', and composed its fifty-nine poems – one for each of the fifty-nine days of the siege of the Tall al-Za'tar refugee camp for Palestinians by the Christian Lebanese Front – over the course of a year through direct experience. Adnan translated *The Arab Apocalypse* herself into English, at first spontaneously, in performance, reportedly without being aware that

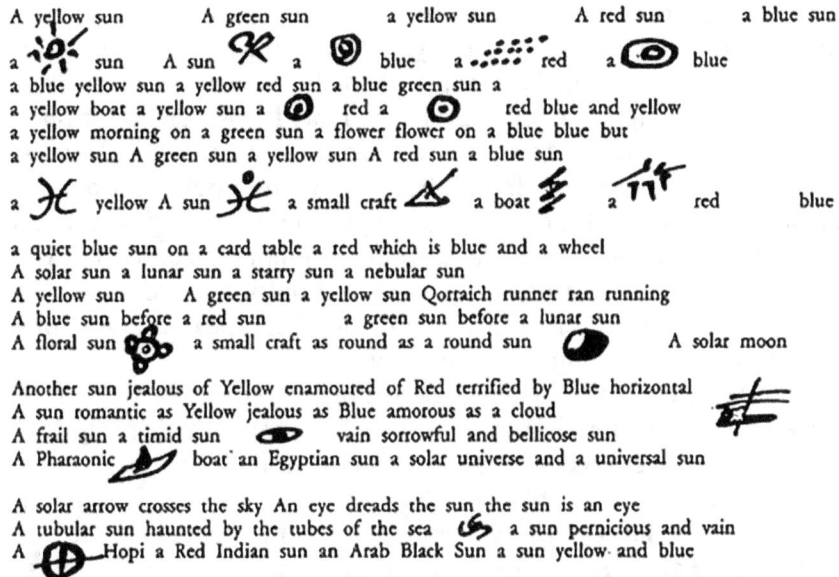

Figure 1.4 Etel Adnan, opening of Poem I of *The Arab Apocalypse* (Sausalito, CA: Post-Apollo Press, 2006), p. 7.

she was doing so, and then formally for Simone Fattal's Post-Apollo Press (1989).[75] It was arguably the urgency of these circumstances of composition that led Adnan to infiltrate the text(s) with a more 'immediate' and universal idiom, that of the semi-apprehensible glyph – each example of which appears to be redrafted with each new edition. The *Apocalypse* is thus in part supralinguistic. This epic work confounds the genres of Adnan's production as codified by criticism: in an interview with Claudia Rushkowsky, she defines it against disciplines, in terms of literal and metaphysical vision: '*The Arab Apocalypse* is not philosophy, it's not traditional poetry: it's really an apocalyptic vision.'[76] Deploying the hegemonic idioms of her education at large, Adnan braids through these languages signs inspired by Egyptian hieroglyphs, Chinese characters, Semitic scripts, glyphs of indigenous peoples of the Americas, proliferating punctuation marks, the signs of symbolic logic and the sheer gesture of action painting, channelling her decades-long practice in abstraction. As gestures, these signs hold out the dream of transparency while in almost every case thwarting definitive decryption. Sonja Mejcher-Atassi reads them merely as emphasising 'the visual aspect of writing', not bringing anything other to the written text; Caroline Seymour-Jorn describes them apprehensively as 'enigmatic symbols';

Aditi Machado reads them as idiosyncratically intelligible, and helpfully points out how much the glyphs change in form from edition to edition, concluding that they 'cannot be "fixed" in the way of linguistic paradigms' and must be recreated.[77] When questioned, Adnan responds that 'the signs are my excess of emotions. I cannot say more. I wrote by hand, and, here and there, I put a word, and I made instinctively a little drawing, a sign.'[78] I would propose that the painted signs invoke ancient and future attempts at codifying experience while falling strategically short of conforming to any single linguistic system or worldview, holding out the hope of transnational communication, and indeed community.

In a foreword to the poem's 2006 English reissue, Jalal Toufic, a writer, film theorist and artist born to a Palestinian mother and Iraqi father who has resided at length in Beirut, identifies *The Arab Apocalypse* as an 'Arab book of poetry in part because it was withdrawn, occulted by the surpassing disasters that have affected the Arab world', and asserts that Adnan's graphic signs are partial translations – possessing the power to 'jolt' the substantial fraction of the adult Arab population that is illiterate, 'for whom Arabic is as illegible as English and French', to read.[79] Finally translated into Arabic in 1990 by Chawqi Abdel-Amir, the book had long remained out of print until its 2006 English-language 'resurrection' amidst the violence of the Second Gulf War: an act that occupies a rich place in Toufic's own oeuvre, following what he calls a post-disaster 'withdrawal of tradition'.[80] Making a bold claim for *L'apocalypse arabe/The Arab Apocalypse* as 'one of the twentieth century's major Arabic books of poetry' notwithstanding its non-Arabic languages of composition, Toufic simultaneously stresses the 'vertiginous extension' of Arabic tradition that takes place in this work of revelation, such that the tradition 'comes to include many a bodhisattva as well as many a schizophrenic/psychotic who is not an Arab by descent and/or birthplace but who exclaims in his or her dying before dying: "Every name in history is I" (Nietzsche)'.[81]

We can extend Toufic's analysis by tracking the way this extension of tradition plays out in the decentralised and proliferating figure of the sun. In Adnan's hands, the condescending French reference to Arabs as '*les enfants du soleil*' is charged with explosive meaning as the technicoloured sun of the covers of *Souffles* that radiated blast and rebellion, and the sun that would light up Salih's depicted *House*, join forces with that of Nietzsche's Apollo, Antonin Artaud's Heliogabalus, and Judge Schreber, whose redemptive transformation from man into woman would be dictated somatically (via the anus), in an 'unfathomable' *Grundsprache*, through divine rays.[82] Like Schreber,

Adnan as queer visionary takes dictation from a grand cosmological scale in haptic fashion, without suturing over the discursive fault lines in the post-apocalyptic tradition the book cobbles together. For Toufic, himself theorist and subject of exile, to invoke tradition in the wake of a disaster requires first resurrecting it, lest one find oneself duelling with its mere counterfeit or double. In *The Withdrawal of Tradition Past a Surpassing Disaster*, which re-collects and contextualises his preface to *The Arab Apocalypse*, Toufic identifies the removal of Arabic script and Sufi culture from early twentieth-century Turkey as one of the most exemplary cases of the withdrawal of tradition, and one that has largely gone unhonoured.[83] Tapping into this historical drama of her late-Ottoman childhood, Adnan's work with unauthorised languages surely resurrects, rather than appropriating them; and according to Toufic's logic, her book itself, being occulted by the disaster about which it writes, becomes part of Arab tradition by virtue of this withdrawal, thereby demanding resurrection.

In the face of neonationalisms such as those stoked in a 2005 Beirut – Toufic's otherwise highly allusive foreword explicitly cites the '100% Lebanese' banners that attended demonstrations following the assassination of former prime minister Rafîk al Harîrî – Adnan's trans- or intra-national calligraphy, paralleling her performative descriptions of a technicoloured, multi-raced sun, implicitly ridicules anyone who would plant this yellow dwarf like a flag. We witness in Poem XII, for instance, the sun invoked in the Latin alphabet evolving, between arrows, from a simple round mimetic form to the precursor of its representation as Chinese characters: 日 (the standard account of this evolution draws a progression similar to this basic one: ○ → 日 → 日), before floating both carnally and unbridledly 'like a tattoo' over a tree on fire.[84] As soon as the poem's first person plants the sun in terrainless sky, we see Adnan's calligraphic representation take off in favour of quivering motion forward that emanates from the belly of women, and veers towards the counterlinear tear (Fig. 1.5).

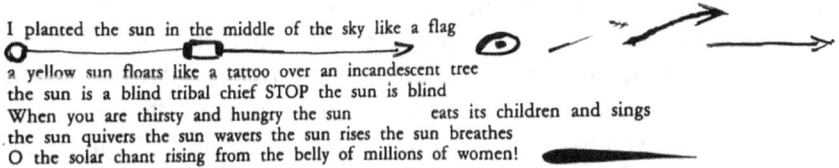

Figure 1.5 Etel Adnan, from Poem XII of *The Arab Apocalypse* (Sausalito, CA: Post-Apollo Press, 2006), p. 30.

Musing on why she used the glyphs in an interview, Adnan suggests, 'Maybe it is because I see these apocalypses ... because my first thought is always explosive. It is not cumulative.'[85] Explosion becomes wedded to painting/drawing as visual transcription, resisting the aggregation of the analytically crafted sentence and accentuating the brutality of experience. 'Yes, light is also terror, the ten thousand suns of Hiroshima,' Adnan admitted in her 1973 contribution to *Intégral*, stressing its transmission through explosives increasingly more deadly and capable of transnational reach; but she insisted on the capacity of artists from North Africa and the Arab East to wrest figurative lightness of it as well, at least ephemerally: 'If, in the end, it must be our catastrophe, for the moment may it also be our happiness.'[86]

Against the aggressive forward velocity of violence apprehended through *The Arab Apocalypse*'s images and signs, we often encounter the word STOP in all caps. Adnan's epic is full of radios, telephones and computers that transmit the sun and sea's apocalyptic messages, and it cites the same technology that inspired Marinetti and comrades into the forging of a wireless imagination: the telegraph, which became not only convenient but fundamental to imperial conquest and management, and the waging of world war.[87] The convention 'STOP' used to end sentences is deployed sporadically as jolt to substitute for standard punctuation, thereby granting the text a simultaneous immediacy and the sense of being transmitted from afar, across the subterranean and subaqueous cables. In our interview, Adnan stressed that this work enabled her own spontaneous, almost unthinking translation into English because it was composed with a basic syntax, antithetical to the 'analytic' quality of French language and literature. It thus falls curiously well into the Futurist call for 'destruction of syntax' (avoiding adjectives, abolishing adverbs and conjunctions, using infinitive verbs, towards production of a continuous image flow unsubordinated to any I) in favor of a more immediate and globally oriented idiom: 'STOP THE VERB'S CREATION STOP' (43).[88] Ultimately, though, the STOP is resolutely anti-Futurist in the imperialist and positivistic sense. It is a cry to halt that jolts the reader out of any complacent comportment rightward: a clamorous demand in an unceasing apocalyptic present tense. In a footnote to another essay, Toufic laments that with the contemporary technologies available to modern journalism, 'gone is the resonant *displacement* of the *stop* from the horrified reaction to an atrocity to the standard punctuation of the telegraphic medium'.[89]

When pressed about what she meant by invoking a 'spherical mental world' in 'To Write in a Foreign Language', Adnan responded by refuting the notion of one-dimensional ethnic identities through reference to the globe and to the radio: 'We all live in a spherical world where things come to us. Every one of us is a radio transmitter that broadcasts and receives.'[90] Adnan implicitly cites the theories of fellow queer Bay Area poet Jack Spicer, for whom poets were radios taking dictation from the Outside.[91] The metaphor of dictation has a history in the avant-garde: Marinetti's 'Technical Manifesto of Futurist Literature' was itself, the Futurist claimed, the result of dictation (from a plane's propeller).[92]

If this 'language-circuit' we rely upon has burned in *The Arab Apocalypse* by force of its destructive suns, what might bring us back together would be the manipulation of a dethroned language by poetherds, its unchaining from the tree of evil that appears to be represented in the right margin of the page in Figure 1.6. The painted glyph below may stand, alternately, for the ancient wisdom of the 'alphabet originated in Ugarit' (43) that accompanies Baudelaire's entrance at the beginning of this poem: for the sign also bears some resemblance to the Ugaritic 's', thereby forcing us to read backwards to ponder whether the forward-moving signs that began appearing in Poem II and at the top of page 43 were indeed arrows propelled forward into an apocalyptic future, or inverted letters of the Ugaritic alphabet compelling us back – or both, in a Benjaminian evocation of the *Angelus Novus* by Paul Klee, one of Adnan's most cherished influences.

Adnan's leporellos have become increasingly exhibited and sought after by galleries as she rises to the status of a nonagenarian artworld star; yet the forms of circulation and viewership that dominate the visual art market threaten to reify or reduce those that function as texts to mere aesthetic marks. Those who have been reading Adnan's politically saturated writing for decades will long for the resonance between her seemingly distinct oeuvres to be elucidated. For while Adnan may have enjoyed relative freedom of movement

sun knower of men the sun is a verb carried by our fingers
sun: herds of poets manifesting the dethroned power of words

BIG PHOSPHORESCENT RINGS CHAIN LANGUAGE TO THE TREE OF EVIL

a yellow sun   a blue sun   a black sun   the language-circuit has burned   STOP

Figure 1.6 Etel Adnan, from Poem XXIV of *The Arab Apocalypse* (Sausalito, CA: Post-Apollo Press, 2006), p. 43.

in recent decades, the political geography of her upbringing remains in violent flux: at the time of writing, the Syrian civil war rages on under the authoritarian Assad dynasty, and Lebanon, host to 1.5 million Syrian refugees, remains on the front lines of one of the largest humanitarian crises of our time; 3.5 million refugees have sought shelter in Turkey, and Greece hosts tens of thousands of asylum seekers in overcrowded camps amidst the aftereffects of a government debt crisis. Against this backdrop, we are pressed to read Adnan's works of writing that verges on drawing beyond, or through, their entrancing or enthralling power to ascertain how they help us remap political belonging.

Adnan's bold deployment of so many languages imposed, elected, lost, and imagined – a language use I have called 'unauthorised' – resonates with the act of 'otherwise belonging', to borrow a term from Ashon Crawley's recent study/manifesto, *Blackpentecostal Breath* (2016). Crawley bases his recasting of socio-political possibility on the aesthetic praxis of the multiracial, multiclass, transnational Christian sect of Pentecostalism, whose hallmark ecstasis was that of speaking (and writing) in tongues – a practice whose performances prompted debates over whether the mysterious language that resulted was glossolalia (nondiscursive and heavenly language) or xenoglossia (natural language that the speakers had not learned). Crawley also looks to the cryptic script at the heart of the so-called Ben Ali Diary (an Arabic manuscript by an African Muslim jurisprudist enslaved in the antebellum US South) as translinguistic matter that disrupts constructs of subjectivity and citizenship as coherent and stable.[93] He refers to such wayward occupations of language as 'centrifugitive': performative acts through which submerged 'otherwise possibilities' resurface under conditions of radical sociality, disrupting reigning configurations of power.[94] *The Arab Apocalypse* ultimately stages a quasi-Pentecostal situation in which 'this tongue smoking like roast-lamb will disappear/make tomorrow's men speak in signs collectively', even as (in the next line) 'They threw the Arabic language to the garbage' and it necessitated resurrection by another species: 'toads took it up'. The act of reading Adnan induces one into the channels of knowledges occulted by provincial political self-interest or the will to spiritual monoliths – and itself promises to become a means of generating this new collective.

Adnan's 'drawn' writings constitute experiments in attachment that are not limited to nativist representation. They compose homages to 'native' language that is imperfectly known, forging solidarity with Arab authors and other colonised peoples forced into various forms of exile, including indigenous peoples of the Americas.[95] In duration – under reading conditions that are not easily enabled by art exhibitions – they performatively alter the act of reading as well, asking us to absorb the imperfectly legible and to seek meaning in expressive forms that transgress the limitations of what we understand to be national languages. Adnan's work ultimately permits us to apprehend the effects of statelessness across generations in terms that expose the holes in political definitions of citizenship, in material gestures that bespeak liberation from political constrictions or denial, however fleeting and rarefied. Across a textual field of mutual defamiliarisation, Adnan's signs herald unsanctioned, intimate collectivities.[96] Her art thereby offers powerful rejoinders to overweening forces of dispossession that normally determine the discourse surrounding the refugee. In this key, we can reinterpret her apologia for not learning Arabic as an active political deportment:

> I did not take time out of everyday life to consecrate all my efforts to acquire Arabic as a full language. When the sun is strong and the sea is blue I can't close my windows and go in and 'study' anything. I am a person of the perpetual present. So I stayed 'outside'.[97]

For Adnan, commitment to daily life comes at the cost of being literate in her 'native' language, yet keeps her doubly 'outside' – both outside culture in the mastered sense, and fully integrated into the immediate landscape. Compare this commitment with that of Édouard Glissant's 'man of the present':

> he claims, protects and perhaps perpetuates the present [*l'actuel*], despite the distances, the sheathings, which exclude him, plunge him into totality. In totality dreamed, where the outline of the landscape and the threatened freshness of its eternal tomorrow shiver together. In totality lived, where opacity opens little by little and sharing is established.[98]

The man of the present stands equally excluded, yet by virtue of this exclusion he is immersed in totality, depicted as a future-oriented landscape. That opacity becomes the medium towards this moment-by-moment process of novel belonging harmonises with the whole of Adnan's body of work. Opacity, in this scenario, participation through a screen or veil, simultaneously preserves the mystery of experience in a way that is not mere obfuscation or orientalisation. For in this conception, 'Some things are not meant to be clear; obscurity is their clarity. Obscurity is as rich as luminosity.' Rather than lack of light, obscurity is comprehended by the painter as 'a different manifestation of light'.[99]

Adnan's commitment to the present tense ultimately forges a new political comportment, and a novel definition of citizenship. 'Time is my country, fog is my land,' she writes in the 2012 *Sea and Fog*.[100] Metamorphic, transubstantial, a 'vertical ocean',[101] Adnan's fog as experienced from the Bay Area of her political and aesthetic rebirth and beyond discloses a geopolitical utopia captured in her painted writing. To live such a landscape fully was to deny herself full entry into the Arab lettered canon, but did not preclude her from painting her own experience of it into Arabic, as in *Rihla ila Jabal Tamalpais* (*Journey to Mount Tamalpais*, 2008; Fig. 1.1). For an inviolate present determined by readers' engagement and attention, the opacity of these painted languages opens a shifting semiotic field of solidarity, enabling a political deportment of mutual confoundment, and of belonging despite.

Notes

1. See Adnan, 'To Write in a Foreign Language'. For useful detailed biographical notes on Adnan, see Suhair Majaj and Amireh Amal, *Etel Adnan: Critical Essays on the Arab-American Writer and Artist*, pp. 15–24, and Wilson-Goldie, *Etel Adnan*. In Tillman and Adnan, 'Etel Adnan: Children of the Sun,' we learn that Assaf Kadri first married a woman from Damascus, with whom he had three children; Adnan hypothesises that he found her mother, a beautiful yet destitute woman of sixteen (twenty years his junior), 'in the street' of Smyrna during World War I, when he was its governor—and that she might have been reduced to prostitution had she not married him. It is not clear when Adnan's mother learned about Kadri's earlier wife and children.

    This essay would not have been possible without the generous time and conversation of Etel Adnan and Simone Fattal. I am also greatly indebted to those who read or heard versions of the piece and provided commentary, in particular Rebecca Walkowitz at Rutgers, Ghenwa Hayek at the University of Chicago, and at Stanford, Alexander Key, Omnia El Shakry, Adrien Zakar and Aamer Ibraheem.

2. This reference to Arab students as '*les indigenes*' hails from an interview that I conducted with Adnan in her Paris home on 23 and 24 September 2017, a lightly edited videorecording of which is published at her new author page at PennSound, the University of Pennsylvania's audiovisual archive of contemporary experimental poetry: <http://writing.upenn.edu/pennsound/x/Adnan.php> (last accessed 17 June 2019).

3. This literalised metaphor adds burdensome new meaning to Frantz Fanon's statement that 'To speak means to be in a position to use a certain syntax, to grasp the morphology of this or that language, but it means above all to assume a culture, to support the weight of a civilization.' See Fanon, *Black Skin, White Masks*, p. 8, <http://pi.lib.uchicago.edu/1001/cat/bib/11185364> (last accessed 17 June 2019; pp. 17–18 in French edition).
4. Interview with Jennifer Scappettone, Paris, 23 and 24 September 2017.
5. I use this term as the nearest English, and thus relatively accessible, equivalent to the term 'al-Mashriq', which is Adnan's preferred term for the region commonly referred to as the Middle East. In both its Italian (*Levante*) and Arabic (ٱلْمَشْرِق) permutations, it refers to a 'land where the sun rises'. Says Adnan, '"Mashriq" means "the place where the sun rises"; it also means the rays of light . . . historically, the Mashriq is the Eastern Arab world. So we can say "the Mashriq and Iran". Arabs themselves say "the Mashriq", but also make the mistake of saying "the Middle East", which is a name that comes from Britain calling it "halfway down the spice route to the Indies". It's a colonial notion.' See Adnan and ibn Khalīfah Āl Thānī, *Etel Adnan in All Her Dimensions*, p. 31.
6. Adnan, 'To Write in a Foreign Language'.
7. See Yildiz, *Beyond the Mother Tongue*, particularly for the German-language tradition as conceived by Herder, Humboldt and Schleiermacher. Yildiz offers a powerful revisitation and revision of Anderson, *Imagined Communities*. The notion of the mother tongue reaches back much further in history than to the romanticism at the basis of Yildiz's account – one need only cite the early recourse to the trope of the mother tongue by which Dante justifies the use of the vernacular in Alighieri, *De Vulgari Eloquentia*. The emotional attachment to the nursing tongue argued for by Dante is inadequately registered in *Beyond the Mother Tongue*, which dismisses the medieval term *lingua materna* as a term used to refer to 'lay peoples' vernaculars'. See Yildiz, p. 10. Braidotti argues that Lacanian psychoanalysis teaches us that there is no mother tongue, 'that all tongues carry the name of the father and are stamped by its register'. She moreover gleans from psychoanalysis 'the irreparable loss of a sense of steady origin, which accompanies the acquisition of language—any language'. See Braidotti, *Nomadic Subjects*, p. 42.
8. Adnan calls Beirut 'a child of WWII': 'In 1920 we had refugees from Armenia. WWII brought foreign armies, not bloodshed. Beirut profited, because when armies are around, there's money.' Tillman and Adnan, 'Etel Adnan: Children of the Sun'.
9. It also enables us to reconceive of diaspora without recourse to flattening accusations of assimilation or cosmopolitanism, to begin answering Yogita Goyal's bid in 'We Need New Diasporas'.

10. Adnan explains that by the time she was sixteen, Beirut became a boom town due to the Second World War, and offices multiplied; the French needed help, inflation was on the rise, and it became acceptable that girls find jobs as secretaries. Adnan took an exciting and politically intense job at the French Information Bureau. See Adnan, 'Growing Up to Be a Woman Writer in Lebanon (1986)', pp. 14–15.
11. See also my entry for xenoglossia in Feinsod et al., *The Princeton Encyclopedia of Poetry and Poetics*. By 'acritical ethnocentrism' I mean to distinguish this habit from forms of ethnocentrism that were mobilised towards political progressivism in the twentieth century, by citing Ernesto De Martino's concept of 'critical ethnocentrism'. For a gloss, see Saunders, '"Critical Ethnocentrism" and the Ethnology of Ernesto De Martino'.
12. See *Acts of the Apostles* 2:1–13, and Richet, 'Xenoglossie ou l'écriture automatique en langues étrangères'. Richet is better known for having won the Nobel Prize for his research into anaphylaxis.
13. Here I use minor in the sense developed in Deleuze and Guattari's analysis of the deterritorialisation of a major language deployed from a marginal position. See Deleuze and Guattari, *Kafka: Toward a Minor Literature*. I am interested in a host of propositions staked out by this seminal work, while being aware of its limits. For the purposes of this essay, I am particularly interested in the assertion that minor literature has no subjects, but only '*collective assemblages of enunciation*' (italics in original, p. 18). The assumption of the collective voice is distressed in this case both by Adnan's status as a queer woman writer and her status as perpetual outsider. To read her is to presume the critiques of subalternisation present in Said, *Culture and Imperialism*, who stresses the need for a 'contrapuntal' reading of imperialism and resistance to it as interrelated processes (p. 79), and in Spivak, *A Critique of Postcolonial Reason*, who underscores the constitutive place of gender in constituting the subject of language and of power. (See also, for example, the legacy of her 1988 essay registered in Spivak, *Can the Subaltern Speak?*). In interpreting Adnan's rigorously interdisciplinary, cross-media, at times 'unlettered' and bohemian body of work, I also find helpful Walter Mignolo's assertion that in 'posttraditional social orders' the defense of tradition must be combated constantly 'at all levels, including the cultures of scholarship and the parochial defense of disciplinarity, even under new paradigms'. See Mignolo, *Local Histories/Global Designs*, p. 203.
14. Villa, 'Cy Twombly: Talento bianco', p. 36. Translation mine.
15. Melehi, 'Questionnaire'.
16. Melehi's quote appears in Melehi, 'Questionnaire', p. 62: 'mobilité et vibration restent les seules intrigues pour le spectateur où se manifestent un message et une éducation visuels. C'est un art qui ne fait pas appel dans sa communication à une culture littéraire ou historique.' See

Nashashibi, *Forces of Change*, p. 36. See also Khatibi, 'A Note on the Calligraphic Sign'.
17. Adnan, 'To Write in a Foreign Language'. Both Ammiel Alcalay and Cole Swensen have built on Adnan's intimations that she turned to painting as a rejection of her French linguistic indoctrination. See their contributions to Donovan and Shimoda, *To Look at the Sea Is to Become What One Is*.
18. See Adnan and ibn Khalīfah Āl Thānī, *Etel Adnan in All Her Dimensions*, p. 73.
19. Adnan's painterly writing helps us continue the work of revisiting a long history of multilingualism stamped out by the theorisation of monolingualism, national languages and the mother tongue emanating from eighteenth-century Europe – a phenomenon well documented by Yildiz in *Beyond the Mother Tongue*.
20. Adnan, 'To Write in a Foreign Language'.
21. Glissant, *Le Discours antillais*, p. 11; Glissant, *Caribbean Discourse*, p. 1.
22. Adnan, 'To Write in a Foreign Language'.
23. Kurjaković and Adnan, 'Etel Adnan: Every One of Us Is a Radio Transmitter', p. 91.
24. Tillman and Adnan, 'Etel Adnan: Children of the Sun'. The pun between sun and son recurs throughout her work.
25. Adnan invokes the first chapter of Fanon's 1952 *Peau noire, masques blancs*. She uses the term 'international' to refer to languages like English in scare quotes within 'To Write in a Foreign Language'.
26. Adnan, 'To Write in a Foreign Language'.
27. Adnan and ibn Khalīfah Āl Thānī, *Etel Adnan in All Her Dimensions*, p. 42.
28. Adnan, 'To Write in a Foreign Language'.
29. Adnan, 'Growing Up to Be a Woman Writer in Lebanon (1986),' pp. 8–9.
30. Adnan, 'To Write in a Foreign Language'.
31. Adnan, 'Growing Up to Be a Woman Writer in Lebanon (1986),' pp. 17–18.
32. Adnan's narrative is consistent throughout her written work and interviews, but this statement appears recently in Adnan and ibn Khalīfah Āl Thānī, *Etel Adnan in All Her Dimensions*, p. 40.
33. Adnan, 'The Enemy's Testament'.
34. Adnan recalls learning about sexual difference through innocent play with this boy. See Etel Adnan, 'Growing Up to Be a Woman Writer in Lebanon (1986),' p. 6.
35. See Adnan, 'To Write in a Foreign Language'.
36. Adnan, 'To Write in a Foreign Language'.
37. 'Yusuf integrated me into Arabic poetry. Before even reading a line. It changed my life.' Adnan and ibn Khalīfah Āl Thānī, *Etel Adnan*

38. Al-Khal's translation from the English was published as *Khams Hawas Li Mouten Wahed*. See also Wilson-Goldie, *Etel Adnan*, p. 93. Wilson-Goldie is likely citing al-Musawi, 'The Republic of Letters: Arab Modernity?'.
39. Adnan, 'On Small Magazines'. Issandr El Amrani notes that the journal's trademark cover (which was designed by Mohammed Melehi), 'emblazoned with an intense black sun, radiated rebellion'; see his 'In the Beginning There Was *Souffles*: Reconsidering Morocco's Most Radical Literary Quarterly'. See also Laâbi, 'La culture nationale, donée et exigence historique', p. 5.
40. On the strangeness of Adnan's name, see Fattal, 'A Few Years in Journalism'. On the adoption of the family surname, see Wilson-Goldie, *Etel Adnan*, p. 50.
41. I am indebted to my Stanford colleague Alexander Key for this connection. See the entry for Adnan in Gibb, *The Encyclopaedia of Islam*.
42. She continues, 'The circulation of the blood. The blood of cities. The blood of a territory.' In Obrist, *Mapping It Out: An Alternative Atlas of Contemporary Cartographies*, p. 182.
43. Adnan and ibn Khalīfah Āl Thānī, *Etel Adnan in All Her Dimensions*, p. 30.
44. For this quote and narration of her discovery see Adnan, 'The Unfolding of an Artist's Book', p. 12, p. 20. Simone Fattal's essay 'On Perception: Etel Adnan's Visual Art,' a pioneering and intimate contribution to the expanding literature on the topic, stresses that 'these books are [Adnan's] greatest contribution to the contemporary visual arts'. See Simone Fattal, 'On Perception: Etel Adnan's Visual Art', in *Etel Adnan: Critical Essays on the Arab-American Writer and Artist*, ed. Lisa Suhair Majaj and Amal Amireh (Jefferson, NC: McFarland & Co., 2002), 101.
45. Al-Sayyab esteemed the writing of T. S. Eliot notwithstanding the latter's condition as 'the poet of death, feudalism, and world imperialism'. Qtd. in Colla, 'Badr Shakir Al-Sayyab, Cold War Poet', p. 257. Colla illuminates the political contradictions in this poet's oeuvre, and his eventual work with the CIA front organisation, the Congress for Cultural Freedom. Colla underscores the way al-Sayyab's 'pan-Arab ideologies could be married with blatantly pro-American positions, and do so in the name of anti-imperialism, art and modernity' (p. 259).
46. Adnan, 'Writing Mountains', p. 57.
47. See Ali, *Modern Islamic Art*, pp. 163–8.
48. Cha, *Dictee*.
49. See Khatibi, 'A Note on the Calligraphic Sign', p. 354. These ideas were fully developed in *The Wound of the Proper Name*: see Khatibi, *La Blessure Du Nom Propre*.

50. I discuss the significance of 'approachability' through LaTasha Diggs's multilingual poetry in Scappettone, 'Phrasebook Pentecosts and Daggering Lingua Francas in the Poetry of LaTasha N. Nevada-Diggs'.
51. Such acts stand in sharp contrast to the tradition outlined in Venuti, *The Translator's Invisibility*.
52. For this and all other readings of the Arabic texts I am immensely indebted to Ghenwa Hayek and Adrien Zakar. Despite repeated requests to the holding parties, I have not been provided access to the complete page spreads of the leporellos under discussion.
53. For more on the adoption of the term 'arts plastiques' or 'al-funun at-tashkiliyya' in the little magazine *Souffles* as a reference to explosives, and its relation to armed anti-colonial struggles throughout the Third World, see Clare Davies, *Decolonizing Culture*, pp. 24–6. For more on *Souffles-Anfas*, see Harrison and Villa-Ignacio, *Souffles-Anfas: A Critical Anthology from the Moroccan Journal of Culture and Politics*.
54. Al-Tayyib Salih, *Bandarshah*, p. 3. I have used my colleague Ghenwa Hayek's translation rather than that of Johnson-Davies, but provide the latter for reference. On the way colonising reading practices have distorted and undermined *Bandarshah*'s reception, see الفيصل هيفاء سعود/Haifa Saud Alfaisal, 'World Reading Strategies: Border Reading Bandarshah/«استراتيجيات القراءة العالمية: قراءة حدودية لـ بندرشاه».
55. Adnan and ibn Khalīfah Āl Thānī, *Etel Adnan in All Her Dimensions*, p. 30.
56. Teresa Villa-Ignacio reads Adnan's *There: In the Light and the Darkness of the Self and of the Other* as imagination of a 'postnationalist, post-terrorist, entirely deterritorialized planet on which national boundaries and global networks are unmade by the resurgence of natural environments. Recognising the historical finitude of the nation-state structure, *There* envisions a deterritorialised future in order to begin that deterritorialization in the present.' Villa-Ignacio, 'Apocalypse and Poethical Daring in Etel Adnan's *There*'.
57. Adnan calls the visual parts of the leporellos an 'equivalence', both response and counterpoint as opposed to illustration or analysis, and embraces the term 'Illuminations'. See Adnan, 'The Unfolding of an Artist's Book', p. 22, p. 25.
58. See Adnan, 'Light: The Ultimate Material for Art' (1973), translated from French by Teresa Villa-Ignacio, in Lennsen et al., *Modern Art in the Arab World*, pp. 355–6.
59. Adnan, 'The Unfolding of an Artist's Book', p. 25.
60. Trithemius, *In Praise of Scribes*, p. 472.
61. Kunin's *Love Three: A Study of a Poem by George Herbert* was published by Wave Books in 2019.
62. Bergvall, *Fig*, p. 65.

63. Ibid.
64. Goldsmith intones that from the 1980s forward, 'artists and writers found it more lucrative—both economically and reputation-wise—to stay in their niche' (Kenneth Goldsmith in João Bandeira and Lenora de Barros, *Poesia concreta*).
65. Adnan and ibn Khalīfah Āl Thānī, *Etel Adnan in All Her Dimensions*, p. 31.
66. Adnan, *Journey to Mount Tamalpais*, p. 32.
67. Adnan, 'The Unfolding of an Artist's Book', p. 22.
68. Robertson, 'Etel Adnan by Lisa Robertson'.
69. Adnan, 'The Unfolding of an Artist's Book', p. 24.
70. Treichl, *Art and Language*, p. 3.
71. Dadi, 'Rethinking Calligraphic Modernism', p. 98.
72. Ibid. p. 111. See also Chakrabarty, *Provincializing Europe*.
73. Robertson, 'Etel Adnan by Lisa Robertson'.
74. I have made a similar argument regarding the first 'English' translation of Ezra Pound's Fascist Italian Cantos in Scappettone, '"Più mOndo i:/ tUtti!": Traffics of Historicism in Jackson Mac Low's Contemporary Lyricism'.
75. On the performed self-translation, see my PennSound interview with Adnan at <https://media.sas.upenn.edu/app/public/watch.php?file_id=223293> (last accessed 17 June 2019).
76. Allen, 'Woman between Cultures', p. 18. Interview with Rushkowsky appears on page 52 of the same volume.
77. See Sonja Mejcher-Atassi, 'Breaking the Silence', p. 208; Seymour-Jorn, '*The Arab Apocalypse* as a Critique of Colonialism and Imperialism', p. 43; and Machado, 'On Etel Adnan's "The Arab Apocalypse"'.
78. Adnan and ibn Khalīfah Āl Thānī, *Etel Adnan in All Her Dimensions*, p. 81.
79. Toufic cites the figure of 38.7 per cent tallied in 1999 when hailing the illiterate fraction of adult Arabs. See Adnan, *The Arab Apocalypse*; Toufic's foreword has no pagination but is reproduced in *The Withdrawal of Tradition Past a Surpassing Disaster*.
80. See Toufic, *The Withdrawal of Tradition Past a Surpassing Disaster*.
81. Ibid.
82. Schreber's *Grundsprache* has been translated as basic language or as 'fundamental' language, emphasising the fundament. See Schreber, *Memoirs of My Nervous Illness*, p. 119. To enumerate the many analyses of Schreber's work here, from Freud to Deleuze and Guattari's *Anti-Oedipus*, would be superfluous. See also Tillman and Adnan, 'Etel Adnan: Children of the Sun'.
83. Toufic, *The Withdrawal of Tradition Past a Surpassing Disaster*.
84. Diagram borrowed from Sensei, 'The Japanese Writing System'.

85. Adnan and ibn Khalīfah Āl Thānī, *Etel Adnan in All Her Dimensions*, p. 81.
86. Adnan, 'Light: The Ultimate Material for Art', p. 356.
87. See for instance Hayles, *How We Think: Digital Media and Contemporary Technogenesis*.
88. Interview with Jennifer Scappettone, <https://media.sas.upenn.edu/app/public/watch.php?file_id=223293> (last accessed 17 June 2019).
89. Toufic, *The Withdrawal of Tradition Past a Surpassing Disaster*, p. 86 n.
90. Kurjaković and Adnan, 'Etel Adnan: Every One of Us Is a Radio Transmitter', p. 91.
91. See 'Dictation and "A Textbook of Poetry"', in Spicer, *The House That Jack Built: The Collected Lectures of Jack Spicer*, pp. 1–48.
92. For an analysis of Marinetti's claim in the manifesto opening, see Schnapp, 'Propeller Talk'.
93. Crawley, *Blackpentecostal Breath*, p. 201. Crawley is building on the analysis of the Arabic heterography and authorial ambiguity offered by Judy in *(Dis)Forming the American Canon: African-Arabic Slave Narratives and the Vernacular*. In my reading, xenoglossia would have been more scandalous to cultural commentators, who were unprepared to believe that Black congregants of multiple classes would find themselves able to read or speak European languages in which they lacked training.
94. Crawley, *Blackpentecostal Breath*, p. 3. Others have read the irregularities of Bilali's manuscript not as cryptic but as innovations deriving from African vernacular usage and oral transcription. See Progler, 'Ben Ali and His Arabic Diary'. Pentecostalism has evolved practices in which, in Fred Moten's terms, the personal becomes much larger, insofar as 'We're sent to one another': 'to be sent, to be transported out of yourself, it's an ecstatic experience . . . it's not an experience of interiority, it's an experience of *exteriority*, it's an *exteriorization*.' See Fitzgerald, 'An Interview with Fred Moten, Part 1'.
95. Adnan was one of the first to make the link between indigenous groups of the Americas and Palestinians in her writings, an analogy that has since become key to political struggles for sovereignty on the West Bank. See Ammiel Alcalay in *To Look at the Sea Is to Become What One Is*, 1:viii. For more on global solidarity with Palestine, see Harrison, 'Cross-Colonial Poetics'.
96. My argument thus resonates with Teresa Villa-Ignacio's ultimate conclusion that 'By . . . commemorating the future of the *you* and the *I* in its present tense, [Adnan] dares the impossibility of community into its tense present.' See Villa-Ignacio, 'Apocalypse and Poethical Daring in Etel Adnan's *There*', p. 333.
97. Adnan, 'To Write in a Foreign Language'.

98. Glissant, *Poetic Intention*, pp. 79–80. The original French text reads as follows: 'Homme du présent, pour ce qu'il revendique, protège et peut-être perpétue l'actuel et, malgré les distances, les enveloppes qui l'excluent, plonge dans la totalité. Dans la totalité rêvée, où frémissent ensemble le contour du paysage et la fraîcheur menace de son éternel demain. Dans la totalité vécue, où l'opacité s'ouvre peu à peu et le partage s'établit.' See Glissant, *L'intention Poétique: Poétique II* (Paris: Gallimard, 1997), p. 85.
99. Robertson, 'Etel Adnan by Lisa Robertson'.
100. Adnan, *Sea and Fog*.
101. Adnan and ibn Khalīfah Āl Thānī, *Etel Adnan in All Her Dimensions*, p. 50.

Chapter 2

Reading Happily with John Cage, Lyn Hejinian and Others
Alex Houen

Because things have been going so badly in the world – from climate change to the political climate – I've recently found myself reading various books on happiness in a bid to come close to it again, and also to think about what it is and can do. There's no shortage of contemporary thinking about the emotion; over recent years, it's gained burgeoning attention not only across various academic disciplines, but also more widely in the public domain. Happiness studies has become a distinct field of research, and there are also a growing number of popular 'self-help' books that exalt the emotion as the ultimate goal of 'well-being' for a person. Governments, too, have increasingly been keen to consider happiness as a social value to foster and measure: in the UK, for example, the former prime minister David Cameron invested in a national 'happiness index';[1] in Bhutan the government calibrates its nation's well-being as Gross National Happiness. There is even a *World Database of Happiness*. The feeling is thus regarded as forming a good *state* (affective and political). When it is valued as such, it's often in terms of people attaining a comfortable 'living standard' through which they can own goods and a nice house by virtue of having a well-paid job and disposable income. The boon of such a good life is also often envisioned as realising *potential* to the extent that a person can (hopefully, ideally) live happily ever after. Yet when happiness is tied to such a *telos* it can become an *end* of potentiality in the sense of terminating it; as Sara Ahmed avers, it 'becomes an exclusion of possibility, and thus a good defense against crisis, as if the decisions about the future are already made'.[2] Consequently, this vision of happy life also 'can be read as involving anaesthetics, a loss of the capacity or will to be affected by anything'.[3] Well-being effectively turns into a form of suspended animation.

Time frozen.

*

Good afternoon sky, opens its bistro of floating
scars – what sense this 'icy present', Reader?
In the early days those words felt
vital, alive as live carp in our hands,
and all hands did stand ready.
So much for year-old ice fudged
with greyer city packs, so much
for the mass, a triangle of concrete,
wound by a brown turning plastic
flow that may once have been gilded.
'It's obviously a monument', she says,
'it's good for nothing'. The crack
between 'useful' and 'necessary'
stretches twelve miles south from here.
*

Like Ahmed, Claire Colebrook reflects on how investing in the ends of happiness can lead a person to become blinkered to the world's trials and tribulations. 'The happiness tradition, from Aristotle to Martha Nussbaum, aims to subordinate knowledge to life and feeling,' she writes; 'It may well be that the motif of happiness [. . .] precludes a recognition of life's generation of malevolence.'[4] In Colebrook's view, that is particularly notable regarding climate change. By investing in happiness as *telos*, she argues, people insulate themselves against the prospect of climate apocalypse and the possibility that human life on earth will end. Even when the 'Anthropocene' era is imagined with a 'posthuman world' on the horizon, this has sometimes entailed portraying the natural world as 'one great thinking, feeling, living' and 'self-forming' organism – Colebrook offers James Cameron's film *Avatar* (2009) as a case in point.[5] The ends of human happiness are thus sublimated and projected onto the natural world as an alternative vast redeeming self.

When happiness is predicated on the exclusion of chance, contingency or potentiality it is dissociated from the intimacy it shares etymologically with what is 'haphazard' and 'happenstance' in what 'happens' (*OED*). For that reason, Ahmed concludes her book *The Promise of Happiness* (2010) by reflecting on the need to put the 'hap' back into happiness so we can refigure the dynamics and values of the emotion. Doing so, she argues, means embracing the happenstance and so 'being open to the possibility of good and bad things happening':

> If we think of happiness as a possibility that does not exhaust what is possible, if we lighten the load of happiness, then we can open things up. [. . .] We can value happiness for its precariousness, as something that comes and goes, as life does.[6]

Well, that's easier said than done. As I've argued in my monograph *Powers of Possibility* (2012), the potentials of individuals in modern society are relentlessly policed and administered – particularly in being forged as labour-power and purchasing-power, both of which inflect what people regard as being concretely possible for themselves.[7] Opening up to wider possibilities in the form of the happenstance and the precarious thus takes effort. What does such an effort look like *in practice*? Ahmed doesn't go into detail on that score, but she does give Mike Lee's film *Happy-Go-Lucky* (2008) as an exemplary artistic vision (the film features a character who maintains her happiness in the face of misfortune that befalls her).[8] It makes sense to offer such an example, for film and literature present viewers and readers respectively with worlds of possibility that also have affective and aesthetic charges. Experimental writing has been particularly effective in opening up intimacies between possibility and the happenstance, and in doing so it's also presented new forms of happiness as a practice.

*

> As I open the door no door and exit the studio, the animals' intoxication is intense: its measure clearly not defined by technical constraint. Although the water clocks operate on a roughly uniform process – the constant flow of cold water down – the parts that show the time are made to change with the seasons, to indicate variable hours. We are 48 degrees, 52 minutes, 2 seconds North, 2 degrees, 22 minutes, 27 seconds East. Every time now I feel the architecture browning to fans, zigzags, and stars of diatomaceous scum, I remember how my nursery experience was made natural co-efficient of the opiates. This joy within me has grown so strong. It's like a cloud. Cannot be scratched by the keenest knife. But my legs belong to a man on a sheet of ice. As soon as he sets foot down in the corridor, he begins to tremble. His icy awkward body, anxious lest it tip.

*

Lyn Hejinian's experimental poetic sequence *Happily* (2000) is a prime example. Preparatory notes she made for the sequence show that she was seeking to explore happiness along the lines that Ahmed later gestures towards. 'Happiness', writes Hejinian, 'erupts in *amor fati* – it is a term for the uproar in one's emotions in response to all that comes to one, good or bad.'⁹ The poem's performance of being open to fate is aimed at materialising the 'etymological link' of 'happiness' to 'happening' and 'haphazardness'.¹⁰ Connecting those things is done through the practice of experiment itself: 'By making sentences as I am – putting down sentence beginnings and sentence ends and then inserting multiple "middles" between those frames – something like "events" occur. Or eventuality (?) is implied. [. . .] Eventuality: a *possible* event.'¹¹ The lines of *Happily* are thus pieced together not to present an experience that has already taken place, but to elicit something unforeseen. The experience happens haphazardly *as an event* of writing and of reading. Happily opening up to the text means embracing *amor fati* as *amor possibilis* and so seeing the syntactical improvisations as forms of affective potential. Let's have a look at an extract:

> Context is the chance that time takes
>
> Our names tossed into the air scraped in the grass before
>   having formed any opinion leaving people to say only
>   that there was a man who happened on a cart and
>   crossed a gnarled field and there was a woman who
>   happened on a cart and crossed a gnarled field too
>
> Is happiness the name for our (involuntary) complicity with chance?¹²

In the second long line here (which runs from 'Our names' to 'field too') we, as readers, are immediately thrown into the happenstance with 'Our names' being 'tossed into the air scraped in the grass'. Does the speaker's 'Our' extend to us readers? How is it possible for the names to be airborne while simultaneously scraping the ground? That makes sense, though, in so far as the line presents the very meaning and identity of the names as being 'up in the air', in suspense, even though they are rooted in a particular context that includes the line's peculiar syntax and its proximity to the adjacent lines. The preceding line points us to the importance of the contextual as 'the chance that time takes'; the sense of a word is always partly determined by the particular context in which it happens to be – for example, look at how 'who' and 'too' colour each other by rhyming in the second line above – such that its meaning and effect take place as a singular situated event each time and so remain open to chance.

For Hejinian, it's not just words that are subject to context; so are people. In her poetic sequence *My Life* (1980, 1987) she asserts as much with charming concision: 'A person is a bit of space that has gotten itself in moments.'[13] That's to say, being a person is a matter of getting yourself into situations and of happening on yourself (getting an insight into yourself) as a consequence. So, in the second line of the extract above we can read it as saying that the 'man' and 'woman' chanced upon a 'cart' in the particular 'gnarled field' they got themselves into, and 'happened' on themselves in the process. And if we're happy as persons to happen on the happenstance in that way, then, yes, we can also say with the poem that happiness does name our 'complicity with chance' – and, yes, that complicity is partly 'involuntary' because the situations in which we find ourselves, often by chance, are indeed irreducible to our own will.

Elsewhere, in her essay 'The Person and Description', Hejinian reflects on how grasping possibilities within given situations requires a certain *practice*:

> sense of being, of selfhood, can only be reached *after* one is in place and surrounded by possibilities. That comes first: the perceiving of something, not in parts but whole, as a situation and with a projection of possibilities. The recognition of those possibilities follows and constitutes one's first exercise of possibility, and on that depends one's realization that oneself is possible. It is in the exercise of *that* possibility that one inescapably acknowledges others, which have in fact already been admitted when and as one initially perceived something. And the exercise of possibilities (including that of consciousness) amid conditions and occasions constitutes a person.[14]

I've already argued that Ahmed's injunction to think of happiness on the basis of opening up to possibility requires practice, and that is exactly what's at stake in Hejinian's emphasis here on working out your 'recognition' of situated possibilities; exercising your ability to admit them is to exercise your own potential as a person. *Happily* is intended to enable just that when we read its lines and remain open to its sequence of textual possibilities.

*

> My frozen legs, my morbid lively spume,
> are so much cover for a pulsing core
> of exaltation, a sort of battery.
> Southing is our desire. We who have taken
> solid, liquid, boiled, unboiled,
> and gaseous shapes of happiness heave

> the frustules we have made ourselves
> by our flagella. But our constructions rank north,
> *Existenzminimum*, so we cook
> in summer, freeze in winter,
> serve as storage. We are drifting
> slowly. Slowly with soundings
> when we get the chance we are so in fee
> to our ears for fathoms, minutes, seconds.
> *

To the extent that Hejinian explores textual possibility to develop powers of personhood, her writing can be characterised as a form of what I've called literary 'potentialism'. As I've argued elsewhere, potentialism doesn't designate a particular literary style or movement; rather, it's a concept of literary or performance practice that draws together various senses of the word 'potential': 1) the possible as opposed to actual; 2) possessing power (potency); 3) a quantity of energy or force; 4) the 'potential' or 'subjunctive' mood. Potentialist writing presents formal and generic experiments with literary possibilities (that can include the utopic or hypothetical) that are aimed at acting constructively as an affective force on readers' capacities (potentials) for thinking and feeling.[15] As the possibilities it presents require a reader to respond imaginatively, it also encourages what I have called a capacity for 'practical imagination', by which a person can respond to particular texts or situations in terms of a 'potentiality principle'.[16] By fostering abilities to admit chance and contingency into one's experience, potentialism like Hejinian's encourages readers not to limit their readings with particular interpretive ends or goals in mind.

Remaining happily open to possibility contrasts with the blinkered well-being that Ahmed and Colebrook depict, and it also differs from the 'paranoid reading' approach that Eve Kosofsky Sedgwick criticises. There's a curious homology between paranoia and *telos*-oriented happiness (which is why investment in one might easily switch to the other): while such happiness covets a stable structure of agency for future fortune, paranoia entails seeing things as symptoms of some destabilising agential structure that's unfortunately already in place. As Sedgwick argues, 'Surprise [. . .] is precisely what the paranoid seeks to eliminate'; 'paranoia requires that bad news be always already known'.[17] In Sedgwick's view a paranoid perspective has become 'coextensive with critical theoretical inquiry' in general, to the extent that a 'hermeneutics of suspicion' has often appeared to be a 'mandatory injunction'.[18] One example she offers is New Historicism's tendency to 'rely on the prestige of a single, overarching narrative: exposing and problematizing hidden violences in the genealogy of the modern liberal subject'.[19] Another example she could have given is Fredric Jameson's influential *Postmodernism* (1992), in which he asserts that 'If we do not achieve some general sense of a cultural dominant, then we fall back into a view of present history as sheer heterogeneity, random difference.'[20]

Like Sedgwick, I don't wish to deny that various kinds of of structure and system (economic, political and otherwise) do exist. But acknowledging them shouldn't mean losing sight of how contingency, chance, randomness and possibility nevertheless continue to be important factors in people's lives. Given the prevalence of the paranoid outlook, Sedgwick suggests that critical theory is sorely in need of other kinds of affective outlook. She doesn't outline an alternative one characterised by a specific affect, but she does describe a form of 'reparative reading' that is notably similar to the kind of happy reading encouraged by Hejinian. In contrast to the paranoid approach, reparative reading means developing your critical and theoretical perspective in the process of negotiating the singular features of a text. It requires close readings and attention to the 'local' while retaining a sense of contingency. For a 'reparatively positioned reader', writes Sedgwick, it can thus 'seem realistic and necessary to experience surprise', and by taking this approach the reader endeavours to 'assemble and confer plenitude' on the text, with the understanding that it 'will then have resources to offer to an inchoate self'.[21] In contrast, from the perspective of paranoid theory, such reparative modes of reading will seem 'inadmissable' or superfluous, 'both because they are about pleasure ("merely aesthetic") and because they are frankly ameliorative ("merely reformist")'.[22] Bearing in mind my readings of Hejinian and Sedgwick, for the rest of this essay I'm going to engage with some of John Cage's experimental writing to continue developing a sense of how happy reparative reading can work. I've stated that experimental writing has been particularly effective in presenting intimacies of possibility and contingency; Cage is exemplary on that score, especially in using 'chance determinations' with his writing to make the happenstance happen.

*

> After the hunger storm the animals will eat everything. One dog has devoured all its leash and kennel – the cardboard, leather, rope, and rivets. Even artists crave a minimum of insulation. I don't know where we

are now, but the transformation of form, which first was meant to transmute matter, has become an end in itself. Sometimes the brash between floes is so thick we don't know if the mirages are work or light play – first the packs are balloons then castles then mushrooms then mosques or cathedrals. In the greyer city packs the infants of the plain are beautiful. Vertical axis: tower. Horizontal axis: ground. The third dimension is too dear, they surge along long walls, past a door, windows, a door, no windows. Where are courtyards, nooks, a high porthole to flood the world with passing clouds? To a blind one as he passes I say 'I am the army now'. The boy retorts that he is its horse. And this was a crucial finding for our science of happiness.

*

In 1952 at Black Mountain College, Cage collaborated in a manifold theatrical event that was a major influence on the development of performance 'happenings': while he read a lecture on Meister Eckhart, the poet Charles Olson pronounced lines of his own poetry from within the audience, the painter Robert Rauschenberg (who designed the set) played records on an old phonograph and Merce Cunningham improvised a dance.[23] The performance thus involved putting the audience in a situation in which they were made to realise that they were, to echo Hejinian, 'surrounded by possibilities' in the form of various things going on simultaneously. As Cage himself stated, 'the happening resulted from the fact that there were many people and many possibilities and we could do it quickly'.[24] In his view, exercising such potential required being 'willing to [. . .] move into a situation in which anything may happen, because one is interested not in expressing ideas or feeling but in increasing one's awareness and curiosity'.[25] Harking back to Hejinian again, the implication of these two statements is that negotiating the potential of situated context can entail exercising possibilities of oneself as a person, and also realising that those possibilities include other people. It's not that Cage is uninterested in 'ideas or feeling'; instead, what he wants to avoid is work that is simply *re-presenting* ('expressing') feelings or ideas that have already occurred. He wants the work itself to generate ideas and feeling afresh *as an event*, a happening. His compositional experiments with 'chance determination' were a means of liberating himself and his work from the limits of personal 'intentions', likes or dislikes. While he acknowledged such practice as requiring self-'discipline', he also saw it to be potentiating: 'If you're nonintentional, then everything is permitted.'[26] By leaving himself open to chance – he liked to describe himself as 'An open

Cage'[27] – he also opened his writing to others' texts by incorporating them through various forms of experiment. Many of Cage's writings can thus be seen as presenting and encouraging experimental forms of *reading*. It's not surprising, then, that he composed many of his writings as 'lectures', given the traditional senses (rooted in the Latin etymology) of a 'lecture' as a 'reading' and 'the action of reading' (*OED*).

*

'I am prepared not to die for you
in particular, but for you in general.'
The bitter taste that found my tongue
is gone now; all that remains is a rimy feel
in my throat and gums, as in a frost
I close my mouth after breathing deep
my love. Is the calving of glaciers no
notion of cruelty? She is singing in the shower
like Venus in her hulking clam,
her stunning grace uncomprehending
as the moist sound clasps its climax,
a sharp crack in the distance, a nearby window
shatters, crashes to the silent street. 'Ugh',
she says, 'an awful place. Let's take it.'

*

Right from his early lectures, Cage was keen to emphasise how his experimental modes of writing were also reading experiments. With his 'Juilliard Lecture' (1952), for example, he wrote it in four parts, each of which involved 'processes of collage and fragmentation to texts which I had written earlier'.[28] Each part was then laid out in four columns, as in the following extract from part III:

			What I am calling	
poetry is	often called	content.	I myself have	
called it	form.	It is the continuity	of a piece of music.	
Continuity,	today,	when it is necessary	,	is a
demonstration		of dis-interestestedness	; that is,	
it is a proof	that our delight	lies in not	pos-sessing	anything
	Each moment	presents what	happens[29]	

Rather than read down the columns, Cage read each line across them 'in order to facilitate a rhythmic reading and to measure the silences'.[30] The musicality of the lecture rests in the 'continuity' it establishes between spoken sound and silence, the pauses also helping to build suspense and turn the words of the syntactically regular sentences into punctual and relatively surprising events. In using texts he 'had written earlier' and rearranging them as a form of music (using columns as idiosyncratic measures of temporal rhythm), the lecture thus transforms the source material as a result of the formal experimentation and so also presents continuity between the 'form' and 'content'. As Cage comments elsewhere, 'An experimental action is one the outcome of which is not foreseen.'[31] Using the columnar mise-en-page to introduce unforeseen changes to each sentence of the source texts is a way for him not to limit the composition to his own tastes. Dispossessing it of his intentions enables the text to generate its own surprises: 'Each moment presents [rather than represents] what happens.' The 'dis-interestedness' at stake isn't a matter of not appreciating anything; rather, it's like the impartial 'disinterest' described by Kant in his 'Analytic of the Beautiful' (1790). People appreciate the beauty of something, Kant argues, when they apprehend it without some fixed concept, taste or utility in mind; it's on this basis that beauty and the pleasure it elicits can so strike a person.[32] Cage's lecture encourages a reparative aesthetics of dispossessive pleasure in which reading what 'happens' results in happy continuities between disinterest and 'delight'.

With his lecture 'Indeterminacy' (1958), Cage again used time measures as a way of transforming the character of textual content. The lecture comprises a series of very short anecdotal 'stories' which relate things that he'd read, or incidents that happened to him or others, all of which he assembled 'in an unplanned way [. . .] to suggest that all things [. . .] are related, and that this complexity is more evident when it is not oversimplified by an idea of relationship in one person's mind'.[33] In performing the lecture, he read out each story in a minute: 'If it's a short one, I have to spread it out; when I come to a long one, I have to speak as rapidly as I can.'[34] The stories convey things that have already happened (they are mostly in the past tense), but in being composed as a haphazard textual set with varying durational intensities they take on a new form of complex happening in the event of reading. Cage offers the stories as resonating with each other by virtue of their haphazard context. In regarding the textual context as open to the situational characteristics of each reading performance, he also amplifies the sense of everything being 'related'. Reflecting on how other people might read 'Indeterminacy', he suggests that it 'be read in the manner and in the situations that one reads newspapers'; 'purposelessly: that is, jumping here and there and responding at the same time to environmental events and sounds'.[35] Not wanting to maintain any barrier between everyday life and his art, Cage implies that reading his lecture can extend to reading the world around you.

While lectures such as 'Indeterminacy' and his Juilliard one each relate an 'aesthetic' in line with Sedgwick's depiction of reparative reading, from the 1960s onwards Cage increasingly aligned his artistic experiments with the kind of 'ameliorative' outlook that Sedgwick also ascribes to reparative reading. His lecture sequence *Diary: How to Improve the World (You Will Only Make Matters Worse)* (written between 1965 and 1982) is exemplary of that: not only was it composed with chance methods of formal experimentation, it also relates environmental issues to prospects of global planning and social revolution. In his 'Foreword' to *A Year from Monday* (1968), in which the first instalment of 'Diary' was published, Cage emphasised the turn in his work: 'I'd like our activities to be more social and anarchically so'; 'Our proper work now if we love mankind and the world we live in is revolution.'[36] That call for revolution needs to be seen in the context of the growing counter-cultural opposition to the Vietnam War as well as to the Cold War politics and ideologies that were being promulgated by governments and media networks around the world. What Cage hoped for was a social anarchism as an alternative to rule by state government, though he also stressed that his aversion to power structures extended to the realm of art:

> The reason I am less and less interested in music is not only that I find environmental sounds and noises more useful aesthetically than the sounds produced by the world's musical cultures, but that, when you get right down to it, a composer is simply someone who tells other people what to do.[37]

That isn't to say that he was uninterested in learning from others; indeed, his 'Diary', as lecture, partly performs an extended reading of writings and sayings from a number of thinkers and artists that Cage had taken to heart, including Marcel Duchamp, Daisetz Suzuki, Marshall McLuhan and particularly the architect and systems theorist Buckminster Fuller – 'He more than any other to my knowledge', Cage stated, 'sees the world situation [. . .] clearly and has fully reasoned projects for turning our attention away from "killingry" toward "livingry".'[38] An early environmental activist, Fuller sought new ways of managing earth's limited natural resources by advocating novel approaches to recycling, energy efficiency, housing and transport. In textually recycling the ideas of Fuller and others in 'Diary', Cage also introduces some anarchy into the process through using chance determinations. By this time Cage's principal method of taking chances involved tossing coins used to consult the ancient Chinese oracular *I Ching* (*Book of Changes*). With 'Diary' he used the method to determine how many sections of the text he would write each day, what typeface they would be in, and how each line would be indented:

```
FULLER: AS LONG AS ONE HUMAN BEING IS
        HUNGRY, THE ENTIRE HUMAN RACE IS
HUNGRY.     City planning's obsolete.    What's
                needed is global planning so Earth
    may stop stepping like octopus on its
own feet.  Buckminster Fuller uses his
    head: comprehensive design science;
inventory of world resources.      Conversion:
                the mind turns around, no longer
                    facing in its direction.  Utopia?
                    Self-knowledge.    Some will make it,
    with or without LSD.    The others? Pray
        for acts of God, crises, power
        failures, no water to drink.[39]
```

As chance operations keep his mind open to events, other people and their potentialities in the world, Cage aligns his experimental approach with Fuller's environmental, ethical and utopic thinking. The utopic vision that Cage's 'Diary' presents through Fuller requires expanding the kind of situational awareness that he encouraged with readings of 'Indeterminacy' to become aware of wider interrelations of 'global' environment as well as possible ways of harmonising them. It's a matter of turning one's mind around by opening it to changes, which is what Cage sees the *I Ching* (as 'Book of Changes') and its coin-tossing as enabling. One consults that text, he writes, 'to discern how to insert oneself into the flow of activity in order to live more harmoniously and thus more fruitfully'.[40] The utopic vision of environmental harmony 'Diary' presents thus contrasts with the insulated and self-interested happiness that Colebrook describes. Whereas she sees such happiness as having potentially apocalyptic environmental consequences (if it prevents people from appreciating the consequences of climate change), Cage wants his work to help open people's minds to their chances of improving world environment. Changing one's mind in this way is also a matter of

'Self-knowledge', which is why *not* gaining some of that might indeed mean becoming apocalyptically blinkered: praying 'for acts of God, crises, power/failures, no water to drink'.

*

We are deep out in it now, and no matter if three thousand times removed, a cousin's still a cousin. The development is at once dynamic and static. It involves ever rising levels, yet the frame is perpetually fresh and frozen. A sky thick as sugar-cube paper, birds chanting invisible from the folds, over the exodus of those bearing back-packs of their lives, full of food containers, lucky charms, hopes, matches, and maledictions. Houses without doors, windows, walls, or roofs. Women and girls in flight without furniture, utensils, succour. Some live on water, others on leaves, and most are taken with new deaths: one the death of hunger, another by her own infection, another by the sweet infection exhaled by those dead around her. Perhaps all are beside themselves with an invisible third that's washed up, has swollen skin, delicate, almost transparent, smells of wild geese or a damp chicken.
*

As the extract above from 'Diary' shows, in thinking socially with others Cage presents an *experimental reading* of their work by turning it into a poem that's full of changes in the form of its chance shifts in lineation, typeface and statement (he also characterised the lecture as a 'mosaic').[41] But as the extract also shows, the formal experimentation in 'Diary' appears to be somewhat secondary to the importance of conveying a clarity of declarative statements. In other words, the 'aesthetic' aspect of the lecture's reparative reading seems to be playing second fiddle to its 'ameliorative' messages. Over the subsequent decades of his life, Cage continued to be outspoken on social and environmmental issues, and he remained a believer in anarchist thinking, as is clear from *Anarchy* (1988), one of his later experimental poetic lectures. While he also continued to hope that his creative work could help to 'produce a revolution in the mind', by 1972 he was expressing scepticism about the possibility of creative revolution leading to any widespread social or political change.[42] Perhaps as a consequence of that, many of his later writings somewhat reverse his 'Diary' approach in re-arranging others' texts and statements to the point of making them 'non-syntactical'.

If Cage was thinking any resulting revolution would take place more in the minds of readers than society in general, that did not mean that the experiments had no political or social import for him or those reading them. Like William S. Burroughs and Allen Ginsberg at the time, Cage regarded social governance to be largely linguistic: 'language controls our thinking: and if we change language, it is conceivable that our thinking would change'.[43] He liked to point out that the word 'syntax' was also originally used to refer to the ordering of troops – 'syntax is the arrangement of the army'[44] – which is why he viewed his non-syntactical writings as a 'demilitarization of language' that is 'conducted in many ways: a single language is pulverized; [. . .] elements not strictly linguistic (graphic, musical) are introduced [. . .]. Nonsense and silence are produced, familiar to lovers.'[45] Cage also regarded these experiments as entailing a transformation of reading itself, as is evident from the instalment of 'Diary' he wrote between 1970 and 1971:

> *To raise language's*
> *temperature we not only remove syntax: we*
> *give each letter undivided attention,*
> *setting it in unique face and size;*
> *to read becomes the verb to sing.*[46]

Altering the 'face and size' of font is one of the things 'Diary' features, but the removal of syntax is more the work of what Cage called his 'mesostics'. The mesostic poems resemble acrostics in having a string of letters spell out a word down the lines; instead of the string being at the beginning of each line and left-justified, though, it runs down the middle with the poem justified neither left nor right, as in this example from 'Writing for the Fourth Time through *Finnegans Wake*' (1983):

> Jist
> dOes
> till bYes will be
> fliCk
> flEckflinging its pixylighting[47]

The words from this stanza are all drawn from Joyce's *Finnegans Wake* (1939), 'JOYCE' forming the mesostic string here that runs down the middle (the name strings alternate between 'JAMES' and 'JOYCE'). This mesostic is what Cage called a 'pure' or '100%' one such that between any two letters of the mesostic string, neither of those letters are allowed to appear (e.g., neither 'J' nor 'O' appears between those first two letters of the name).[48] That rule thus becomes a form of chance determination for selecting which words and phrases will work with the name string, and also which letters in the lines' central words will be capitalised. The inventive spirit of Joyce's text is thereby complemented by Cage's novel rewriting of it, which produces curious splicings of syntax and surprising graphic emphases. 'bYes' here, for example, introduces a 'yes' into 'byes' so that the word effectively presents an internal half-rhyming eye-rhyme with itself. Although we rarely find end-rhymes in the poem's lines, all its stanzas can be seen as rhyming with each other through the corresponding name strings. While all the stanzas thus rhyme with 'JAMES JOYCE', each one also forms a new chance expression of his name and so builds different linguistic potentials from it. The name effectively instances how someone 'is a bit of space that has gotten itself in moments'. Bearing Hejinian's sense of a person in mind, we could also say that such a mesostic exercises possibility by relating to others' work by reading and rewriting it creatively.

*

Through the window the neighbour house
wrinkles and its chimney veers off, wet and shiny,
into the sky. Working remains labour time
to us, but will be frozen out, superfluous.
48° 52' 2" N,
2° 22' 27" E,
our dead reckoning naturally uncertain.
At each send of swell the ship bangs her bows
on the floe before us. We have forgotten warmth
of dusty tea, can't recall the smell
of bitter cabbage cooled, the last trace
of social life. Another gorgeous left-hand sun-
dog. I don't always know the parhelion a reflex
of myself. One final example from Europe:
*

In another mesostic work, 'Themes and Variations' (1982), Cage exercises possibilities again with Joyce, as well as fourteen others 'who have been important to me in my life and work':[49] Norman O'Brown, Marshall McLuhan, Erik Satie, Robert Rauschenberg, Buckminster Fuller, Marcel Duchamp, Jasper Johns, Henry David Thoreau, Merce Cunningham, David Tudor, Morris Graves, Mark Tobey, Arnold Schoenberg and Daisetz Suzuki. Those names are used for mesostic strings in the text, but unlike his previous mesostics the stanzas in this work 'are exceptionally not about the men named at all, except coincidentally'.⁵⁰ Rather, the various stanzas draw on 110 'ideas' that Cage noted as being prominent in his own work, including 'DEMILITARIZATION OF LANGUAGE (NO GOVERNMENT)', 'IT IS, IS CAUSE FOR JOY', 'PURPOSEFUL PURPOSELESSNESS', and 'A WORK SHOULD INCLUDE ITS ENVIRONMENT, IS ALWAYS EXPERIMENTAL'.⁵¹ Using *I Ching* chance operations to determine which of the ideas should be used for each name string, he wrote a set of mesostics for each name and then took inspiration from the Japanese form of renga to rewrite them non-syntactically. He explains that form and its significance in the 'Introduction' to the poem:

> Traditionally renga is written by a group of poets finding themselves of an evening together and having nothing better to do. Successive lines are written by different poets. Each poet tries to make his line as distant in possible meanings from the preceding line as he can take it. This is no doubt an attempt to open the minds of the poets and listeners or readers to other relationships than those ordinarily perceived. In Buddhist thought all creation is a network of cause and effect; everything causes everything else; everything results from everything else. Buddhism is utterly ecological [. . .]. Thus an intentionally irrational poem can be written with liberating effect.⁵²

While 'Themes and Variations' is an exercise in the Buddhist beliefs that Cage had long held, it is also a collective effort through which he composes the text as a 'group' with the fifteen people whose names all play a part in determining choices. Composition becomes a way of experimenting with how you can be composite. That has implications for the 110 'ideas' Cage uses. Although he draws the ideas from his own work, they are themselves composite in being informed by other thinkers and bodies of thought, including anarchism and Buddhism. In addition, rather than writing the text simply to re-present these ideas, his renga approach reorders them as fresh composites; it is, as Cage states, 'a way of writing which though coming from ideas [. . .] is not about ideas but produces them'.⁵³ That sounds as though it's all about intellection, though, which it isn't, for the mesostics and non-syntactic writing are very much about foregrounding musical and graphic elements, too, and so happily drawing the aesthetic, affective and experiential more generally into the mix. All of those things are part of Cage's composition process. But a text is not itself a sentient, feeling being; instead, the composition opens the aesthetic, affective and experiential to chance, drawing new composite possibilities for them as a series of textual forms. The experiential potentiality of the text is its openness to being realised singularly with each act of reading. It's like a musical score that takes on a different character with each performance.

*

A clock driven by a weight, attached to a wheel, split into compartments, partly filled with mercury, acting as inertial brake. The setting is a public performance on a park lake. In its colossal silence the blows of the silver hammer raise suffocated echoes from the waters' depths to the trees' branches, all the birds crowding to listen. The agitation is weird. A compact mass surrounds the engine. Helmets are visible then vanish. 'Did you see?' 'We'll be late again.' 'It's the head, it's horrible.' A boy laughs, too brightly. He burns the banknotes he rips from his pocket. We haven't forgotten the start of the battle, the lake covered in gondolas, surrounding the triremes, gracious and arbitrary. Here in the place called 'The Tomb of Narcissus', the battle finished to a happy stupor; the bells that briefly shook the birds were never meant to reckon a constant unit of time.
*

It just so happens that numerous mesostics in 'Themes and Variations' require a reader to grapple with the 'just' not only in terms of immediacy in the reading experience (*what just happened?*), but also with regard to how such grappling is right (*justified*) and involves particularities (*just this, just that, just so*):

>   Just
>   pregnAnt fluent
> or did we pull ourSelves
>   on the Part of
>   is possiblE
>   even to youRself
>   of Just what happened[54]

These lines are drawn from one of the mesostics using 'JASPER JOHNS' as name string, and just when I'm reading the first lines in terms of how it makes sense to think of oneself as a composite, as 'ourSelves' – and so, in a way, pregnant with others – an ant ('pregnAnt') interrupts my flow of thinking, prompting me to wonder just how 'fluent' I am. Its interruption makes me change tack, reflect on how the personal and interpersonal are open to happenstance aspects of context and environment that extend to the nonhuman. If reflecting on such possibility in this context of the mesostic is also to exercise my potential as a person, then yes, I suppose I have pulled off something of myselves as 'Part of' what 'is possible', part 'of Just what happened'.

The word 'pregnant' has certainly just taken on a different sense for me in terms of both meaning and aesthetic charge. That's because the poem helps to see that it's not only the non-syntactical expression that plays a part in producing ideas; they also arise from giving attention to the graphic and musical and quirks:

>   in a final waY
>   of sounD
>
>   to tAke the final step
>
>   riVulet
>   happIly[55]

These lines are from a mesostic featuring 'HENRY DAVID THOREAU' as name string; thinking on my feet ('tAke the final step'), I take them as encouraging me to go with their flow, to form with them a 'riVulet' of composite experience – one by which I end up seeing an 'I' arise in 'happIly', the final syllable of that word also putting me in mind of an 'Ill'. The mesostic here enables you to chance on unusual possibilities for that final syllable; stressing its significance would be unlikely if you were drawing on conventional scansion and so reading the word as a dactyl.

Having been following Ahmed in happily seeking more 'hap', seeing some 'Ill' in 'happIly' brings us back to the happiness Hejinian describes as an eruption of *amor fati*: 'the uproar in one's emotions in response to all that comes to one, good or bad'. Let's consider that with these lines from another 'JAMES JOYCE' mesostic:

>   not a funny Jest
>   the decisiOn
>   base all the laws on povertY
>   plaCing imagination
>   livE with happily
>
>   these interruptions are Just
>   for eAch and everyone[56]

A 'Jest', a joke, can be funny by virtue of its recasting something as absurd or ridiculous. It can thus work as a form of defamiliarisation, which is how Hejinian has characterised the work of comedy: 'The comedian is antinomian [. . .] by virtue of being a foreigner, that is, the comedian makes the familiar foreign by regarding it from a foreign point of view.'[57] Cage's mesostics perform as comedy at times because the anarchic changes they perform with language and syntax do produce absurdities, 'nonsense' and defamiliarisation. As Paolo Virno has argued, social mores and beliefs are also 'linguistic customs' which make up 'the *grammar* of a form of life'; a joke can thus be 'a performative example of how the grammar of a form of life can be transformed'.[58] The anarchy of Cage's text is 'antinomian' (from the Greek: 'against the law') in not settling for any conventional perspective (personal or social) so that the text itself can present a 'foreign point of view' that's intended to be transformative to the point of cultivating a 'revolution in the mind'. In using chance determinations to break convention, the collectively minded spirit of Cage's work runs counter to 'laws' based 'on poverty' (whether financial or of the imagination) which are, indeed, 'not a funny Jest'. Such laws may also not be a jest to the extent that they are a reality; in which case, yes, 'plaCing imagination' on the line (by joking about the situation with dark humour, for example), might be a way of dealing with them in order to judge them according to a potentiality principle, and so not accept them on their own terms. Doing so involves getting to grips with how your chances are rooted in a context that often happens to be out of your hands, whether because of things that are constraining, or haphazard, or interruptive. Trying to accept that 'these interruptions are Just / for eAch and everyone' means trying to 'live with' the 'happily' as *amor fati*.

For Cage, as we've seen, opening up to eventualities means not reducing them to one's own ego, ideas or feelings. Happiness means affirming how you *happen to feel* in a situation, which means grasping how the feeling itself is not actually limited to the personal; it is instead a composite affective event that arises as an interaction between you and the world in a given context. If practising a certain 'dis-interestestedness' helps one to be happily open to 'all that comes to one, good or bad', it also means that such a happy comportment admits mixed feelings:

    maKing behavior

      no deSire no dislike
    with pleAsure

  or do you find iT
      producIng
     laughtEars[59]

These lines from one of the 'ERIK SATIE' mesostics echo the extract I quoted earlier from the the 'Juilliard Lecture', in which 'disinterestedness' becomes 'proof that our delight lies in not possessing anything'. In the mesostic lines here, one possible outcome of disinterest ('no deSire no dislike') is 'pleasure', but another alternative is 'laughtears', which Joyce coins in *Finnegans Wake* to denote a mixture of tears and laughter. The mesostic's twist is to suggest that this mixed feeling brings an ability to make sense of it – brings, as it were, new 'Ears'.

Joan Retallack is right to argue that by enacting 'a tolerance for, and a delight in complex possibility', Cage's work fosters 'poethics': 'a practice or form of life in which ethics and aesthetics come together'.[60] In experimenting with chance operations to compose new affective and aesthetic potentials for readers, Cage offers a form of potentialism that helps to develop what I've called 'practical imagination'. Ascribing an 'ism' to his work does not mean reducing its complexity; after all, Cage was happy to ascribe 'Indeterminism' to his work. To call it potentialist also does not mean to say that it's identical with Hejinian's approach; as I've shown, Cage has his own various influences and modes of experiment, which is also why the potentialism of a text such as the 'Juilliard Lecture', for example, is not identical with that of 'Themes and Variations'. I do think that the Cage writings I've discussed are similar to Hejinian's *Happily*, though, in performing and encouraging a 'reparative' reading practice along the lines called for by Sedgwick. Not only do the texts eschew any happy blinkering of self that Ahmed describes, they also work counter to any paranoid investment in fixed narratives or social structures. How reparative happiness might work in relation to politics or environment is clearly questionable, though, if it were to amount simply to a form of *amor fati* that is reducible to accepting with resignation whatever happens in the world. But that is not the tenor of either Hejinian's or Cage's potentialism, both of which are more about remaining *open* to fate and how one happens to feel as a consequence, whether that involves an 'uproar in one's emotions' (Hejinian), or the possibility of 'laughtears' as much as 'pleasure' (Cage). Reparative happiness means trying not to close yourself off from any aspect of what's going on, while also weighing what's happened (fate) in terms of alternative possibilities for thinking, feeling and performing. It's true that although Cage saw his creative work as an artistic 'activism' fostering 'revolution in the mind', he pursued no part in the activism of any political movements or organisations. There's no reason for seeing the two forms of activism as mutually exclusive, though; one can read work like Cage's to potentiate powers of collective personhood, while acting on that potential by participating in some form of social or political activism or movement.

Because Cage's texts as experimental readings encourage readers to be aware of aesthetic and affective possibilities that arise, I've presented some of my reading experiences in the first person. I don't see the result to be a strictly 'subjective' set of readings, for my readings and the 'I' involved are composites that have arisen as interactions between me and the text. In responding to Cage's experiments, then, I've experimented with my own style and stance of reading, and that's included interspersing throughout this essay the asterisk-sandwiched stanzas of poetry that you might have been wondering about. The stanzas are from a poem, 'Sun-Dog Express' that I co-wrote with Geoff Gilbert over a year before writing this essay. We wrote it much like a renga, drawing on a variety of source texts to write lines or sections of lines in turn, and so variously complementing or undermining each other's efforts. Co-writing it (and our other poems) has thus resulted in some of my happiest moments. As the poem also offers up a series of critical situations, interpolating it somewhat haphazardly in this essay after the essay was written enabled me to see some of my phrasings and arguments differently – particularly those about context and environment – and I rewrote them accordingly to ensure the texts are resonating with each other.

*
All the mirrors are snow covered. The fibreglass
Vesuvius triggers its artificial fire
and incandescent rocks. When they beat
their wings something falls from the sky:
a brown powder, absurd response
provoking the absurd frame.
Another slab calves from the Barrier.
Powder veils the windows, the wrinkles
of plaster, no windows, a door. She declares
she likes this dusty public street,
and is believed. These bits of happiness I've placed
before you, like a beautiful infant, teasing
a dog. Like ginger, sugar, hot water.
Like Venus back in her shell.
*

Notes

1. Bentley, 'First annual results of David Cameron's happiness index published', p. 1.
2. Ahmed, *The Promise of Happiness*, p. 217.
3. Ibid. p. 207.
4. Colebrook, 'The Once and Future Humans', p. 65.
5. Ibid. p. 75.
6. Ahmed, *The Promise of Happiness*, p. 219.
7. Houen, *Powers of Possibility*, pp. 1–21.
8. Ibid. p. 220.
9. Hejinian, 'Background Notes for *Happily*', p. 1.
10. Ibid. p. 2.
11. Ibid. p. 3.
12. Hejinian, *Happily*, p. 5.
13. Hejinian, *My Life*, p. 163.
14. Hejinian, 'The Person and Description', p. 203, Hejinian's emphases.
15. See Houen, *Powers of Possibility*, p. 16.
16. Ibid. p. 254.
17. Sedgwick, 'Paranoid Reading and Reparative Reading', p. 130.
18. Ibid. pp. 126, 125.
19. Ibid. p. 139.
20. Jameson, *Postmodernism*, p. 6.
21. Sedgwick, 'Paranoid Reading and Reparative Reading', pp. 146, 149.
22. Ibid. p. 144.
23. See Kirby, 'Happenings: An Introduction', p. 19.
24. Cage quoted in Kostelanetz, *Conversing with John Cage*, p. 110.
25. Cage quoted in ibid. p. 119.
26. Cage quoted in ibid. p. 223.
27. Cage, 'Diary [. . .] Continued 1973–1982', p. 160.
28. Cage, 'Juilliard Lecture', p. 95.
29. Ibid. pp. 106–7.
30. Ibid. p. 95.
31. Cage, 'Composition as Process', p. 39.
32. See Kant, 'Analytic of the Beautiful', pp. 90–6.
33. Cage, 'Indeterminacy', p. 260.
34. Ibid.
35. Ibid. p. 261.
36. Cage, 'Foreword', in *A Year from Monday*, pp. ix–x.
37. Ibid. p. ix.
38. Ibid.
39. Cage, 'Diary [. . .] 1965', p. 5.
40. Cage quoted in Revill, *The Roaring Silence*, p. 130.
41. Cage, 'Diary [. . .] 1965', p. 3.
42. See Kostelanetz, *Conversing with Cage*, p. 282.

43. Cage quoted in ibid. p. 155.
44. Cage quoted in Revill, *The Roaring Silence*, p. 248.
45. Cage, 'Foreword', in *M*, p. x.
46. Cage, 'Diary [. . .] 1969', in *M*, p. 107.
47. Cage, 'Writing for the Fourth Time through *Finnegans Wake*', p. 3.
48. See Cage's discussion of '100%' versus '50%' mesostics in *I–VI*, pp. 1–2.
49. Cage, 'Themes and Variations', p. 55.
50. Ibid.
51. Ibid. p. 56.
52. Ibid. p. 65.
53. Ibid. p. 63.
54. Ibid. p. 107.
55. Ibid. p. 80.
56. Ibid. p. 143.
57. Hejinian, Letter to Susan Howe, p. 1.
58. Virno, *Multitude*, p. 94.
59. Cage, 'Themes and Variations', p. 86.
60. Retallack, 'Poethics of a Complex Realism', pp. 268, 243.

Chapter 3

Experiment, Inscription and the Archive: Kathy Acker's Manuscript Practice
Georgina Colby

> In research libraries and collections, we may capture the portrait of history in so-called insignificant visual and verbal textualities and textiles. In material details. In twill fabrics, bead-work pieces, pricked patterns, four-ringed knots, tiny spangles, sharp-toothed stencil wheels; in quotations, thought-fragments, rhymes, syllables, anagrams, graphemes, endangered phonemes, in soils and cross-outs.
>
> Susan Howe, *Spontaneous Particulars: The Telepathy of the Archive*[1]

Susan Howe's words here, in *Spontaneous Particulars: The Telepathy of the Archive* (2014), point to the material epistemology of the archive, a body of knowledge unique to the works that both precede a published book, and those that often remain unpublished. Archival knowledge is hardly the sole preserve of scholars of avant-garde literature, yet Howe's landmark 1985 work *My Emily Dickinson* illustrates in irrefutable terms the importance of the archive to an understanding of an experimental writer's compositional practices.[2] Howe's creative work and critical scholarship exemplify that which she elucidates in interview in the *Paris Review* in 2012 as the 'porous border between the visual and the verbal'.[3] It is for this reason that I take Howe as the starting point for an exploration of experiment, inscription and the archive in the work of Kathy Acker. Acker's body of work, which spans three decades from the 1970s to 1997, is the product of a vast array of compositional materials. A recent landmark exhibition held in November 2018 at the Badischer Kunstverein Gallery in Karlsruhe, titled 'Get Rid of Meaning', curated by Matias Viegener and Anja Cassar, offered a timely retrospective of Acker's works. Many of the materials on display were archival materials: the original notebooks Acker used for her 1973 work *The Childlike Life of the Black Tarantula* (now housed in the Fales Library and Special Collections, New York University); the original drafts of 'The Persian Poems', 1972; the original proofs of *Blood and Guts in High School*, 1978; the large-scale dream maps for *Blood and Guts in High School* and *Pussy, King of the Pirates* (1996); Acker's original drawings from Shinichi Segi, *Yoshitoshi: The Splendid Decadent* (1983), which she appropriated and included in *In Memoriam to Identity* (1991); Acker's concrete poems; and many other works. The exhibition coincided with an international resurgence of interest in Acker's oeuvre, a revival that has been complemented by the scrutiny of the archive by Acker scholars.[4] Utilising blibliographic scholarship alongside the work of visual theorist and book artist Johanna Drucker, I look at the relation between experiment, inscription and the archive in Acker's body of work, with a particular focus on the visual medium of writing. Addressing a number of materials housed in the archive, I argue in this chapter that Acker's works can be read as diagrammatic in form and as continuing a modernist lineage of diagrammatic texts. In Acker's texts the diagrammatic is experimental composition, and the generative nature is heightened when the original materials in the archive are taken into account.

Proponents of the importance of materiality to an understanding of works, such as N. Katherine Hayles,[5] insist that the formal features of a work are intrinsic to the production of meaning in and by a text. In Acker's compositions formal features work to imbue the materiality of the works with active resistance against conventional meaning. Acker's feminist experiments are the sites of the production of new forms of voice. An exploration of the archive materials housed in the Kathy Acker Papers at Duke University, the Fales Library collection in New York, and the Kathy Acker Reading Room at the University of Cologne yields unique insights into the processes and acts of composition inherent to Acker's experimental works at both the structural large-scale level and the local lexical level. A prolific annotator of the literary works she owned, Acker's extensive library of works housed in the Kathy Acker Reading Room at the University of Cologne offers insight into the process of her experimental practices. In her copy of Jean Genet's *The Screens* (1961), Acker notes 'WRITING IS EXPERIMENT NOT EXPRESSION'. In her edition of Georges Bataille's *Visions of Excess*, by the section titled 'The Heterological Theory of Knowledge', Acker has written 'why literature must not make sense. And that doesn't mean the avant-garde.'[6] Gertrude Stein's *Everybody's Autobiography* (1937) seems to have provided material for Acker's experiments with life-writing. In her annotations on the work, Acker explicitly refers to imposing two parts of her life over each other. On the back inside cover the annotations read: 'I give up caring/about slogans/I'm a woman I'm/a dekeanarchist etc/ impose 2 parts/of my life/on each other/I live with arma (sic) or and ma sis'. In the chapter of Teresa de Lauretis's *Alice Doesn't: Feminism, Semiotics, Cinema* (1984) titled 'Desire in Narrative', Acker notes 'structure as content'.[7] Such marginalia gesture to Acker's process of reading and developing her compositional techniques. In *Philosophical Investigations* (1953) Ludwig Wittgenstein states of a passage: 'With different training the same ostensive teaching of [these] words would have quite a different understanding.' Acker has written next to this sentence: 'meaning of a word depends on the way it is learnt'.[8] The contingency of language and meaning is critical to Acker's experiments and extends to the reading of her works, which dislocate and free words from their conventional referents. In other texts, Acker wrote pieces that would find their way into her works. In the work of the *Tel Quel* writer Philippe Sollers, *Writing and the Experience of Limits* (1968), Acker writes an extensive passage on the need to free language from meaning: 'on the model of nature/The book must be/is a machine which breaks down [therefore] allows/the uncontrolled reconstitution of that & expression. All other books simply/express.'[9] A variant of this passage eventually found its way into the unpublished drafts for her work *Don Quixote* (1986) titled 'Description of a Female Weight-Lifter'[10] and the passage is clearly preliminary material for her 1993 essay on bodybuilding: 'Against Ordinary Language: The Language of the Body'. Acker's annotations reveal a continuous intertextual process of writing whilst reading.

The archive renders visible the composition of Acker's works, writing processes that are not always immediately apparent or tangible when looking at the published works. Acker wrote in notebooks, many of which are housed in the archives. She composed her works from these notebooks and other materials, producing first drafts that she would then draft and redraft into the final manuscripts. Acker's compositional stages are, for example, evident in the numerous notebooks and the revised drafts housed in the Kathy Acker Papers that became *Eurydice in the Underworld* (1997). The handwritten notebooks reveal the preliminary materials for the work. Long passages of prose, some struck through to denote erasure, constitute much of the material. Acker also includes small maps sketched in pen in the notebooks that became large-scale artworks, the Xeroxes of which were then included in the final published version of the work. The preliminary materials include a notebook marked 'Eurydice/Electra

Notebook', which begins with handwritten drafts of Act III; another notebook, 'Eurydice Speaks', contains the handwritten drafts of Eurydice's monologues; and there are a number of sets of typed drafts with copious revisions titled accordingly, such as 'Memories of Electra', and 'Requiem Revised'. Acker meticulously revised the drafts of her works, altering grammatical registers (in the case of *Eurydice in the Underworld,* a change from present tense to past tense) and omitting adjectives, to create the form of the final works. The material for the section 'Diary written by Eurydice when she's dead' first appears in the notebook titled 'Eurydice Speaks'. The first handwritten drafts are long passages of writing, many of which take the form of life-writing written as a stream of consciousness. Often Acker has eliminated material by striking it through with a clean diagonal line. For example, at one point in the notebook Acker has crossed out a line that reads, 'Who's I, who's Eurydice?'[11] Such omissions reveal Acker's continual concern with the politics of identity. In the drafts this material appears revised and formatted. These drafts reveal the excisions and truncations Acker made to the prose to yield a more minimal and more visual poetic prose. The draft of the section titled 'Diary written by Eurydice when she's dead' reveals the changes Acker made in the editing process. In the draft the original typed script reads 'I'm free to begin travelling/ With three or four other girls./into the countryside: Silver here is everywhere an object, and swamps. Pale green and browns mix with the branches; here objects and colors have the same status. Bits of sky can be seen either through, or falling through, wood, colors, inside which is a house.' On the drafts, Acker has made amendments in fountain pen that alter the text to read: 'Now I'm free to begin travelling, with three or four other girls. The countryside: silver here is everywhere an object, and swamps. Pale greens and browns mix with branches; in this place objects and colors have the same status. Sky can be seen either through, or falling through wood, inside the colors is a house.'[12] The minor amendments made to prose here by Acker increase the visual medium of the work. Such revisions heighten the text as a mode of perception. In the first version the house is located in a wood; in the revised version the house is suspended in colours, located in an abstract space. Attention to these avant-textes reveals new relations between surface and non-verbal, non-conventional meaning. In my work on Acker's archive, I explore new modes of attention and intention brought to light by archival knowledge.

As I have argued elsewhere, composition in Acker's work is not extrinsic to the production of non-verbal meaning.[13] In this chapter, I utilise bibliographic scholarship, most notably the work of D. F.

McKenzie and the proponents of genetic criticism, Louis Hay and Jean Bellamin-Noël, to explore the relation between Acker's experimental writing, manuscript practice and aesthetic protest. Genetic criticism emerged in France in the early 1970s. Louis Hay defined genetic studies as 'studies dealing with the production of writings, especially of literary texts'.[14] Genetic criticism, Jed Deppman, Daniel Ferrer and Michael Groden explain, 'grows out of a structuralist and poststructuralist notion of "text" as an infinite play of signs, but it accepts the teleological model of textuality and constantly confronts the question of authorship'.[15] Similar to philology, genetic criticism looks at 'tangible documents such as writers' notes, drafts, and proof corrections, but its real object', they argue, 'is something much more abstract – not the existing documents but the movement of writing that must be inferred from them'. Genetic criticism then 'strives to reconstruct, from all available evidence, the chain of events in a writing process'.[16] In a similar vein, Jean-Michel Rabaté terms the scholar who engages in genetic criticism a 'genreader', 'a textual agent that actively confronts a new type of materiality and temporality'. For Rabaté, 'texts have to be read in the context of an expanding archive that also creates its own sense of pedagogy'.[17] It is through this approach as a genreader that I bring Acker's avant-garde practice into dialogue with the 'avant-texte' to contend that the relation between archive materials and local and major form in experimental work allows for a new understanding of Acker's feminist experiment as diagrammatic. Such a reading illuminates the relation between textual value and the feminist force of Acker's works.

The archive brings to light the complex materiality of Acker's works. Encountering these works in their original forms, often merely as elements of the final works that Acker would then compose for the printed editions, increases both the modernist difficulty of Acker's texts and the generative nature of her works. As a means of articulating these forms of amplification yielded by the archive, I address Acker's work in relation to Johanna Drucker's recent work on diagrammatic writing and performative materiality. For Drucker, diagrammatic writing is a modernist form; the diagram has the potential to be 'the paradigm of poetic production'.[18] Drucker remarks that in contrast to Pound's concept of the ideogram that has dominated Anglo-American modernism, the diagrammatic operations of Mallarmé's works, most notably *Un coup de dés jamais n'abolira le hasard*, 'offer a radically different set of possibilities for poetic expression'. Instead of depending on 'the representational and concrete vision of the ideogram', Mallarmé's works 'suggest a kinetic mobilized field of articulated *relations* that expresses the belief that the very condition of poetic form is its suspension between the arbitrariness of language ("hazard") and the temporary configuration of meaning ("constellation")'.[19] As such, Mallarmé's works are paradigmatic of the diagrammatic format, 'one that uses fragments and phrases suspended in a field of dynamic possibilities – the poetic problem staged by the work'.[20] By comparison, through diagrammatic experimental composition, *Blood and Guts in High School* stages a linguistic problem: Janey's failure to find meaning and self-expression in ordinary language. Drucker is not alone in understanding an alternative history of Anglo-American modernism through the diagrammatic rather than the ideogram. The art historian John Golding in his seminal work *Visions of the Modern* (1995) highlights the 'mysterious diagrammatic images of Tanguy';[21] he interprets the 'colouristic abstractions' of Balla produced between 1911 and 1914 as being 'to do with the diagrammatic movement of light'.[22] For Golding, in the modernist period: 'Alchemy, which dealt with concepts of a cosmic and esoteric nature . . . had been forced at certain stages to render these in terms of diagrammatic and visual images.'[23] The diagrammatic also characterised the abstract portrait of James Joyce by Constantin Brancusi that the writer himself chose for the frontispiece of his *Tales Told of Shem and Shaun*, published by the Black Sun Press in 1929, suggesting a relation between the diagrammatic and Joyce's literary experiment.[24] Tracing modernist art and writing through the concept of the diagrammatic, Drucker and Golding offer an alternate understanding of modernist experiment that challenges the existing modernist history.

Drucker defines the diagrammatic as 'the condition of any poetic work in its inscriptional instantiation'.[25] The prime example of the diagrammatic is Aristotle's squares of logic: 'diagrams are schematic drawing that *work* – they *do* something rather than *represent* something. The squares of opposition used in classical and medieval philosophy to construct syllogisms are diagrams – drawings that can be used to advance an argument. They are generative because they are structural possibilities for thinking.'[26] Looking closely at Acker's acts of composition, in particular her use of images in *Blood and Guts in High School*, I argue that Acker's works are diagrammatic in Drucker's sense of the term, and that Acker's works open up new 'structural possibilities' that are socio-political gestures. *Blood and Guts in High School* not only offers a rewriting of Mallarmé's *Un coup de dés*, it echoes the composition at a wider level, employing experimental tactics of alignment, non-conventional typography and disjointed syntax. Drucker observes that the poetic problem at work in Mallarmé's

Un coup de dés 'is repeatedly expressed as a tension between the probabilities of meaning production and those of entropic dissipation held in play by the structure of the poem whose main – perhaps only – objective is to reflect upon the way poetry can be expressed in a linguistic form as a field of potential meaning'. For Acker, Mallarmé's central concern with indeterminacy is applicable to her own interest in the inadequacy of ordinary language. As Drucker remarks, 'Mallarmé shifts our engagement with philosophical questions of necessity (mechanistic determination) onto the field of language, where the problems of chance are all posed to challenges to meaning as form.' Drucker argues: 'If deterministic models of linguistics actually explained the operations of language (they do not), then the problems of the arbitrariness of language would never have reared their scary heads with such vengeance.'[27] *Blood and Guts in High School* engages with the problems of the arbitrariness of language, and the impossibility for a woman of making meaning within the symbolic, extending Mallarmé's preoccupations into the late twentieth century.

Rather than being representations, Acker's experimental compositions are generative through the 'play of elements' in the work. Indeed, Acker's works are anti-representation – they are concerned with a feminist form of language that, Acker states in her essay 'Seeing Gender', 'is not constructed on hierarchical subject-object relations'.[28] Acker's practice of experimental inscription can be read as a feminist practice concerned with the visual features of language. Charles Bernstein comments on Drucker's insistence that 'the place for woman is not as the Other but as the one that shows that the Other has always been present'. Bernstein observes that this is 'a position that is to a remarkable degree, analogous to her view about the material features of language'.[29] Such a correlation points to the feminist power of materiality, which is critical to an understanding of Acker's experimental inscription. The diagrammatic nature of Acker's texts necessitates a form of reading distinct from conventional forms of reading. In Acker's works the reader encounters what Drucker understands as the 'performative materiality' of a work. Performative materiality accompanies diagrammatic texts. Drucker explains that in the context of diagrammatic writing, in which the diagrammatic is a source of knowledge production, 'the performative is the term under which the reception practice of constituting a text might be identified'.[30] Exploring such reception practice, the performative materiality at play in Acker's works emerges as a politics of materiality that is intrinsic to the radical, revolutionary politics of Acker's writings and inextricable from the avant-textes housed in the archives.

The Avant-Garde and the Avant-Texte

The term 'avant-texte' derives from the genetic criticism of Jean Bellamin Noël, who defines the avant-texte as 'the totality of the material written for any project that was first made public in a specific form'.[31] Pierre-Marc de Biasi, another key proponent of genetic criticism asserts: '[a] work's manuscripts are clearly distinct from the text, although they lead to the text, they also keep reminding us that they are prior and external to it'; he argues that 'to attend to an avant-textual document is *to read, continuously with the text and without any presuppositions, the totality of formulations that, as previous possibilities, have become part of a given work of writing*'.[32] This idea of the avant-texte can be brought into relation with the avant-garde composition of Acker's works. The proof manuscript of *Blood and Guts in High School* is perhaps the most striking example of an avant-texte that differs significantly from the published text, not in content but through its material aesthetic form. The experimental form of the work explicitly yields the textual properties Drucker explores in *Diagrammatic Writing*, which, she remarks, 'is designed to demonstrate that a book is not a static object but a dynamic space, not a fixed and final expression but an organized arrangement of elements whose spatial arrangements encode semantic value'.[33] Revealing the book's material status as a collagist artwork, the proofs of *Blood and Guts* that Acker sent to Grove Press are hand set in a lined Citadel Notebook with various parts of the text: images, handwritten text, typed text and Xeroxes of the large-scale materials pasted onto its pages.[34] Illustrations are stuck onto the pages between text fragments, the sections titled 'Parents Stink' and 'Outside High School' are assembled from magazine cuttings, and the Janey/Father play scripts are typed separately and pasted into the notebook between the 'Parents Stink' pages. The manuscript is in many places composed of recycled found materials. For instance, the 'Outside High School' title section is pasted on the back of a letter from Ken Dollar dated 1 August 1978. The very notion of the 'text-book' is significant here, not just for the fact that *Blood and Guts in High School* is quite literally a text-book in its original form, and in content is Janey's self-reflexive text-book in which she writes, amongst other texts, her linguistic exercises, 'The Persian Poems'. The material form of the proof manuscript in this regard echoes the Standard French Schoolbook Gertrude Stein used for *Sentences* (1931), as well as the ATLAS Cahiers of Hélène Cixous.[35] Writing by hand is a modernist form of composition. It is significant that the materials that Acker produced in her notebooks that were then cut up and used for her texts were handwritten. Acker's notebooks that she kept throughout her career are similarly 'text-books'. The proof copy of *Blood and Guts in High School* is literally a textbook with items pasted in. The aesthetic artefact of the original proofs is then also the symbolic form of the work.

The materials in the Kathy Acker Papers inform an understanding of Acker's acts of experimental composition. Housed as separate objects, it is clear that Acker consciously arranged the materials with great attention to details and the effect of textual collage. Many of the notebooks are long pieces of prose, streams of consciousness, diaries and rewritten version of texts. In a taped interview with Peter Greenaway, Acker stated that she used up to five notebooks at a time to compose her works.[36] Acker's acts of composition involved cutting up her notebooks and arranging them alongside the other materials such as images and maps to create indeterminacy. There are, for instance, twenty-five notebooks containing materials for *Pussy, King of the Pirates*. One contains loose-leaf drafts and sketches of the dream maps 'The Place of Transformations', 'Pirate Island', and 'The Flying and Dying of Artaud' that were to become large-scale artworks which would then be Xeroxed for the published book.[37] Nowhere are Acker's compositional intentions clearer than in the 'Instructions' she sent to Grove Press alongside the proofs of *Blood and Guts in High School*. The heading of Acker's typesetting notes: 'INSTRUCTIONS FOR PUTTING THIS DAMN BOOK TOGETHER' – which stands alone on its own page in the Citadel Notebook – discloses the anxiety the author experienced in the act of assembling the materials for the publisher. On the following page, under the heading 'DUMMY FOR BLOOD AND GUTS', nineteen very detailed handwritten directions stipulate exactly the way in which Acker wanted the book to be assembled.[38] Meticulously detailed and fraught with tension between the experimental writer and their materials, Acker's typesetting requirements expose the strict arrangement of text and image and highlight the authorial intentionality present in the book at the level of experimental composition.

The modes of indeterminacy and process found in genetic criticism and the avant-texte can productively be brought into dialogue with the avant-garde indeterminacy and process found in Acker's works. The question of authorship that arises from the indeterminacy inherent to the shifting temporal nature of the archive is significant to Acker's works. A genetic criticism approach reveals a new form of intention inherent in Acker's works. Arguably, Acker's authorial presence is asserted not through the I, which is pluralised and destabilised to the point of non-identity in her texts, but through the composition of the text. It is worth here pointing to the difference between textual criticism and genetic criticism that the editors of the volume *Genetic Criticism* highlight: 'a textual critic will tend to see a difference between two states of a work in terms of accuracy and error or corruption, whereas a genetic critic will see meaningful variation'. They extend this thinking further: 'One could even say that genetic criticism is not concerned with texts at all but only with the writing processes that engender them.'[39] For genetic critics, an understanding of the 'process' by which a text came into being is fundamental to the integrity of the work. The emphasis placed here by genetic criticism on the importance of process speaks to Acker's avant-garde concern with process. For Acker process was crucial to experiment. In her 1990 essay 'Critical Languages', she reflects on her early adult years in the New York art world, recalling 'being taught that it's not an art work's content, surface content, that matters, but the process of making art. That only process matters.'[40]

Acker's emphasis on process has a number of antecedents. In *Blood and Guts in High School* Mallarmé's work is perhaps the most significant point of reference. Typographic signification is a fundamental component of Acker's avant-garde practice. My work claims the materiality of the text as an activist discourse resistant to, and in flux with, linguistic meaning and traditional grammatical structures. The presentation of *Blood and Guts in High School* as a collage, and the new relations generated between text and image by the work, positions *Blood and Guts in High School* in a lineage of illustrated works by Charles Baudelaire, Mallarmé and Arthur Rimbaud. These avant-garde writers, whom Acker engages with at numerous points in her works, were the progenitors of the avant-garde experiments with text and image at the beginning of twentieth century. Acker's debt to Mallarmé is overtly evident in her rewriting of Mallarmé's 1896 *Un coup de dés* in *Blood and Guts in High School*. Illustration, experimental typography, non-referential language and the use of the poetic function in *Blood and Guts in High School* as sites of an alternate language that emerges through compositional form and experimental forms of rewriting. This often non-verbal language runs counter to ordinary language. Acker's practice of *récriture*, in which she rewrites the works of César Vallejo and Mallarmé, merges the practice of rewriting and experimentation with typography to produce a linguistic performativity. In *Blood and Guts in High School*, illustration, the use of hieroglyphics and the experiments in typography empower inscription, visual depiction and writing, over linguistic transparency and conventional grammar structures.

Acker was arguably not only influenced by the experimental typography and radical literary politics of the *poète maudits*. As well as their shared use of experimental typography, Mallarmé's approach to the literary work in terms of composition is significant when considering Acker's experimental practice and the materiality of her works in the archive. 'For Mallarmé,' Deppman observes, 'the literary work was essentially open: it depended more on the structural indeterminacy of language than on the universality of a speaking or reading subject.' It was for Deppman the relaying of Mallarmé's works through modernism and postmodernism that created 'the conditions of possibility for books that celebrate the many signifying states and auras of texts'.[41] Similarly, Paul Valéry placed importance on process. In his 1922 Cahiers he highlights: 'The making, as the main thing, as whatever product constructed as *accessory*.'[42] Scholarly interest around the Mallarméan and Valéryan conceptions of text and genesis increased in the late 1960s, when Acker first started to experiment. Such a line of enquiry speaks to the bibliographic scholar D. F. McKenzie. McKenzie's 1986 work *Bibliography and the Sociology of Texts* sought to highlight the role of form in determining the meaning of a text. He believed that 'bibliographers should all be concerned to show that forms effect meaning'.[43] It is this relation between form and meaning that drives McKenzie's study, in which he interrogates 'whether or not the material forms of books, the non-verbal elements of the typographical notations within them, the very disposition of space itself, have an expressive function in conveying meaning'.[44] McKenzie's perusal of the 'relation of medium to meaning' and the assumption that 'forms effect sense' can function as co-ordinates to examine the avant-textes in the Kathy Acker papers. This notion of the text and its inherent instability recognises that 'no text of any complexity yields a definitive meaning'. McKenzie argues: 'The ostensible unity of any one "contained" text – be it in the shape of a manuscript, book, map, film, or computer-stored file – is an illusion. As a language its forms and meaning derive from other texts; and we listen to, look at, or read it at the very same time we re-write it.'[45] The Mallarméan linguistic indeterminacy and the Cagean indeterminacy operate in Acker's works alongside this textual indeterminacy that McKenzie points to.

The Avant-Texte and Visual Epistemology

The archives at Duke, NYU and the University of Cologne house the original drawings for Acker's works, which Acker then reproduced in her published works. The text/image composition is one way that

Acker creates indeterminacy; and it is through the use of images in the final section of *Blood and Guts in High School* that Acker is able to realise transformation. Visual language offers Acker a form of breaking free from ordinary language; an objective that drove her literary experiment. Acker's 1993 essay on bodybuilding, in which she theorises a language of the body, is concerned with positioning the material and visualisations in opposition to ordinary language. For Acker the only way to approach the language of the body, which, echoing Wittgenstein, she defines as 'a language game which resists ordinary language',[46] is to use the indirect route of Elias Canetti's discussion of 'geography that is without verbal language'[47] – the Marrakesh in which the writer is unable to understand what people are saying. Canetti's experience of being in Marrakesh allows Acker to articulate the non-verbal material language of bodybuilding and breath. For Acker, in bodybuilding the material body provides a route to 'a complex and rich world' that stands in contrast to the syntax generating ordinary languages prevalent in the world outside the gym. 'In a gym', Acker writes, 'verbal language or language whose purpose is meaning occurs, if at all, only at the edge of its becoming lost.'[48] The visual is one way in which Acker resists and moves away from ordinary language towards a speechless language. In *Empire of the Senseless* Acker uses the aesthetic of the tattoo, including ink drawings of tattoo art. *In Memoriam to Identity* she reproduces works from Shinichi Segi's *Yoshitoshi: The Splendid Decadent: The Last Master of Ukiyo-E*.[49] *Pussy, King of the Pirates* comprises a number of dream maps related to the pirates' feminist quest to find 'the place of transformations'. *Blood and Guts in High School* remains Acker's most experimental work in terms of visual language. Acker incorporates pencil drawings throughout *Blood and Guts in High School*, captioning these images with lines from the text alongside complex dream maps, ink illustrations, handwriting (Fig. 3.1) and experiments with typography. Whilst Acker's works use images, they are anything but pictorial or representational compositions. Acker's experiments break the pictorial and visual referent, just as they challenge and resist conventional referential relations in language.

This aspect of Acker's experimental practice in *Blood and Guts in High School* is directly related to the avant-texte, as in 1978 the incorporation of the verbal and visual was possible only through the cut-and-paste technique and then the reproduction of the collaged pages. This is evident in the final two sections of the work, titled 'The World' and 'The Journey', which form illustrated books that are parts of the overall work. The original proof pages of these works comprise twenty-four pages, most of which are text/image collages. In

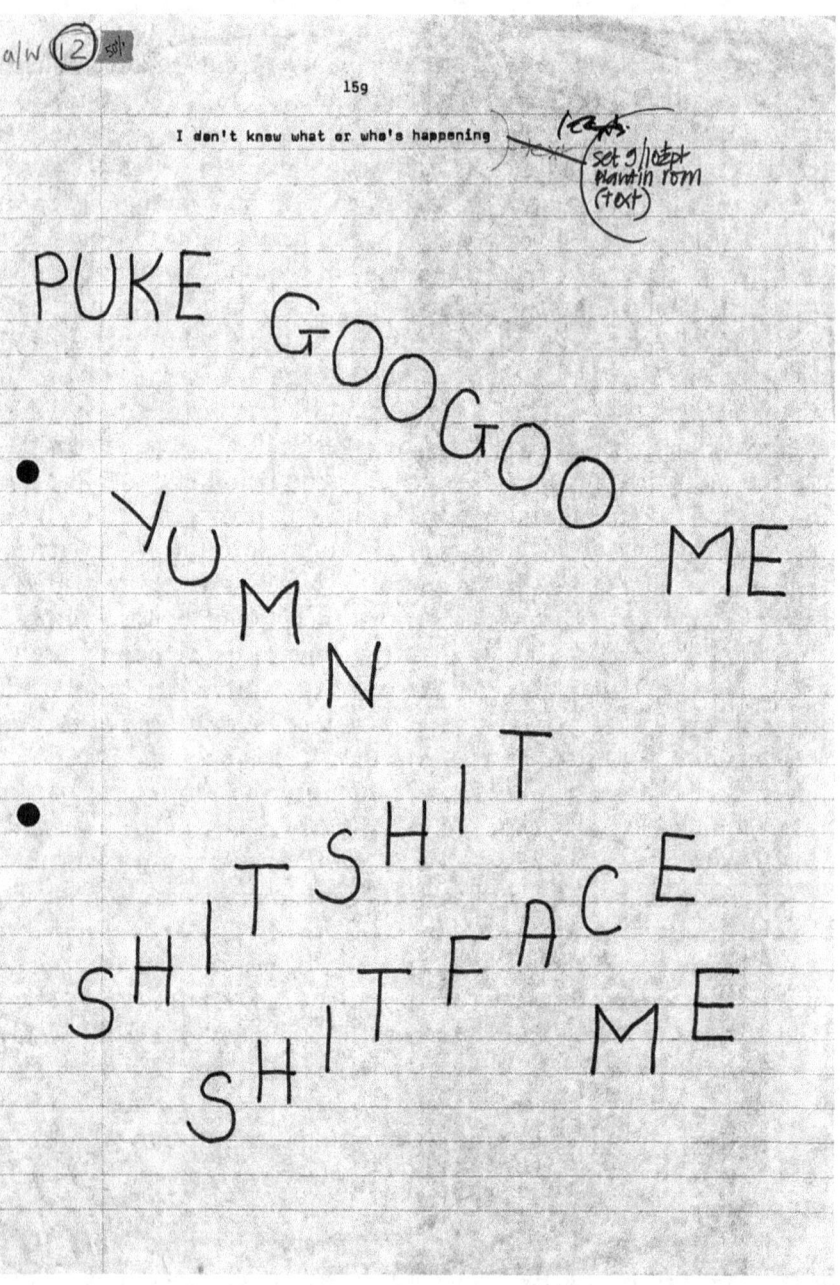

Figure 3.1 Kathy Acker, page from the original artwork for *Blood and Guts in High School*. Box 29, Folder 1. Kathy Acker Papers, David M. Rubenstein Rare Book & Manuscript Library, Duke University.

'The World' and 'The Journey', Acker moves from experimenting with majuscules in the early part of the book to working with early writing systems, most notably Egyptian hieroglyphics, in the latter part of the book. Acker begins 'The World' by juxtaposing phonetic language (the English alphabet in the form of grammar exercises) with a form of hieroglyphics. Impossible to recreate in their aesthetic complexities and idiosyncrasies, the elaborate inscriptions of Egyptian hieroglyphs are perhaps the ultimate avant-texte. Here Acker enacts a feminist experiment that engages with the materialities of seeing. As Drucker remarks: 'There are many aspects of hieroglyphic writing that are not, in a sense, pronounceable, or meant to be pronounced. It's not a script for speech; it's its own written code the way that pictorial representations are their own code. We don't look at a picture and imagine that we are supposed to speak it out loud. We receive that information visually.'[50] Hieroglyphs in 'The World' demand a reception practice that is visual rather than verbal. This form of visual knowledge production stands counter to the verbal knowledge production of language that Janey wrestles with in *Blood and Guts in High School*; it is one of the registers Acker uses to create feminist inscription that offers a language outside of ordinary language.

This non-phonetic nature of hieroglyphs was also important to William Burroughs, to whom Acker stated she was indebted in much of her work. In her essay on Burroughs, Acker wrote: 'For me, William was the American writer who wrote by thinking about how language is used. Who dissected the relations between language and power. Especially political power.'[51] In his essay 'Hieroglyphic Silence', published in his 1978 collaborative work with Bryon Gysin, *The Third Mind*, Burroughs remarks: 'I've recently spent a little time studying hieroglyph systems, both the Egyptian and the Mayan [. . .] Words – at least the way we use them – can stand in the way of what I call nonbody experience.'[52] The first page of the 'The World' refers to the conception of the world: 'The forms of the ancient arts of Egypt this is the time that wolves come out of the trees.' This typed passage is pasted onto the page. Below it, a list of exercises, which relates animal nouns to drawings that resemble Egyptian hieroglyphs, is pasted adjacent to the sentences (Fig. 3.2). Acker's use of images and handwritten inscriptions gesture to the original material writing systems that predate and form the alphabet: Egyptian hieroglyphs and cuneiform forms. As Allan H. Gardiner observes: 'in the eyes of the old Egyptians the hieroglyphic writing always remained a system of pictorial representation as well as a script.'[53] Acker's work echoes the indecipherability of Egyptian

THE WORLD

A light came into the world. Dazzling white light that makes lightness dazzling burning Happiness. Peace. The forms of the ancient arts of Egypt this is the time that wolves come out of the trees.

This is a wolf.

This is a dog.

This is a horse.

This is an elephant.

This is a kangaroo.

This is a snake.

Figure 3.2 Kathy Acker, page from 'The World', original artwork for *Blood and Guts in High School*. Box 29, Folder 1. Kathy Acker Papers, David M. Rubenstein Rare Book & Manuscript Library, Duke University.

hieroglyphs and she offers combinations of pictorial signs to generate new non-verbal meanings. The avant-texte allows for the inclusion of hand-drawn images, which are a form of feminist inscription that resists verbal language. Here the Mallarméan spatial practices found in the rewriting of *Un coup de dés* in the earlier part of *Blood and Guts in High School* emerge in pictogrammatic compositions, the visual field of which exceeds that of the verbal language. This is evident in the part of the illustrated book that tells of the journey of the giant bird at night (Fig. 3.3). The language is very simple, written in a child's register: 'At night the wolves snap at the flying bird/The alligators lie in wait to yump him up/And huge snakes wait/The alligators are the biggest.' Aesthetically, the images inscribe more than the words denote. The flying bird resembles a human; the candle and moon, symbols to denote the night, serve to create a disjunctive perspective, and the alligators are abstract shapes rather than literal depictions. The abstracted material denotation of such inscription and the non-verbal nature of the hieroglyphs offer a counter script to the reference system of ordinary language.

For Burroughs, the image was a vehicle for moving outwards and silencing the inner voice. 'Translating the connection between words and images', his experiments with scrapbooks enabled Burroughs to think in images, without words.[54] The cut-up method facilitated Burroughs' visual experiments, leading to a widening of perception. 'Cut-ups', he states, 'establish new connections between images, and one's range of vision consequently expands.' Acker uses the cut-up method in *Blood and Guts in High School*, and her other works, to both break from the constraints of ordinary language and to create new relations between text and images, culminating in *Blood and Guts in High School* in 'The World' and 'The Journey'. In her 1971 diary, Acker wrote 'USE only words which directly correspond to images.' This reflection comes into a feminist spatial and temporal practice in 'The World' and 'The Journey'. These two final sections are composed of text/image cut-ups. Burroughs defined the cut-up as 'a juxtaposition of what's happening outside and what you think of'.

This idea of the cut-up is prevalent in Acker's works most notably in the dream maps. 'The World' includes a dream map titled 'All over the earth' (Fig. 3.4). The map juxtaposes places in the city – the dress store, the bank, the shoe store – with imaginary places such as 'an island' which is also 'the land of skulls'. Text pasted below the circular visual depiction of the island offers political critique: 'There are no trees on the island due to capitalism.' Other parts of the map include the South of Calcutta, Thailand, China

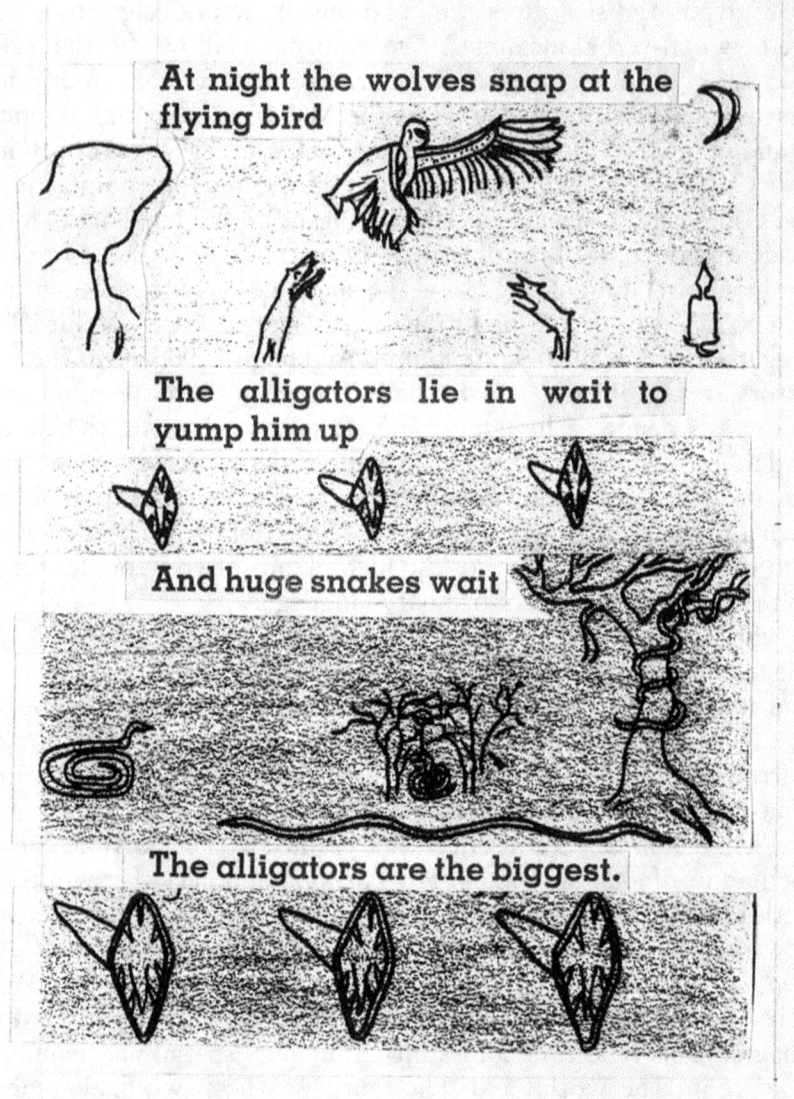

Figure 3.3 Kathy Acker, page from 'The World', original artwork for *Blood and Guts in High School*. Box 29, Folder 1. Kathy Acker Papers, David M. Rubenstein Rare Book & Manuscript Library, Duke University.

and Algeria. The images, a number of which are taken from the earlier section of the world that depict alligators and other animals, function to abstract the map and to create a surrealist space that fuses the imagination with the everyday. 'A human', the text of

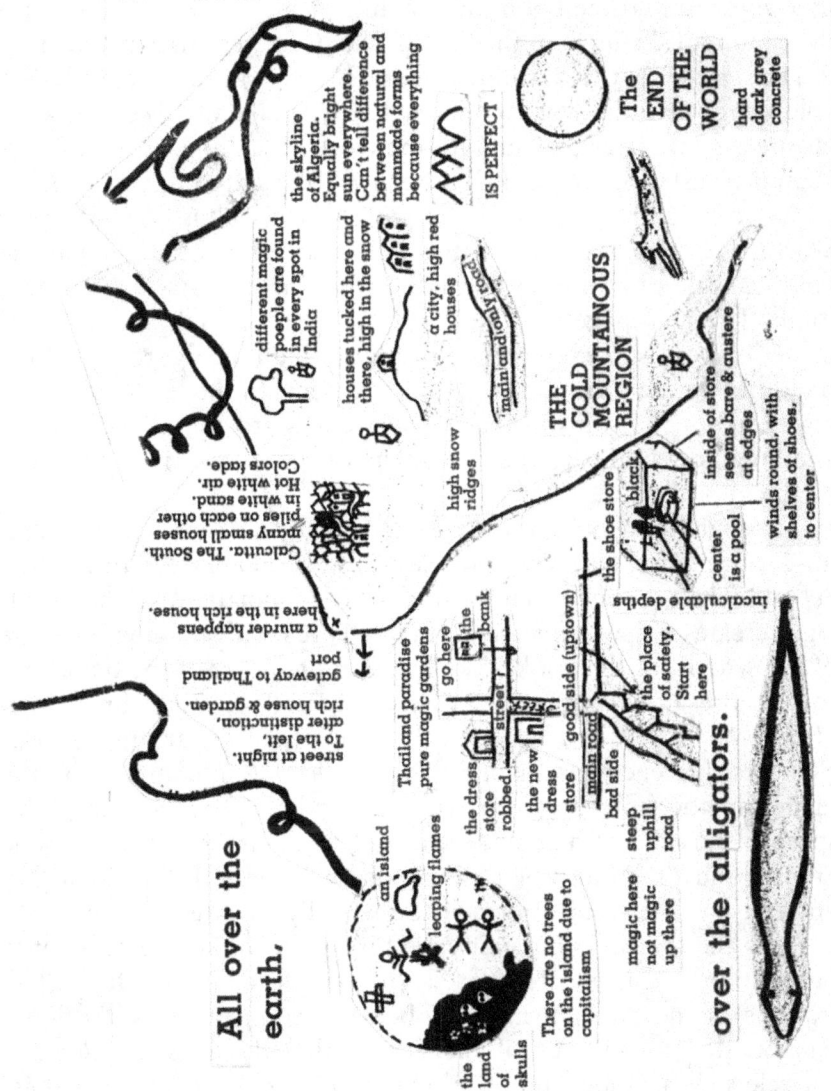

Figure 3.4 Kathy Acker, page from 'The World', original artwork for *Blood and Guts in High School*. Box 29, Folder 1. Kathy Acker Papers, David M. Rubenstein Rare Book & Manuscript Library, Duke University.

'The World' tells us, 'is a being halfway between an alligator and a bird who wants to be a bird.' 'The World' is an exercise in world-making through text/image experimentation. It is also the preliminary text to 'The Journey', which tells an illustrated surrealist tale of a quest to find the book on human transformation, hidden with the corpse of Catullus in the Saba Pacha Cemetery in Alexandria.[55] Acker read widely in Catullus's work. Acker's library houses three volumes of Catullus's poetry dated 1969, 1970 and 1976.[56] Acker's most extensive engagement with the work of Catullus is her experimental translation of Catullus's Poem VIII in *Don Quixote*.[57] Journeys are a central theme in the works of Catullus. Acker's 'The World' and 'The Journey' create an illustrated book that depicts the mythical tale of a journey to find a book that resides in Catullus's tomb. The final page of 'The World' is purely visual, a non-verbal depiction of a surrealist image of a god-like bird figure, of which the other animals are a part (Fig. 3.5). Beneath the figure, a drawing sketches the transformation of a corpse to the alligator-bird, and an arrow points to the final stage of the transformation to the mythical bird figure.

Through the visual and the cut-up technique, Acker creates a feminist temporality in the final two sections of *Blood and Guts in High School*. The non-linear nature of the diagrammatic text/image collages creates a new temporality that accords with the mythical tale of the search for the book. Like Drucker's concept of the book that she explores in *Diagrammatic Writing*, the collages in the final pages of *Blood and Guts in High School* are 'an organized arrangement of elements that encode semantic value'; reflecting in composition the diagrammatic features of the work as a whole. The cartographical space blends the architectural space of Catullus's tomb, the Magic House, and the House of Disjunctions with Saba Pacha Cemetery and Alaska. The visual language aesthetically narrates a journey that exceeds the text in complexity. Text/image relations create at once disjunction and new referential relations. On one page, four illustrations of the book in multiple boxes accompanied by the lines: 'Surrounded by swarms of the desires that drive us mad,/desires encircled by a golden bracelet whose ends are joined,/in the East River' abstract and mythologise real space (the East River of New York) (Fig. 3.6). The shapes drawn in pen surrounding the box inscribe desire; the golden bracelet is a metonymical reflection on the opening of 'The World'. The limited vocabulary and the repetition of symbols and language throughout the illustrated book create a self-referential homogeneous space. Shifting into Catullus's journey to the East River, the proceeding collages depict the poet's quest for the book. 'The Journey' ends with a subversion of the creation myth: 'So we create this world in our own image'. The two illustrated books that complete *Blood and Guts in High School* engender

Kathy Acker's Manuscript Practice 93

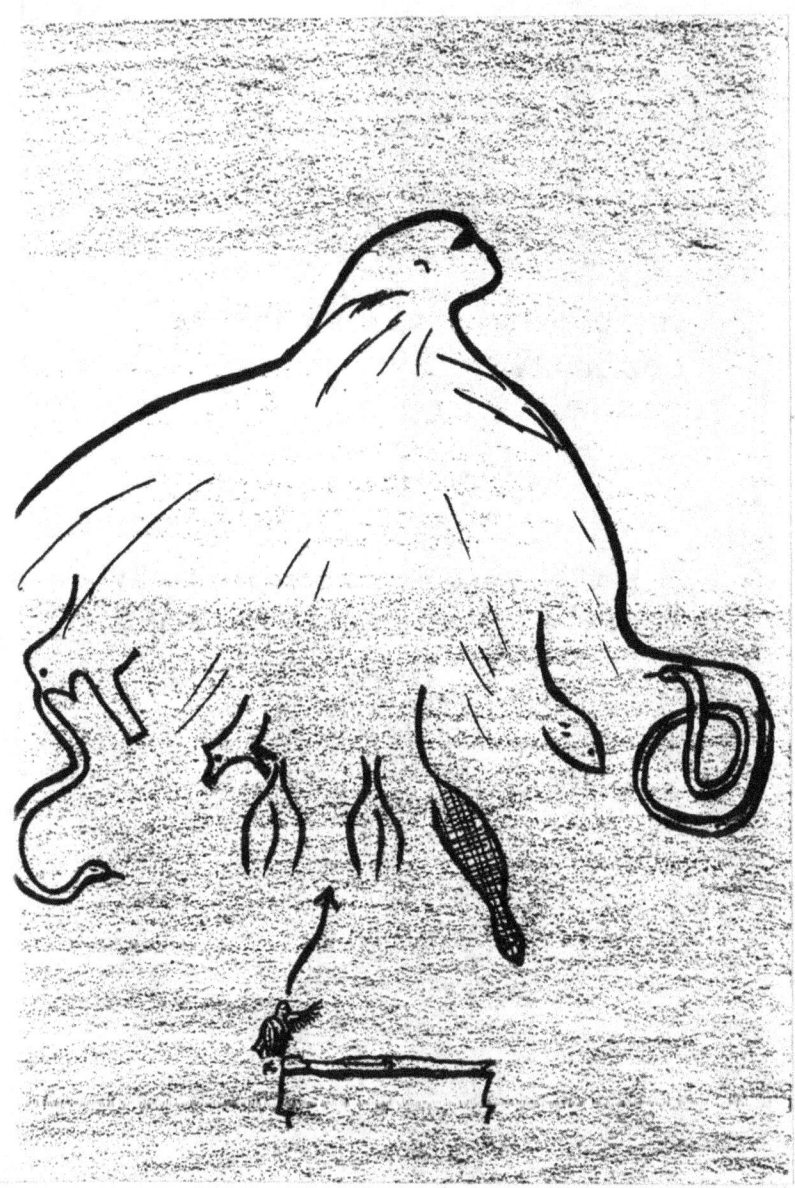

Figure 3.5 Kathy Acker, page from 'The World', original artwork for *Blood and Guts in High School*. Box 29, Folder 1. Kathy Acker Papers, David M. Rubenstein Rare Book & Manuscript Library, Duke University.

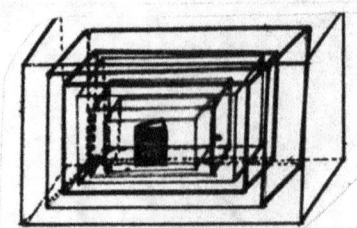

surrounded by swarms of the desires that drive us mad,

desires encircled by a golden bracelet whose ends are joined,

in the East River.

Figure 3.6 Kathy Acker, page from 'The Journey', original artwork for *Blood and Guts in High School*. Box 29, Folder 1. Kathy Acker Papers, David M. Rubenstein Rare Book & Manuscript Library, Duke University.

a performative materiality that extends the previous experiment with majuscules and line drawings in the earlier parts of the book. The sections move the work away from verbal language to a visual text that creates a feminist visual epistemology and liberation from the syntactical and referential constraints of ordinary language.

The archive materials magnify the generative nature of Acker's works and reveal Acker's material practices. In an interview with Linda Kinnahan, Caroline Bergvall refers to Kamau Brathwaite's explanation of how 'he wants his strongly graphic and visual poetry to blind the reader to force up another kind of reading, of comprehension'. For Bergvall, 'this is a useful metaphor for much current multilingual writing'.[58] Acker's work similarly forces up new ways of reading through graphic and visual experimental writing. All of Acker's works are, arguably, diagrammatic. Here, I have focused on instances of the diagrammatic that are inextricable from the material inscription of the avant-texte. In the dream maps and the text/image collages of 'The World' and 'The Journey', Acker's experimental inscription exhibits a diagrammatic structure and yields performative materiality. Like Drucker's stochastic poetics, in Acker's work we have an indeterminate 'field of language activity', 'a non-linear and non-deterministic system of signification'. Drucker states that what the 'diagrammatic and stochastic share is the instability of the field of production that then loops into the instability or generative conditions of reception'. For Drucker, '[t]he performative dimension of reading exists in every encounter between reader and text but diagrammatic aspects expand the possibilities of poetic form and the changing conditions of documents and text.' In the final sections of *Blood and Guts in High School* non-verbal meaning is produced in a performative engagement with the diagrammatic form. The original artworks for 'The World' and 'The Journey' offer a feminist performative materiality that demands a new form of reading resistant to linear form. Performative materiality emerges in the reception of the text. The visual cut-up texts in 'The World' and 'The Journey', and Acker's dream maps in *Blood and Guts in High School* and, later, *Pussy, King of the Pirates* (1996), create a diagrammatic space in which the reader finds affectual significance in the dynamic structure of the experimental work. Through Acker's experimental practices in these works, knowledge is created in the act of receiving the text, in its disruptions. The performative materiality that arises from our engagement with these avant-textes constitutes a radical literary politics which is at once the means by which Acker gets rid of conventional meaning, and gives rise to new non-conventional non-verbal expression that resists the semantic field of ordinary language.

Notes

A version of this paper was presented at a symposium on 22–24 November 2018, held as part of the landmark exhibition 'Kathy Acker – GET RID OF MEANING', curated by Matias Viegener and Anja Cassar. My thanks go to Matias and Anja for allowing me to reproduce the work that I presented here. As always I am deeply indebted to Matias Viegener for his generosity in granting me permission to reproduce materials housed in the Kathy Acker Papers at the Sallie Bingham Center for Women's History and Culture at the David M. Rubenstein Rare Book and Manuscript Library at Duke University.

1. Howe, *Spontaneous Particulars: The Telepathy of the Archive*, p. 21.
2. Howe, *My Emily Dickinson*.
3. Howe, 'The Art of Poetry No. 97'.
4. This includes a recent exhibition at the ICA, London, '*I, I, I, I, I, I, Kathy Acker*', 1 May – 4 August, 2019.
5. See Hayles, *Writing Machines*.
6. Bataille, *Visions of Excess*, p. 97. These works are housed in the Kathy Acker Reading Room, University of Cologne, which is curated by Daniel Schulz.
7. Teresa de Lauretis, *Alice Doesn't: Feminism, Semiotics, Cinema*, p. 131. Kathy Acker Reading Room, University of Cologne.
8. Wittgenstein, *Philosophical Investigations*, 5e. Kathy Acker Reading Room, University of Cologne.
9. Acker's annotation on the first unpaginated page of Sollers, *Writing and the Experience of Limits*. Kathy Acker Reading Room, University of Cologne.
10. Acker, 'Rejects from *Don Quixote*' (annotated typescripts).
11. Acker, 'Eurydice Speaks' (notebook).
12. Acker, *Eurydice in the Underworld*, excerpts.
13. Colby, *Kathy Acker: Writing the Impossible*.
14. Hay, 'Genetic Criticism: Origins and Perspectives', p. 18.
15. Jed Deppman, Daniel Ferrer, and Michael Groden, 'Introduction: A Genesis of French Genetic Criticism', *Genetic Criticism*, p. 2.
16. Ibid.
17. Jean Michel Rabaté, *James Joyce and the Politics of Egoism* (Cambridge: Cambridge University Press, 2001), p. 196.
18. Johanna Drucker, 'Diagrammatic Writing and Stochastic Writing and Poetics', *The Iowa Review*, Vol. 44, Issue 3, Winter 2014/15, pp. 122–32; p. 124.
19. Drucker, 'Diagrammatic Writing and Stochastic Writing and Poetics', p. 126.
20. Drucker, 'Diagrammatic Writing and Stochastic Writing and Poetics', p. 127.

21. John Golding, 'Visions of the Modern' (California: University of California Press, 1994), p. 261.
22. Ibid. p. 162.
23. Ibid. p. 302.
24. Ibid. p. 191.
25. Drucker, 'Diagrammatic Writing and Stochastic Writing and Poetics', p. 124.
26. Drucker, 'Diagrammatic and Stochastic Writing and Poetics', p. 122.
27. Drucker, 'Diagrammatic and Stochastic Writing and Poetics', p. 127.
28. Kathy Acker, 'Seeing Gender', *Bodies of Work: Essays* (New York: Serpents Tail, 2006), p. 166.
29. Charles Bernstein, Introduction to Johanna Drucker, *Figuring the Word: Essays on Books, Writing, and Visual Poetics* (New York: Granary Books, 1998), xiii.
30. Johanna Drucker, 'Diagrammatic Writing and Performative Materiality', Volume 19, Issue 2: *Disrupting the Humanities: Towards Posthumanities*, Fall 2016. Unpaginated.
31. Jean Bellamin-Noël, 'Psychoanalytic Reading and the Avant-texte', *Genetic Criticism*, p. 31.
32. Pierre-Marc de Biasi, 'Toward a Science of Literature: Manuscript Analysis', *Genetic Criticism*, p. 38.
33. Drucker, 'Diagrammatic and Stochastic Writing and Poetics', p. 123.
34. Kathy Acker, *Blood And Guts In High School*, annotated proofs. Box 4, Folder 2, Kathy Acker Papers, David M. Rubenstein Rare Book & Manuscript Library, Duke University.
35. Helélène Cixous, *Mother Homer is Dead*, trans. Peggy Kamuf (Edinburgh: Edinburgh University Press, 2018).
36. Acker, K. and P. Greenaway (1990). Interview with Peter Greenaway by Kathy Acker – Tape. Kathy Acker Reading Room, University of Cologne.
37. Kathy Acker, 'Dream Maps' (2 notebooks and 5 hand-drawn maps), undated, Box 13, Folder 7. Kathy Acker Papers, David M. Rubenstein Rare Book & Manuscript Library, Duke University.
38. For a full discussion of Acker's instructions see Georgina Colby, *Kathy Acker: Writing the Impossible*, pp. 77–8.
39. Deppman et al., 'Introduction', in *Genetic Criticism*, p. 11.
40. Acker, 'Critical Languages', in *Bodies of Work*, p. 83.
41. Ibid. p. 6.
42. Paul Valéry, *Cahiers 8*, p. 578; *Cahiers/Notebooks*. 'Ego scriptor' 2: 1922; 475' cited in Deppman et al., *Genetic Criticism*, p. 6.
43. McKenzie, 'The book as an expressive form', p. 13.
44. Ibid. p. 17.
45. Ibid. p. 8.
46. Kathy Acker, 'Against Ordinary Language: The Language of the Body', in Acker, *Bodies of Work*, pp. 143–52; p. 147.
47. Ibid.

48. Ibid. pp. 144–5.
49. Yoshitoshi was a Japanese artist born in 1839 in Tokyo, Japan, whose works comprise innovative forms of the ukiyo-e genre of woodblock printing and painting. The stencils of the images are on display and are housed in Acker's copy of Shinichi Segi, *Yoshitoshi: The Splendid Decadent*, in the Kathy Acker Reading Room, Cologne.
50. 'Dr Johanna Drucker – Art Meets Technology: The History and Effects of the Alphabet', <https://childrenofthecode.org/interviews/drucker.htm> (last accessed 17 June 2019).
51. Acker, 'William Burroughs' (typescript).
52. Burroughs and Gysin, *The Third Mind*, n.p.
53. Gardiner, *Egyptian Grammar*, p. 438.
54. Burroughs and Gysin, *The Third Mind*, n.p.
55. Chris Kraus observes in *After Kathy Acker* that Acker in fact intended to end *Blood and Guts in High School* with the page of 'The World' that tells of the mythical book on human transformation in Catullus's tomb in Alexandria's Saba Pacha Cemetery. The final line of the page read: 'Shall we look for this wonderful book? Shall we stop being dead people? Shall we find our way out of all expectations?' See Kraus, *After Kathy Acker*, p. 154.
56. Acker owned *Catullus: The Complete Poems for American Readers* (New York: Dutton, 1970); *Catullus, Tibullus, and Pervigilium Veneris* (London, Cambridge: W. Heinemann, Harvard University Press, 1976); and *Catullus (Gai Valeri Catulli Veronensis liber)* (London: Cape Goliard Press, 1969). These works are part of the collection at the Kathy Acker Reading Room, University of Cologne.
57. For an extensive discussion of Acker's translation of Catullus's Poem VIII in *Don Quixote* see Colby, *Writing the Impossible*, p. 126.
58. Kinnahan, 'An Interview With Caroline Bergvall', p. 239.

Chapter 4

Rereading Race and Commodity Form in Erica Hunt's *Piece Logic*
Chris Chen

Contemporary experimental poet Erica Hunt has long been interested in exploring imaginative spaces that, in the poet's words, 'teeter on the verge of legibility, blur public and private, set boundaries anew'.[1] As part of a body of contemporary black experimental poetry endeavouring 'to expand the range of the thinkable and sayable',[2] in the words of Anthony Reed, Hunt's writing restlessly interrogates the conditions or terms of social legibility that regulate differential incorporation into a postwar US political, economic and social order organised around what the poet describes as rigid and mass-produced social roles. The poet models an investigatory poetics that consistently troubles or complicates the normative boundaries of such roles, even and especially when they are framed in oppositional terms. In my reading of Hunt's 2002 chapbook, *Piece Logic*, I argue that the poet reimagines an oppositional poetics and politics by synthesising historically segregated antiracist and anticapitalist political imaginaries.

Hunt's poems have appeared in various influential anthologies, from Language Poet Ron Silliman's *In the American Tree* (2002), *Gathering Ground: A Reader Celebrating Ten Years of Cave Canem* (2006), to Aldon Lyn Nielsen and Laura Ramey's *What I Say: Innovative Poetry by Black Writers in America*, vividly demonstrates how Hunt's writing occupies a kind of liminal space between a historically Anglo-American avant-garde or experimental poetic tradition on the one hand and contemporary black poetry and poetics.[3] Drawing inspiration from a range of sources, from bop improvisation to Oulipian procedural writing, Hunt's poetry could be read as a pioneering example of contemporary black experimental writing that in the words of poet and critic Evie Shockley has been 'dismissed, marginalized, and misread: first, in relation to the African American poetic tradition, because its experiments were not "recognizably black"; and second, in relation to constructions of the avant-garde tradition, because they were'.

The poems contained in *Piece Logic* question ideals of desegregated access to mass consumer culture as a measure of racial progress, though the poet treats race as fundamentally entangled with other forms of social differentiation. In this chapbook Hunt explores how relations between subjects within and beyond the boundaries of the US have been continuously shaped and reshaped by what Arjun Appadurai has called 'the social life of things'.[4] As processes of commodification have come to remake a range of previously uncommodified areas of social life, *Piece Logic* investigates how race and gender appear in what I want to call the mirror of commodity form. It is a distorting mirror that does not simply reflect pre-existing realities but radically reshapes them. Illuminating a society where nation, home and workplace are interlinked through circulating objects and a dream of consumer abundance, Hunt's collection draws attention to the intersection of processes of racialisation and what Karl Marx has called 'the fetishism of the commodity'.[5]

The social order reflected in the mirror of commodity form does not simply describe hierarchically segmented populations or material objects but a seemingly all-encompassing measure of comparative social valuation that extends to both persons and things. By telling the story of disposable objects whose value is continuously fluctuating, *Piece Logic* also narrates the fate of individuals and groups threatened with an analogous form of devaluation and disposability. Persons excluded or expelled from the postwar economy are subsequently compared to 'broken' commodities.

In presenting an allegory of 'broken' things, the chapbook reveals how the 'brokenness' of the postwar economy has been consistently displaced onto specific 'broken' populations. The meaning of 'brokenness' has within the postwar period been thoroughly freighted with racial meaning and symbolised through persistent tropes of 'broken families'[6] and black cultural pathology in particular contained in the controversial 1965 'Moynihan Report', for example, penned by sociologist and senator Daniel Patrick Moynihan. *Piece Logic* stages a simultaneously antiracist and anticapitalist critique of the mirror of commodity form itself as evidence or 'proof' of the pathological character of a social order organised around a single measure of abstract value. Hunt's collection can thus be read, I argue, as a radical revision of the image of a 'tangle of pathology'[7] whose origins lie in the organisation of black households. Hunt's collection reimagines this 'brokenness' not in terms of subjects but broken objects that mark the boundaries of a postwar consumer imaginary that the historian Charles McGovern has dubbed 'material nationalism'.[8] The poems diagnose the pathological character of contemporary explanations for the intergenerational reproduction of black poverty and civic marginalisation contained in documents like the Moynihan Report, I argue, and reorient the object of that report's critique away from 'broken' subjects and towards a 'broken' general economy of objects.

This critique depends upon the poet establishing a kind of continuous parallel between the life cycle of commodities and the fluctuating economic value of persons. Hunt represents radically devalued persons and objects as stamped with the spectral imprint of an entire society-wide process of abstract value production that is both racially organised and organising. While the chapbook's rare explicit references to race often appear in the form of oblique euphemisms, the chapbook presents a seemingly 'colour-blind' vision of consumer abundance in order to denaturalise how things become the measure of the value of persons. It is a measure that embeds racial divisions within other processes of social differentiation and converts what Hunt calls the 'statistical likelihoods'[9] and 'rigged destiny'[10] of racial life chances into the intrinsic characteristics of racial groups. The seven interconnected poems collected that comprise *Piece Logic* dramatise how the boundaries between national citizen-subjects and mass-produced objects blur as national and domestic space are increasingly remade by market imperatives. The 'social life of things', Hunt suggests, positions individuals and groups within a general logic of value production that sets the measure of racial progress, sharply delimits the material boundaries of civic rights and complexly structures an evolving global division of labor.

Material Nationalism and the 'House of Broken Things'

Piece Logic thus exposes racial inferiorisation as a defining feature of what the poet calls a 'House of Broken Things' – a figure that describes the US not only as a nation, but as a combination of a home, laboratory and factory where objects are made, warehoused and destroyed. Over the course of seven poems, the chapbook likens what I take to be a Cold War national consumer imaginary to a household, department store, warehouse and supermarket stocked with 'miles of appliances,/lining the intestinal maze of its imposing architecture'.[11] The inhabitants of this nation are likened to an immense collection of goods whose value is constantly recalculated through seemingly unknown and unknowable market processes. Consumer subjects are pushed to the margins of the poems, appearing only as ghostly adjuncts to animate objects invested with great political and epistemic 'Object Authority'.[12]

Organising people and things, and people *as* things, such processes are represented in these poems in terms of expulsion from a kind of chiasmic structure of personification and reification that Karl Marx has famously characterised as 'commodity fetishism', in which 'the definite social relation between men themselves . . . assumes here . . . the fantastic form of a relation between things'.[13] The poems that make up *Piece Logic*, however, do not simply trace a general commodity logic that Marx and subsequent Marxist theorists have identified as a constitutive feature of contemporary capitalist social formations. The poems also describe how postwar economy reproduces racial, gender and class distinctions in relation to each other through simultaneously atomising and aggregative market relations. *Piece Logic* then arguably functions as a description of a form of political and economic rationality that paradoxically binds together groups precisely through the same logic that divides and continually disaggregates them. What the poet calls *Piece Logic* binds as it separates, positioning atomised subjects within relations of market interdependence mediated by things. The social life of things, then, establishes the normative terms of racial inclusion and exclusion within the nation.

While Hunt is careful not to claim that categories of difference that delimit social roles are reducible to political economy, the poems in the collection explore how the increasing commodification of postwar social life powerfully alters the meaning of national belonging, the gendered division of domestic labour and the lived experience of legible and illegible social roles. Human subjects in Hunt's poems are forced to exist in the curiously vacant negative space around things, where readers only catch momentary glimpses of human activity in the form of labouring hands seemingly disconnected from bodies, or in fragments of a formulaic, ambient language of advertising and journalistic reportage.

The collection traces how the seemingly intrinsic value or valuelessness of mass-produced objects is generalised, becoming a measure of the value of persons including but not limited to economic quantification. Racial difference then reappears as 'brokenness' at the far side of a process of reification that invokes a seemingly objective discourse of economic value that both conceals and naturalises complexly interwoven histories of racial oppression, capitalist imperatives and communal survival and social reproduction. Hunt's collection thus endeavours to capture the market-mediated dimension of postwar processes of racial differentiation in a collection of poems that compels readers to place existing accounts of contemporary racial formation in conversation with critiques of postwar mass consumer culture.

Nation, Naturalization and Generic Citizens

The first poem of *Piece Logic*, 'A House of Broken Things', describes the principles of social cohesion that knit together the inhabitants of an unnamed nation, where the formal equality of national citizens is mirrored by the abstract exchangeability of goods. Both are examples of a peculiar way of structuring the relationship between parts and wholes, the poet suggests, that reveals the imprint of an entire 'wounded social body'[14] in each isolated person or thing that constitutes that larger collective body:

> In a country that is not one but several.
>
> In a country where it is common to assume that a new name gives you a new origin, leading to a different set of partners and possibly more exalted purpose. In a country that lives by its headlines, where explanations are clocked to correct enormity. In a country where a foreigner is welcome as long as s/he is generic. Or naturally naturalized and numbered.[15]

These opening lines stipulate a number of mechanisms that establish and then regulate relations between 'generic' and seemingly formally equivalent national subjects: from the rules governing the adoption of surnames and the audiences called into being by mass print media, to shifting immigration and naturalisation policy. These institutional mechanisms come to signify both the potential rewards and the civic boundaries of national belonging. What defines national subjects in these opening stanzas are a kind of 'piece logic', I want to argue, in which iterative procedures can produce 'several' subjects from 'one'. The collection will go on to explicitly liken this process to the mass production of goods.

Even the 'foreigner' can be rendered legible and calculable through 'naturally naturalized' pathways to citizenship based on assimilability to a regime of state and economic quantification. Within the context of US immigration policy, the lottery and national origin quota systems, along with per country numerical limits, have historically determined the maximum allowable number of immigrants and refugees granted citizenship in any given year. Already in these opening stanzas, the poem begins to map the basic institutional mechanisms that can enforce racial boundaries at the intersection of two forms of quantification: state recognition of national citizenship and the national economic demand for labour.

The 'generic' character of the national citizenry functions in the poem both as a reference to enforced, disciplinary homogeneity, but also to an expansive liberal democratic right of free association seemingly unburdened by historically entrenched status hierarchies. This capacity is exemplified, the poem suggests, in the possibility of constructing new kinship ties and adopting different surnames – acts that bestow upon subjects 'a new origin, leading to a different set of/ partners and possibly more exalted purpose'. Here the poem seems to trace a process of assimilation through tied to the promise of individualised social mobility represented by the possibility of choosing 'different partners' within a new country. As scholars of the politics of names and naming observe in relation to early twentieth century waves of immigration from southern and eastern Europe, surnames often indicated professions, places of origin and kinship relations,[16] and so changes to these names could conjure alternate familial histories and therefore different potential futures. The Anglicisation of both surnames and primary names – whether the result of voluntary decisions often made during the process of naturalisation or of the actions of immigration officials at Ellis Island and Galveston, Texas – often signalled a desire on the part of initially stigmatised, non-Anglo Saxon European immigrant groups for cultural assimilation into an imagined American mainstream as well as a method of preempting xenophobic prejudice and historically codifying a white racial identity.[17] The poem's stray reference to the politics of names and naming seems to allow for individuals to obscure or 'forget' their origins in order to identify with the 'more exalted purpose' of a sense of national mission.[18] Of course, this process of establishing national unity through what one might call the historical forgetting of origins is not unique to the United States. In one of the earliest attempts to define the basic components of the nation-form, nineteenth-century French scholar Ernest Renan has argued that 'Forgetting, I would even say historical error, is an essential factor in the creation of a nation.'[19] If for Renan nations often obscure or 'forget' their own violent origins, such forgetting becomes a precondition for the assertion of nationhood as a spiritual principle of unity that must be continually ratified by what he has famously called a 'daily plebiscite'.[20]

An Imagined Community of Objects

Hunt's poem draws attention to how such acts of forgetting are repeated in the lives of national subjects as the basis for an associational freedom that paradoxically constitutes a formative principle of what political theorist Benedict Anderson has famously called the 'imagined communities'[21] of modern nations. The poem suggests that the freedom to alter personal narratives of origins and ends are nevertheless established in relation to the time of the nation. The poem's reference to 'headlines, where explanations are clocked/to correct enormity' suggests that print media may be one particularly powerful mechanism for synchronising the experiences of disparate, spatially dispersed subjects.

The poem's reference to headlines in particular echoes Anderson's observation that the consolidation of national identities has been facilitated by emergent print technologies – from newspapers to novels – capable of creating and sustaining mass reading audiences and promoting vernacular languages. For Anderson, such languages have frequently been tied to territories and imagined homelands and have thus played a key role in cohering national populations by interpellating them as vernacular audiences, but also by suturing together otherwise seemingly disconnected events – marriages, deaths, political appointments and commodity prices. For Anderson, the newspaper functions as a vehicle for imagining the lived experience of national subjects as parallel and simultaneous despite the absence of direct social ties. The poem's brief reference to headlines draws attention to the generic journalistic conventions that project an image of national belonging as a horizontal community of equals. It is a community renewed through what Renan calls a 'daily plebiscite'[22] and what Anderson describes as a kind of collective subject moving through 'homogeneous, empty time'.

Hunt's chapbook instead represents the nation as an 'imagined community' of objects that not only mediates social life but becomes a normative model for it:

> It is customary to give every object its count: To number
> the citizen and her possessions. Each object passing
> through enumeration is certified, and citizens are
> surrounded by certified belongings, a horde of things
> indemnifying identity.[23]

Citizenship is here not simply defined through the possibility of acquiring a different name, or of being situated within a national history, but through the acquisition of commodities. Both citizen and 'her possessions' are forced to pass 'through enumeration', testing and certification – a process likened to the language government agencies, corporate inspectors and consumer groups use to describe quality control procedures for determining the safety and saleability of consumer goods. That such testing typically involves verifying the industrial origins of these goods echoes the poem's earlier mention of the genealogical implications of names and naming. The 'horde of things' that seem to surround and determine the relative value of the citizen at the same time seems to sever the relation between things and human labouring activity. The passage reveals a latent tension between the demand for consumer goods, whose quality and authenticity is dependent upon traceable origins, and citizens, whose genealogies are revisable.

The fact that such products serve the function of 'indemnifying identity' doesn't simply draw attention to the similarities between product testing and establishing the economic boundaries of national citizenship, but also to the systematic reproduction of identity as a kind of commodified object. As a legal term indicating insurance against risk or payment for loss, indemnification presupposes a contractual obligation binding legal parties together. In the poem, however, this contractual relation is also a fantasmatic one where objects compensate for the incompleteness and finitude of 'identity'. How commodities secure identity against loss, the poem suggests, renders the value of identity calculable. Persons and things can be submitted to the same measure of abstract value capable of surviving a succession of perishable material forms:

> The objects arrive shrink wrapped, adamant, brilliant,
> resembling an illuminated text, ready to be admired.
> The tags claim the high ground of indestructibility,
> shamelessly wrapping themselves in the symbols of
> great empires, pyramid, halo, iron cross, to disguise
> their true membership in the atomic kingdom, with
> its currency of rust, dust, and ashes.[24]

Here product packaging can significantly alter the meaning of mass-produced objects that 'shamelessly' wish to obscure their origins by invoking traditional symbols of authority. The comparison of commodities with illuminated manuscripts suggests that value possesses a seemingly metaphysical, quasi-religious character. These new 'shrink wrapped' objects conceal their secular, modern and mass-produced origins through the association of their production with the painstaking and costly artisanal labour of earlier eras.

We may read what such objects 'illuminate' as not only ancient Egyptian or Christian 'great empires' but also decidedly more modern space of the nation. The personified object's claim to 'indestructibility' reveals one way in which subjects might compensate for their own finitude through identifying with nations, empires or symbols of divinity. The fact that these commodities are both new and 'adamant' while clearly being susceptible to damage and decay, however, exposes the purportedly timeless and transcendental sources of spiritual or political authority as a human invention. The claim to permanence, the poem maintains, conceals not only the object's 'true membership in the atomic kingdom, with its currency of rust, dust, and ashes', but also the transience of empires and nations.

That this 'atomic kingdom' possesses a kind of currency of its own reveals that these objects are not simply reducible to their 'atomic' materiality after all, but are also implicated in a system of human production and exchange that invests such objects with abstract, immaterial value. Here, Hunt's poem shifts towards an investigation of the split character of commodity form that Karl Marx famously made a central component of his analysis of the history and structure of capitalism. By mixing the language of value with references to an 'atomic kingdom' of objects, the poem counterposes two distinct philosophical conceptions of materialism: ancient atomist theories of the world, and later analysis of the 'metaphysical subtleties and theological niceties'[25] of the commodity, or what Marx called 'the economic cell-form'[26] of developed capitalist societies. Though one may read these lines from the poem as an ironic commentary on the limits of attributing permanent value to evanescent things, the decomposition of things nevertheless reveals the essential exchangeability of things with 'rust, dust, and ashes'. Things are different configurations of the same underlying atomic order. Likening the atomic structure of reality to a peculiar form of currency highlights the social function of currency itself as a medium of exchange and index of relative value that does not inhere in the specific mutable form of objects. Which is to say that the metaphorical currency of 'rust, dust, and ashes' invokes two incommensurable ways of conceiving of the value of things: as a literal atomic property of objects, or as a socially constructed measure governing the exchange of the products of human labour.

The poem's telescoping or superimposition of these forms of value, I would argue, exposes a peculiar feature of capitalist social relations where, as Marx has famously observed, social relations between persons assume the 'fantastic form of a relation between things'.[27] That the poem represents commodities as passing through a life cycle ending in the brokenness of 'object death',[28] mirroring the lives of the subjects who consume and own them, echoes Marx's description of the process of what he characterises as 'the fetishism of the commodity'[29]:

> The mysterious character of the commodity-form consists therefore simply in the fact that the commodity reflects the social characteristics of men's own labour as objective characteristics of the products of labour themselves, as the socio-natural properties of these things. Hence it also reflects the social relation of the producers to the sum total of labour as a social relation between objects, a relation which exists apart from and outside the producers. Through this substitution, the products of labour become commodities, sensuous things which are at the same time suprasensible or social . . . . It is nothing but the definite social relation between men themselves which assumes here, for them, the fantastic form of a relation between things. In order, therefore, to find an analogy we must take flight into the misty realm of religion. There the products of the human brain appear as autonomous figures endowed with a life of their own, which enter into relations both with each other and with the human race. So it is in the world of commodities with the products of men's hands.[30]

For Marx, the exchange of commodities within developed capitalist societies can invest objects with seemingly intrinsic value that conceals the fact that what is being exchanged is in fact heterogeneous forms of human labour that are subject to ongoing market comparison expressed in the fluctuating prices for goods. Having first encountered the concept of fetishism in the eighteenth-century scholarship of Charles de Brosses on religious development, Marx describes commodity fetishism in terms of the personification of the products of human labour – a process similar to the attribution of an independent existence to imagined beings that inspire religious belief. In societies organised around generalised commodity production and exchange, Marx argues, commodity fetishism thus describes how products not only hide their origins in human labour but also how commodity exchange establishes an abstract measure of value through a mysterious 'social process that goes on behind the backs of the producers'.[31]

In Hunt's poem, commodity form is animated by the 'spirit' of abstract value that seems to call up the authority of ancient empires or religious symbols. At the same time readers are reminded of 'the truth of things, that they/self-destruct from the day they roll off the assembly line,/moving guilelessly toward object death'.[32] That these products are presented as simultaneously perishable and imperishable reveals how in Marx's words they possess both a sensible and 'supersensible' form. They are physical objects with specific material properties on the one hand, and on the other they express relations between persons mediated by economic value. The abstract value that regulates the exchange of these products and that renders different forms of human labour commensurable is ultimately for Marx measured through the ever-shifting average time it takes to produce specific commodities – or what the theorist calls 'socially necessary labor time'.[33]

Echoing Marx's critique of commodity fetishism, Hunt's draws on the language of metaphysical or religious 'incarnation' in order to compare the abstract dimensions of commodities as eternal. Things are animated by seemingly immutable, 'suprasensible' forces that, in the absence of a theoretical elaboration of *what* is being exchanged through commodities if not the commodities themselves, can only be described in mystical terms:

> The objects are tested and assigned an incarnation, and
> > Objects so tested are given a seal, an assignment of limited
> durability, by the House of Broken Things, a holy affiliated
> division of its original.[34]

Images of product testing circulate throughout the chapbook as a reminder that physical commodities can break down at any point in their life cycle. In a deeper ontological sense, the passage suggests that these products are already 'broken' precisely because they are perishable instances of an endlessly recreated social form in which the ghostly or spectral imprint of a whole system of economic organisation appears. Testing, then, becomes more than simply an act of determining the functionality of objects but of calculating their value through exchange. Even the figure of a 'House of Broken Things' itself, which may here refer to a lab where product testing occurs, seems to obey a similar market logic that renders it a 'holy affiliated/ division of its original' – one of many 'incarnations' of an enduring abstract form. The poem's punning mixture of the language of corporate subdivisions and wholly owned subsidiaries underscores how the 'House of Broken Things' is itself, like the objects it contains, a material copy of a 'suprasensible' original.

Hunt's poem arguably splits the page into upper and lower halves in order to separate the sensuous, material properties of objects from the processes of economic abstraction that invest these objects with agency. Printed in noticeably smaller text, the elliptical, staccato textual fragments that comprise the poem's lower portion differ markedly from the language of product testing and bureaucratic state regulation on display in the upper portion of the poem. The bottom half offers impressionistic descriptions of the home as a kind of sensorium disarticulated by discrete acts of consumption:

> Stewing in my own juice
>
> Minty, sour, strong, medicinal, narcotic, chalky, bitter,
> burnt, hint of frost, caramelized, envious, enchanted, dazzled,
> undressed, musky, briny, soapy, salty, oiled, interrupted,
> frozen, sticky, mucilaginous, squeaky, gritty, frothy, volcanic,
> round, wrinkled, shoe leather.[35]

The catalogue of details here arguably reduce affect-laden, sensory experience to the isolable, commodified attributes of things. The passage engages not only the senses, from taste to texture, but absorptive emotional states like envy or enchantment that describe distinct subjective orientations towards that experience. Here the language of experience is supplanted by the rhetoric of advertising. 'Stewing in my own juice', the speaker has seemingly undergone a process of self-objectification that compels them to understand their experience in terms of the disarticulated, consumable attributes of things.

The 'House of Broken Things' is represented as a kind of managed sensorium where the material qualities of things are both regulated by and spatially separated from the abstract logics structuring commodity exchange and national citizenship traced by the upper portion of the poem. Over the course of the poem, the proper classification and management of commodities comes to thoroughly remake repetitive domestic tasks, industrial manufacturing and the civic life of the nation.

The Cold War Kitchen and the Machinery of Race and Gender

The material logic of production, exchange and consumption that connects domestic and national space posits the nuclear family as a kind of basic unit of national belonging. The historically gendered labour of social reproduction is presented in the chapbook as a fundamental mechanism of racial differentiation. Likening a subject overwhelmed by domestic tasks to 'broken' labour-saving appliances evokes both the invisibility of domestic labor and what historian Kate Baldwin has called 'The Racial Imaginary of the Cold War Kitchen':[36]

> The Cold War kitchen was a surprisingly frequent point of reference not only for architects and politicians, but also for writers, filmmakers, advertisers, and others for whom this dynamic space was both a place of departure and an end, both restrictive and inspiring. As such the kitchen offers a lens through which to interrogate the reigning ideals of postwar American exceptionalism and the broadcasting of this ideology, as well as Cold War rhetoric about women and minorities during the late 1950s and early 1960s.[37]

Perhaps no incident more dramatically demonstrated the Cold War politicisation of consumer culture than the July 1959 'kitchen debate' between then Vice President Richard Nixon and Soviet Premier Nikita Khrushchev. After an agreement to host national exhibits in Moscow and New York, Nixon and Khrushchev engaged in a recorded and broadly publicised debate over the relative merits of both countries. One widely broadcast portion of the debate took place in the kitchen of an American model suburban ranch home constructed within the US Trade and Cultural Fair in Moscow's Sokol'niki Park. Within an exhibition hall featuring products from several hundred American companies, and against a backdrop of kitchen appliances meant to represent the average standard of living of US citizens, the model kitchen provoked a heated exchange between the two figures on the comparative material productivity and technological development of capitalist and communist countries. At the same time this exchange revealed that the two political leaders took for granted the structure of the heterosexual nuclear family as a basic economic unit of society.

At the same time, the figure of the Cold War kitchen that would come to symbolise the technological sophistication of US domestic space for the designers of the Moscow exhibition placed the hidden, repetitive and racially segregated character of domestic labour in competition with new labour-saving devices:

> The exhibition presented a kind of science fiction of technological advancement. In the presence of automated appliances, labor became a kind of clutter to be expunged from the scene. The paradox of presence and absence is central to the Cold War kitchen: like the new technological innovations, women also are present there. But their work

can be hidden behind labor-saving devices and, to a large extend, women and minorities were the 'machines' removed from sight in the Moscow kitchen.[38]

The impact of the 'labour-saving' automation of human labour within the home and factory fundamentally altered the meaning of racial difference, pitting racialised populations against technological processes that threatened to render their labour ever more superfluous.

For Hunt, this image of the Cold War kitchen at the center of a 'House of Broken Things' also becomes a figure for both a laboratory and a nation in crisis, collapsing an opposition between the public and private sphere that has long constituted a locus of feminist theorisation.[39] The 'House' is described in the poem as a lab where objects are tested until they are broken, revealing the limits of the material properties of both objects and the consumers of objects. The breaking point of objects, I want to argue, also describes the boundaries of prescribed racial and gender roles more broadly. Whether understood in terms of nation, domestic labour or laboratory, the 'House of Broken Things' arguably describes the increasing penetration of commodity form into all areas of public and private life, and the emergence of a web of market-mediated activities linking sites of industrial production with what feminist theorists have called the labour of social reproduction.

The repeated references to broken objects in *Piece Logic* function as a kind of refrain characterising brokenness in terms of an ever finer segmentation of social life and language into elementary and intricately standardised modular components: from 'broken links'[40] and 'a line of never broken nouns'[41] to the generalised separation that constitutes 'a broken world'.[42] What constitutes proof of 'brokenness' within this postwar consumer imaginary is, in my reading, fundamentally constituted by a contested and irreducibly gendered discourse of cultural pathology and 'broken families'[43] promoted by the 1965 'Moynihan Report'.[44] Penned by sociologist and four-term US Senator Daniel Patrick Moynihan, the report was a policy planning document commissioned to offer explanations for the obstacles to full civic and economic integration for black Americans often turned on explanations of pathological group culture and non-standard family structures headed by single mothers. Moynihan identified 'at the center of the tangle of pathology' of black poverty, youth delinquency and crime, not deeply racialised and gendered labour markets, police violence and pervasive de jure state-sanctioned discrimination, but a 'weakness of family structure':[45]

There is no one Negro community. There is no one Negro problem. There is no one solution. Nonetheless, at the center of the tangle of pathology is the weakness of the family structure. Once or twice removed, it will be found to be the principal source of most of the aberrant, inadequate, or antisocial behavior that did not establish, but now serves to perpetuate the cycle of poverty and deprivation.[46]

While Moynihan insisted that white bigotry played a significant role in the continued social marginalisation of black Americans, the report nevertheless insisted on labelling as pathological not simply fatherless families but the matriarchal structure of both single and dual-parent households that were marked by the 'often reversed roles of husband and wife'.[47]

Leaked to the public in advance of its release, the report drew almost immediate criticism from liberal pundits and influential civil rights figures like Congress of Racial Equality member William Ryan. In the 1965 'The New Genteel Racism' published in the pages of the journal of the NAACP, *The Crisis*, Ryan called into question the empirical data used to establish the report's conclusions – conclusions that seem to invert the causal relations between family structure and poverty. Ryan would later coin the phrase 'blaming the victim' in his book-length response to the report, *Blaming the Victim*. The report's own findings suggested that, in Ryan's words, 'unemployment and poverty cause "family breakdown" rather than vice-versa'.[48] Moynihan's conclusions have continued to elicit polarised critical commentary in the decades following its publication. The report has continued to figure heavily in continuing debates over whether structural racism or group cultural norms, or what anthropologist Oscar Lewis in 1959 called a 'culture of poverty',[49] adequately explain the persistence of not only a black 'underclass' but also intergenerational white precarity.[50]

The Automatic Subject of Domestic Labour

In Hunt's chapbook, this segmentation and modularisation of objects seems to record the impact of Fordist production methods on domestic labour, resulting in the latter's rationalisation and standardisation, as well as the absorption of increasing numbers of women into wage work. The latter process has recreated socially reproductive labour as what Arlie Hochschild has called a 'second shift'[51] for working women now left with significantly less time to complete domestic tasks beyond the boundaries of the workday. The resulting 'speedup' of the pace of domestic tasks provides a crucial context for interpreting why the speakers of these poems are frequently described as product testers of appliances inevitably broken by the performance of devalued and monotonously repetitive tasks. The physical and psychological limits of subjects performing labour inside of the home are repeatedly likened to the point at which commodities 'shatter'[52] and become inoperable.

The collection thus frames the labour of social reproduction as structurally embedded in a demand for ever-increasing productivity that also shapes the Fordist assembly line and its continual drive to reduce the labour time allotted for the completion of specialised tasks. Trapped within a stultifying domestic routine, the speaker of the opening poem suffers through a 'windowless calendar workday',[53] where 'egg timers ration my phone calls'[54] and where the socially unrecognised and unwaged work they perform requires an explanation of 'How it's done./First of all/Son./365/Hot/Meals/On the table./Every day./No reheats./No cold plates./When you get there –/Hot. Second.'[55] What is produced in this passage is not only a series of meals, but an experience of standardised units of time – a 'Hot. Second'.[56] The house is described as a kind of workplace extensively regulated by the 'time management'[57] it requires to perform the repetitive tasks of social reproduction – tasks that bear the traces of workplace routines outside of the home. Domestic work as product testing that breaks the tester in *Piece Logic*.

The chapbook poses the question of just how the productivity of domestic labour might be quantified and how one might understand the structural relationship between labour performed in the home and in the workplace. The precise structural role played by unpaid domestic labour, including slave labour, in not only reproducing workers within capitalist economies but contributing to the profitability of business became the subject of ongoing debates among feminists – from Angela Davis[58] to Martha Gimenez[59] – about the possibility or desirability of constructing an integral 'unitary' theory of capitalist exploitation and systematic racial and gender subordination.[60]

In the 1970s, a number of Italian and US-based feminist activists and theorists – Silvia Federici, Selma James, Mariarosa Dalla Costa and others, would form the International Wages for Housework campaign in order to draw attention to the significance of the historically unwaged and socially unrecognised character of domestic labour. The campaign drew inspiration from 1970s Italian autonomist theory and politics, or 'operaismo', while challenging the limits of traditional Marxist analysis in accounting for the gendered division of labour and the restructuring of work within highly industrialised postwar societies like Italy and the United States.

The co-organisers of the campaign drew on the concept of what Italian autonomist theorist Mario Tronti called the 'social factory'[61] – a term used to describe the increasing subordination of social life beyond the workplace to the needs of capitalist profit-making. As feminist theorist Silvia Federici has written, the campaign co-organisers understood the home as a space where business could rely on 'the free appropriation of immense areas of labor and resources that must appear as externalities to the market',[62] and therefore a potential site of political struggle and transformation around socially reproductive work:

> Equally important for the development of our perspective was the Operaist concept of the 'social factory'. This translated Mario Tronti's theory, in *Operai e Capitale* (1966) according to which at a certain stage of capitalist development capitalist relations become so hegemonic that every social relation is subsumed under capital and the distinction between society and factory collapses, so that society becomes a factory and social relations directly become relations of production. Tronti referred here to the increasing reorganization of the 'territory' as a social space structured in view of the needs of factory production and capital accumulation. But to us, it was immediately clear that the circuit of capitalist production, and the 'social factory' it produced, began and was centered above all in the kitchen, the bedroom, the home – insofar as these were the centers for the production of labor-power – and from there it moved on to the factory, passing through the school, the office, the lab.[63]

The concept of the 'social factory' that feminist theorists and activists like Federici, James and Dalla Costa extended to the home provides a suggestive framework for reading the complex figure of the 'House of Broken Things' in *Piece Logic* as an amalgam of home, nation and factory. Adopting Tronti's concept of the 'social factory' and its subsequent feminist reformulation, Hunt's 'House of Broken Things' can be read as a space that produces a range of socially stigmatised 'broken' subjects.

In 'House of Broken Things', the erosion of boundaries between private and public spheres renders escape from the rule of objects increasingly difficult, though the speaker repeatedly attempts to do so:

> Disconnect, to invent this life in phantom objectivity
> Step outside, as if the leash could reach that long, and
> Look back in, the heap uncoils a pile of props,
> Instruments for measuring speed useless for this atomic measure[64]

The backward glance into the interior of the house reveals a heap of objects that, like theatrical props, expose the artificiality of images of domestic harmony and what the poet calls 'object theater'[65] of automated abundance promised by the labour-saving appliances. This 'object theater' that I would like to read as, among other things, a description of the Cold War kitchen arguably conceals the continued need for domestic labour despite its partial mechanisation. It is not objects but time that functions as a relevant 'atomic measure' for socially reproductive labour that in the poem seems to resist both commodification and automation. The invention and increased access to labour-saving appliances that could partially automate routine domestic tasks and increase domestic 'output' could thus be situated within an unfolding postwar process of automation and superfluisation fundamentally reshaping the racial and labour politics of what Lizabeth Cohen has called an emergent 'consumers' republic'.[66]

The difficulty of getting 'outside' of the home takes on a distinct political resonance in the context of the occupational confinement of black women in particular to domestic service work. The increasing commodification of social reproduction in the postwar period allowed white families to transfer caretaking duties to a labour pool composed predominantly of black women and women from the Global South.[67] Such forms of occupational segregation had far-reaching implications for Sixties-era black and woman of colour feminist critiques of the presumption that 'typical' gender roles involved being confined to unwaged family labour in books like Betty Friedan's *The Feminine Mystique*.[68] 'Of the black women who earned wages in the late nineteenth century,' historian Jacqueline Jones observes, 'fully 90 percent of them laboured as domestic servants in private homes or in commercial settings such as hotels and boardinghouses.'[69] 'The cheapness of domestic labour,' Jones continues, 'meant that all but the poorest white families considered some sort of "help" an affordable necessity.'[70]

> By 1950, 60 percent of all black working women (compared to 16 percent of all white working women) were concentrated in institutional and private household service jobs, and 40 percent of all white working women (compared to 5 percent of black women) had clerical or sales jobs.[71]

Despite a gradual convergence of employment rates among black and white women, the over-representation of black women in domestic and low-wage commercial service work has persisted well into the twenty-first century.

While at this point in Hunt's collection, the racially segregated character of this labour is not explicitly mentioned, the home is nevertheless clearly represented as a kind of capitalist enterprise increasingly subject to market pressures to cut costs and accomplish tasks more speedily. What historian Lizabeth Cohen called a postwar 'consumers' republic' is also a 'world of objects we/have made, and their silent rebel-/lions are conducted under our very/eyes. The inventory gets out of/line.'[72] It is a world where previous processes of intergenerational reproduction are recreated in the image of a Fordist assembly line where occasional acts of rebellion, stoppages or slowdowns lead to 'unauthorized/breaks on the line between one/thing and another'.[73] Radically estranged from both the 'object theater' of the home and from the normative gender roles associated with domestic labour and biological reproduction that the multiplication of commodities appear to mimic, the speaker notes how even the intergenerational transmission of historical memory, in the form of family heirlooms, are subject to commodification:

> I didn't even understand lactation
>
> I inherited many small items and I go from house to house
> expecting to find a use for them. It is a long and tedious
> process but rather than belabor it, I believe in them. I discover
> money in quotes, and suddenly, these items amass tremendous,
> disproportionate value, amassing piles of appliances for some,
> and yards of lace. I wonder if the people of this place are at all
> in their right minds or if I stir admiration and desire to sell
> through the windows what cannot be obtained even in the dint
> of so much constant wage peonage, caged foliage, long work
> weeks, blank stock options, branded cars, the empty nights of
> the ice age.[74]

The progressive colonisation of the space of the household by a form of economic rationality attributes 'disproportionate value' to heirlooms that cannot be put to any practical use. It seems to put the entire notion of abstract value in question and to place 'money in quotes' as a peculiar relation with no obvious relationship to the utility of things. The pun on how the speaker does not 'belabor' the lack of usefulness of some objects underscores how such objects bear an uncertain relationship to work and expose monetary value as a peculiar product of 'belief'. Here 'money in quotes' might refer to its unavailability but also to its virtuality and what the poem calls 'phantom objectivity'.[75] Placing 'money in quotes' also suggests that money behaves as a kind of linguistic signifier whose semantic and material referent is in question. If money is in the poem represented as a principle of commensuration capable of translating things into quantities of other things – 'amassing piles of appliances for some, and yards of lace'[76] – it also embodies unequal and quantifiable relations between the owners of commodities that expressed as status differences evoking 'admiration and desire'.

The passage depicts the existential emptiness of the home as part of a kind of 'ice age' that extends to the waged work that makes this vision of domestic life possible. The condition of possibility for the sublimated violence of the good life',[77] the poem suggests, is 'constant wage peonage, caged foliage, long work weeks, blank stock options, branded cars'.[78] The striking off rhymes that reverberate through 'wage peonage' and 'caged foliage' sonically embed a creeping 'ice age' across the workplace, home and perhaps even an emergent carceral space. The home is not a refuge from wage labour but part of an expanded 'social factory' designed to reproduce a glut of objects whose social value is unclear.

The reference to 'wage peonage', or debt peonage, connects the existential vacuity of this 'consumers' republic' to earlier forms of racialised unfree labour – in particular a specific post-Civil War labour regime of sharecropping, tenant farming and convict leasing imposed upon formally emancipated slaves that entrapped black labourers through debt. The poem's association of unpaid labour in the home with a notoriously exploitative postbellum labour regime that preserved key coercive features of enslavement underscores how the commodification of socially reproductive labour that takes place within private households has formed a crucial though often neglected part of post-emancipation labour history. The largely unrecognised labour performed in Cold War kitchens not only reproduced patriarchal gender roles, but forms of racially typed labour historically excluded from Social Security, pensions and unemployment insurance. The 1935 Social Security Act notoriously excluded low-wage and irregularly employed agricultural and domestic labourers from eligibility even though they constituted nearly one third of the existing labour force of the country, and despite lobbying efforts at the time by the NAACP and Urban League.[79]

In 1974, Margaret Prescod and Wilmette Brown co-founded Black Women for Wages for Housework, 'a network of Black/Third World women claiming reparations for all our unwaged work including slavery, imperialism and neo-colonialism' (*The International Wages for Housework Campaign*). Over a decade later, Prescod would go on to confront then Senator Daniel Patrick Moynihan during 1987–8 congressional proceedings over welfare policy that resulted in the establishment of work requirements for Aid to Families with Dependent Children (AFDC). After being denied the opportunity to speak before a congressional committee deliberating over these changes, Prescod took the stage with three other members of the Black Women for Wages for Housework campaign. 'Black women have been paid for generations for doing housework in white people's houses,' Prescod argued. 'When we did that work for no pay, it was called slavery.'[80] Analysing how race and gender came to shape assumptions about the dependence and autonomy of black women in ways that otherwise passed without comment during the congressional proceedings, Nancy A. Naples has pointed out that Prescod was not only 'committed to centering the value of women's work in the home'[81] but to exposing the racial subtext of an emergent consensus on welfare reform derived from the conclusions of the Moynihan report.

Hunt's *Piece Logic* can be read as an intervention into these older debates over capitalist forms of socially reproductive labour as a mechanism of racial formation. The book compels its readers to reread the meaning and value of commodities not as evidence of abundance but as proof of the pathological sociality of capitalist value itself as a historically specific measure of social belonging. As the chapbook implies, it is also a form of value marked by a racialised and gendered division of labour and the 'ice age'[82] of pervasive social atomisation. *Piece Logic* calls into question the political horizon of visions of racial and gender inclusion within a 'House of Broken Things' that inevitably produces brokenness itself as a kind of mass-produced object.

Notes

1. Hunt, *Piece Logic*.
2. Reed, *Freedom Time*, p. 18.
3. The poet and critic Aldon Lynn Nielsen's investigation of the nature of poetic 'experiment' within contemporary black poetic tradition argues that much contemporary black experimental writing troubles dominant narratives of that tradition that privilege a vernacular orality as the singular reference point for black poets' longstanding exploration of the expressive possibilities of a 'writerly' textuality.

4. Appadurai, *The Social Life of Things*.
5. Marx, *Capital*, p. 163.
6. Moynihan, *The Negro Family: The Case For National Action* (1965), p. 2.
7. Ibid. p. 29.
8. McGovern, *Sold American*, p. 104.
9. Hunt, 'Notes for an Oppositional Poetics', p. 200.
10. Hunt, *Piece Logic*, p. 15.
11. Ibid. p. 11.
12. Ibid. p. 10.
13. Marx, *Capital*, p. 165.
14. Hunt, 'Notes for an Oppositional Poetics', p. 201.
15. Hunt, *Piece Logic*, p. 1.
16. Clark-Oates et al., 'Understanding the Life Narratives of Immigrants through Naming Practices'.
17. Jacobson, *Whiteness of a Different Color*.
18. Renan contends, 'and it is for this reason that the progress of historical studies often poses a threat to nationality. Historical inquiry, in effect, throws light on the violent acts that have taken place at the origin of every political formation, even those that have been the most benevolent in their consequences.'
19. Hutchinson and Smith, *Nationalism*, p. 17.
20. Ibid. p. 54.
21. Anderson, *Imagined Communities*, p. 13.
22. Hutchinson and Smith, *Nationalism*, p. 17.
23. Hunt, *Piece Logic*, p. 2.
24. Ibid. p. 4.
25. Marx, *Capital*, p. 163.
26. Ibid. p. 190.
27. Ibid. p. 165.
28. Hunt, *Piece Logic*, p. 5.
29. Marx, *Capital*, p. 163.
30. Ibid. pp. 164–5.
31. Ibid. p. 135. The trajectory of the critique of commodity fetishism in Marx emerges from not only religious mystification but from a critique of the limitations of the ostensibly materialist critiques of religious idealism offered by Young-Hegelians like Ludwig Feuerbach at the time.
32. Hunt, *Piece Logic*, p. 5.
33. Marx, *Capital*, p. 129.
34. Hunt, *Piece Logic*, p. 3.
35. Ibid. p. 4.
36. Baldwin, *The Racial Imaginary of the Cold War Kitchen*.
37. Ibid. p. 5.
38. Ibid. p. 10.

39. The latter division also reproduces an ancient philosophical opposition between *polis* and *oikos* that distinguished Greek city states from the private households taken to be the basic units of Greek civic life. For an account of how this fundamental division, and 'the premise of the properly productive household' (p. 28), structures the capitalist reproduction of 'the nexus of race, gender, class, sexuality and nation' (ibid.), see Mitropoulos, *Contract & Contagion*.
40. Hunt, *Piece Logic*, p. 10.
41. Ibid. p. 14.
42. Ibid. p. 16.
43. Moynihan, *The Negro Family*, p. 21.
44. For an extended discussion of the mixed reception of the report, and the divergent ways in which its findings were interpreted, see Geary, *Beyond Civil Rights*.
45. Moynihan, *The Negro Family*, p. 30.
46. Ibid.
47. Ibid.
48. Ryan, 'The New Genteel Racism', p. 623.
49. Oscar Lewis, 'The Culture of Poverty', *Scientific American* 215.4 (1966): 19.
50. As Daniel Martinez HoSang and Joseph E. Lowndes observe, there 'has been a growing tendency to advance cultural and even biological explanations for the expansion of white vulnerability, placing a greater number of whites in discursive categories once reserved for people of color as white poverty is increasingly framed through explanations of dependence, criminality, family disorganization, and genetic deficiency'. Daniel Martinez HoSang and Joseph E. Lowndes, *Producers, Parasites, Patriots: Race and the New Right-Wing Politics of Precarity* (Minneapolis: University of Minnesota Press, 2019), p. 58. 'The anti-Black tropes of cultural and familial degradation proposed by Moynihan's 1965 *The Negro Family*', HoSang and Lowndes continue, 'now circulate in explanations of white poverty' (p. 58). For a recent example of the application of these tropes of cultural pathology as an explanation for white poverty, see Charles Murray, *Coming Apart: The State of White America, 1960–2010* (New York: Crown Forum, 2013).
51. Hochschild, *The Second Shift*.
52. Hunt, *Piece Logic*, p. 7.
53. Ibid. p. 8.
54. Ibid.
55. Ibid. p. 6.
56. Ibid.
57. Ibid. p. 8.
58. Davis, 'The Approaching Obsolescence of Housework'.
59. Gimenez, 'The Dialectics of Waged and Unwaged Work'.

60. For two influential attempts to theorise double or multiple 'jeopardy' within the context of contemporary black feminism, see Beale, 'Double Jeopardy', and King, 'Multiple Jeapordy'. For an overview of Marxist and socialist feminist debates over whether capitalism and patriarchy constitute a unitary or 'dual system', see Arruzza, 'A Queer Union', and Young, 'Beyond the Unhappy Marriage'. For attempts to bridge a Marxist analytic with theories of the specificity of black women's labour under capitalism, see Jones, 'An End to the Neglect'; Cooper, 'The Negro Woman Domestics'; Davis, 'The Approaching Obsolescence of Housework'; and 'The Combahee River Collective Statement'.
61. Tronti, 'La Fabbrica e La Società', p. 20.
62. Federici, *Revolution at Point Zero*, p. 140.
63. Ibid. pp. 7–8.
64. Hunt, *Piece Logic*, p. 9.
65. Ibid. p. 10.
66. Cohen, 'A Consumers' Republic'.
67. For a post-Civil War history of black women's labour in the south, see Hunter, *To 'Joy My Freedom*. For an analysis of the contemporary social organisation of care work within the United States, see Glenn, *Forced to Care*.
68. Friedan, *The Feminine Mystique*.
69. Jones, *Labor of Love, Labor of Sorrow*, p. 110.
70. Ibid. p. 111.
71. Ibid. p. 198.
72. Hunt, *Piece Logic*, p. 13.
73. Ibid.
74. Ibid. p. 5.
75. Ibid. p. 9.
76. Ibid. p. 5.
77. Ibid. p. 6.
78. Ibid. p. 5.
79. For an analysis of the racial consequences of these exclusions within a broader history of the development of the US welfare state over the twentieth century, see Fox, *Three Worlds of Relief*.
80. Naples, 'The "New Consensus"'.
81. Ibid. p. 934.
82. Hunt, *Piece Logic*, p. 5.

Chapter 5

Contemporary Experimental Translations and Translingual Poetics
Sophie Seita

To write in a language that is not considered your own because you weren't officially born with it or within the borders that define its purview, its realm of belonging, is always to confront that question of belonging, of one's own tongue (the metaphors we use to describe nation states could give us pause, too). In other words, to use or not to use one's mother tongue is to signal or betray origin – or not. Words can also feel foreign when you write in a language that is supposedly 'your own', in which case, as the German poet and translator Uljana Wolf puts it in an essay on the Korean American artist and writer Theresa Hak Kyung Cha: 'The reading ist not master in its owl house.'[1] Through a displaced consonant, the owner becomes a wise owl in this ole house of the poem. How do we translate these old and new *hows* and *whys*, but also the *whos* of language? Masterfully, but without being mistress over them? In this chapter, I want to attend to the nuances and difficulties in reading and translating contemporary multilingual and translingual poetry. My main example is the poet I have translated: Uljana Wolf, who has traversed the language barriers between German, English, Polish and Belarusian in conceptually and linguistically innovative ways in her multilingual and politically engaged poems and translations.[2] I contextualise Wolf's experimental translational poetics by making reference to such innovative English-language and multilingual poets as Rosmarie Waldrop, Theresa Hak Kyung Cha and M. NourbeSe Philip, some of whom have a first language other than English or who grew up bilingually. Wolf is very much in conversation with the work of these writers and with anti-colonial discourses more broadly. Their and my intention is to reconceive translation as a radically inventive and collaborative practice that complicates access to the 'foreign' it is usually supposed to facilitate.

As a critic who has written about transhistorical literary communities but also as a poet and artist, translation – for me – is another practical (or delightfully impractical) way to address the need for an inclusive contemporary experimental literary and artistic community. Translation is generative: it generates conversations and transnational communities. At least, ideally. Antena, 'a language justice and language experimentation collaborative founded in 2010 by Jen Hofer and John Pleuker', write in their 'Manifesto for Ultratranslation': 'Who we choose to translate is political. How we choose to translate is political.'[3] The subject positions of both *whos* matter: poet and translator. Analogously, John Keene, himself a translator from Portuguese, French and Spanish, argues that we need 'more translations of work by women, by LGBTQ peoples, by Indigenous writers, by working class and poor writers, by writers with disabilities' and 'more translation of literary works by non-Anglophone black diasporic authors into English'.[4] We need this diversity for a more inclusive present, but also with an eye to how the future might read the past, which is our present.

In a printed conversation in the magazine ON: *Contemporary Practice* in 2008, poet-translators Jen Hofer and Sawako Nakayasu discuss this very awareness of futurity and a revision of the past. For them, translation 'intervenes in typical forms of canonization' and runs 'potentially even counter to it', but only 'if we manage to successfully navigate around its imperialist trappings'.[5] While a critique of such trappings is not already halfway to undoing imperialism (if only), it can certainly change our habits of reading. We become more hospitable readers in spending time with work in different languages and with work in translation, moving away from monolingualism and the cultural monopoly of English. Thinking through Derrida's writing on the conditions of hospitality, Derek Attridge describes what such 'hospitable reading' could mean for scholars, namely, to uphold 'the unlimited, unpredictable force of unconditional openness to whatever might arrive' in a literary work.[6] Translators, he argues rightly, already practise this openness, because translation is a 'peculiarly intensive mode of reading'.[7]

Before I analyse what it means to read and translate without being the wise mistress with her owl pen, with examples drawn from my own writing-as-reading practice as Uljana Wolf's translator, I want to mention the recent translation anthology *Currently & Emotion*, edited by Sophie Collins and published by the London-based press Test Centre in 2016, which tries precisely to offer routes into such a new hospitable and translational reading. Translators are routinely ignored or completely obliterated from acknowledgement in reviews or prizes. The translator's name usually appears in a smaller font, or sometimes doesn't even appear on the cover of a book at all. *Currently & Emotion* tries to rectify this cultural invisibility of the translator in bringing translational practices and voices right to the centre of our contemporary literary and political debates. It does this by foregrounding the creative work of the translator, briefly introduced by Collins herself, sometimes complemented by the source text, and framed by essays by translator-poets Erín Moure and Zoë Skoulding. The anthology also expands traditional notions of translation and includes different *kinds* of translations (based on Roman Jakobson): firstly, the interlingual (translations from one language into another); secondly, the intralingual (English-to-English translations); and thirdly, the intersemiotic, which are translations that 'operate between different mediums'.[8] I salute this broadness of definition, because it highlights that translation is just another form of writing, of creativity, rather than the lesser copy to the more brilliant and allegedly authentic original.

That said, there is perhaps a different responsibility to another text and language, which is not quite in place when I translate a picture into a poem. This has a lot to do with how we think about authorship and intellectual property on the one hand, and about language and identity on the other. But it also emerges from the widespread belief in equivalence: that a translated work in English *is* that German work. But whose work are we reading? In reading a translation, Kate Briggs cautions in her excellent book-long manifesto for translation, there is a difficulty but also necessity of 'holding and maintaining a relation with both writers, a sense of both writing practices, in their shared project and in all the important ways those projects differ, in the head, and somehow together'.[9] I am really reading two works, two authors, when I read a translation. This double presence is especially the case with experimental work. It's this conceptual multiplicity, these constraints, responsibilities and possibilities, that fascinate me in translating the multilingual poetry of Uljana Wolf. And while the translator, as Briggs writes, might disappear from a reader's mind precisely because of her 'investment' in making the sentences seem 'right' and smooth for a reader's experience,[10] in my own experimental translation of Wolf's experimental translingual and translational work, I was very invested in *not* quite letting the reader forget that they are reading a translation. Emily Apter urges writers and readers to endorse 'the importance of non-translation, mistranslation, incomparability and untranslatability' (and I will return to this aspect again later with regard to M. NourbeSe Philip).[11] As a translator, I have the responsibility to translate both the translatable and untranslatable, and to decide which one is which.

Uljana Wolf's poetry cannot be seen outside her work as a translator (of poetry in English, Polish and Belarusian into German). To translate, she writes, means to practise 'transformations and goodbyes'.[12] In its farewell to the original, translation, or poetry that is informed by translation, also represents a unique opportunity to question origins on more than a textual level. Developing a migratory poetics that engages with social issues, Wolf's work demonstrates how contemporary hyphenated identities can be expressed in poetry – by navigating the silences in the maps of German-Polish history, as in her first book *kochanie ich habe brot gekauft* (*kochanie i bought bread*), or exploring so-called grammatical and ideological 'false friends' and immigrant narratives in her second book *falsche freunde* (*false friends*), or the multilingual subversions of historically pathologised 'hysterical' women, of asylum seekers and of bilingual children in *meine schönste lengevitch* (*my most beautiful lengevitch*).

Considered within the 'transnational turn' in literary studies, Wolf's work lends itself to a critique of borders, nationality and 'mother tongues', but crucially this critique is performed not only thematically but also poetically, i.e. by way of neologisms, unusual syntax and prefixes, and by splicing a number of languages into the texture and prosody of her 'German' poetry.[13] Such an approach to multilingualism – as a formal feature with political stakes and a concomitant rejection of an idealised originality – invites a similarly multilingual alertness and rigorous playfulness from a translator like myself. Let's look at an example. One poem from Wolf's latest collection *meine schönste lengevitch* begins, or shall I say, I begin, in English: 'i went to the tingel-tangel to angle lengevitch.'[14] In German, 'angeln' means 'to fish' or 'catch a fish' – I went to catch language – but in English the word arrives at an angle, it is slanted, already corrupting language into a deliberately misheard, bilingual and hybridised lengevitch. The word 'lengevitch' in our book's title is taken from Kurt Stein's humorous poetry pamphlet, published in Chicago in 1925, which presents a Germanised and mispronounced version of the word 'language'. In this set-up of the German-English mash-up of Wolf's poem, the 'tingel-tangel' (a cheap dance hall) also suddenly gets tinged, tingled and tangled into sing-song in English; it rings differently, even though the word remains untranslated from the German.

Uljana Wolf's translingualism shows itself most often in small modifications of a prefix, by swapping vowels and inserting unexpected consonants into words. For example, 'sich äußerlich zuerst' (which combines 'sich äußern', to express or manifest itself, and 'äußerlich', outward or external, but also contains the word 'Licht', light) becomes 'first transfires' in my translation, swapping the expected p for an f.[15] Sometimes lines miss a full verb and have only the auxiliary, and since German grammar allows for the verb to appear at the end of a sentence, the syntactic guessing game requires reading textual and contextual clues – always with a sense of dilation or semantic hovering (see Fig. 5.1). A similar hovering occurs in 'tatting' (Fig. 5.2 and Fig. 5.3).[16] Since verb placement at the end of a line is uncommon in English, in my translations I introduced interruptions, absences and disturbances of the otherwise often happily flowing and flip-flapping rhythm of Wolf's prosodic investigations.

That Wolf would coin the term 'Babeltrack' for a series of poems is apt: the track is both the musical track, but also the track of the train of translation, huff-puffing its way through the landscape of multilingual 'valley-ripples of frog-throats'.[17] What would a poetic Tower of Babel look or sound like today? Well, it might sound something like this: 'such crochet things, slings, loops and bubbles built in saliva, be-sputtered, a-babbled, meaning a sort of air-bubble-speak, cheering and clicking, balloon-like, without skeins'. And the last stanza of the sequence reads:

> molars, myriad mobiles – star, and the child sleeps in her bed again, and around it a valley, volley or *voll* it may be called, where i practice my blicken through palm-gaps, berry bad and anderersights, while the frog-track ripples through the banana valley, quack-quack, with its multi-tracked croaking surrounding the child, who grows, and i now at her bed, encircling attrition, the spot where structures collapse and where the surface cracks, something for becoming permeable, for a napping tooth to nag, with quadrants, querulants, for the babeltrack in the trail-vale, ribbit, repeat, repeat[18]

The poem's language needs this bubbly lace-making, spinning forth, making translational and translingual threads and loops.

In German, the first couple of lines read: 'molare, unzählige mobiles – stern, und schläft das kind im bett again, und liegt ein tal darum, wallt oder walleh, wo ich mein blicking durch palmenlücken treib, berrybad und otherweiß'.[19] In my translation, I was able

ANNALOGUE ON ORANGES

when it is time for oranges, ist keine zeit, no time at all, für nichts. i only eat oranges, at least they exist, even if not much else is, no things at all, not much. petite little boats and stringy thin skin! i suck on them for hours. keeps me busy. free run for the tongue, looking for thread between teeth, interlace-space, and rooms to own, not much. oranges or existence all round. oranges or residence all round. with weighty curtains and rooms that step together conspiring, brother, mother, doctor, and the wardress, daily a session, that's how they planned it all, wall to wall around my standstill arms. but oranges exist, as transportation, outside my window, orange busses, orange trains, over cobbled headstone pavement, rattling through the ages. and on my bed those glimmering signals—peel, swinging segments, white skinned bridges! i lay them out for hours. keeps me going drüber. while the wardress brings fresh water fresh sheets, all the unemptied glasses, cups. daily a warding off for repair, nicht wahr, that's how they planned it all. later ten rooms on each floor, servants galore, with bow and tie marriage and tea. marriage and in the evening a little riot, then tea. but when it is time for oranges, ist keine zeit, no time at all for thirst, für wasser, for being thus arranged. because oranges are their own maneuvering material. because trains, bridges, and little glimmering glitches keep me going unallayed. go lack go lack use to her. because oranges communicate through the ages. oranges or restricted residence all round. oranges or a rather limited range of vision. oranges or it's like we're in prison. just trees and animals, we're at the **Ende der Welt**. when it is time for oranges, ist keine zeit, no time at all, for world-endings, padlock-curtains, paper measures for sure. because oranges are center-residence for life. for a lack, for want, go go be good, of use to her, go sweep the chimney, so that the doctor comes again. that's what they figured: that they wander and then go astray. get stuck in the body, block vocal tracts, good manner tracts. o range of things. because storage, and organs, organs. because collect yourself, then wander. glimmering bright and lacking. against

I, a native something-or-other-girl

"solide

"geistige Nahrung and she digested

          mit affektiver athletik

                      und orangenpoetiqqqq

or as you say   ein organ haben

"Starting from or with an orange, all travels are possible.
All ways of the voice that lead across it, are good."

or as you say   eine parole haben :

                      you tell me what it means

or french   a lengevitch on parole

(dry up in mid-speech

          stuck : repeat :

a)   ich have krämpfe in my calves
b)   my teeth klappern

Figure 5.1 Uljana Wolf, 'Annalogue on Oranges', in *Subsisters: Selected Poems*, trans. by Sophie Seita. Belladonna, 2017.

is called   *süstikpitsi süstikpitsi*   syllables repeat   like little shuttles
through secret eyelets etc.   in how many endless loops   does she dream
of *departure*   in how many languages   do the ropes of the sailor
(as a matter of lace) coil   & is it called   *working on the little ship*
in departing translation   but t t in french   (my little lip)
like a slip of the tongue   sl sl   sloped breakwater   is it a *frivolité*
in the sense of care   free   (tho with so much care   was made)   or
fragile   (because the end   *très fragile* bends)   or
crumbled   because of latin *friare*   like crumbling
of the indo-germanic   tribe   from ⟶drilling   belongs (to it)

[with tools sharpened and laced, handle it, cut, then hit, kill, the board, bordure, bordello, bread crumbs]

heißt sie   *süstikpitsi süstikpitsi*   wiederhole   die silben   wie schiffchen
durch heimliche   ösen usw.   in wie vielen bögen   träumt eine
vom *ablegen* in wie vielen sprachen   winden sich (tat
sache) die seile des seemanns   u heißt sie   nach dem übersetzen
arbeit am schiffchen   abrr eben auf französisch   (mein kl. bisschen)
wie ein versprecher   prrr prrr   wellenbrecher   ist sie eine *frivolité*
im sinne von leicht fertig   (wo das so bedacht gemacht)   oder
zerbrechlich   (weil das ende   *très fragile* wände)   oder
zerrieben   weil doch lateinisch *friare*   wie zerreiben
der indogermanischen   sippe von   ⟶bohren   (dahin) *gehört*

[mit scharfem oder spitzem werkzeug bearbeiten, pflügen, schlagen, töten, brett, bord, bordell, brosame]

Figure 5.2 Uljana Wolf, 'Tatting', in *Subsisters: Selected Poems*, trans. by Sophie Seita. Belladonna, 2017.

or in some   languages or regional dialects "spitze"   also means

"pierce"   & "spit"   &   now no longer with sealed lips

the lace-stitching girls: form holes   between

white threads   or form silences   between   strains of saliva

or   an unformed silence   also disputed   i need to

puke   cecilia   i said   i have to   swallow it &

conversely   lace would mean "spitting"   silently in stitches

for (botched up) hours   having a pinch of hunger   would then mean

"to stuff

  lace"

oder heißt in manchen   ihrer mund-   oder landarten   speichel

„spitze"   u speien „spitzen"   u   nu das mündige   an spitze

stickenden mädchen   sind zwischen weißen fäden   gebildete

löcher   oder zwischen   speichel fäden   gebildete

stille   oder ungebildete stille   auch gebrochen   ich muss mal

brechen cäcilie sagt ich   muss es runter   schlucken anders

rum heißt   spitzen „speien"   in schweigend verstickten

(vergeigten) stunden   einen hunger leiden   aber heißt

„spitze

  schlingen"

Figure 5.3 Uljana Wolf, 'Tatting', in *Subsisters: Selected Poems*, trans. by Sophie Seita, Belladonna, 2017.

to add another alliterative word to the first section 'molars, myriad mobiles'. The noun Stern (star) in German reads in English both like a noun and a verb – the mobiles and molars star in this dreamscape of the child, of Wolf's 'multilingual fantasia' to quote from an earlier section in the poem.[20] I chose to un-translate or back-translate Wolf's blicking into 'blicken' ('looking', 'glancing'), which is the word Wolf hints at in her anglicised version of it. To me, 'blicken' in English sounds a bit like 'blinking' and maintains the state of sleepily peeking through language. Whereas Wolf approximates 'blicking' and 'lücken' (gaps), my 'practice' and 'blicken' in turn approximate sound-wise such glancing through palm gaps. Wolf's choice of the word 'otherweiß' (half English, half German) turns 'otherwise' into another white baby tooth and drop of milk which she's been describing earlier in the poem, which I then inverted and translated as 'anderersights'. These *other sights* function yet again as a comment on Wolf's poetic practice of multilingual blinking: to *see* the gaps within and between languages.

Translation can make something lucid temporarily, as is so wonderfully captured in Juliana Spahr's and Jena Osman's *Chain* issue on 'Translucinación', a topic suggested to them by Cecilia Vicuña, who took the word from Andrés Ajens. It is this 'chain', this 'dialogue' that translation invites with its 'relentless utopian drive' to enable intercultural 'rigorous conversation' and exchange.[21] But the title also captures a view of translation I very much agree with: that as an experimental and conscientious translator I must 'not treat the original work as a completely knowable object'.[22] In the afterword to my translation of Wolf's *Subsisters*, I write:

> Uljana and I share a belief that translations of poetry cannot attempt a pure or perfect congruence, but must instead afford an investigation of the slippages, moments of misunderstanding and ambiguity, from which a new articulacy emerges. Uljana's work enacts the 'plurilingual poetics' that Caroline Bergvall detects in Rosmarie Waldrop and Theresa Hak Kyung Cha, arguing that '[d]isplacement is not here envisaged as exile but as the very condition for a positive understanding of relocation across and against the unifying, mythicized, and frequently exclusionary principles of national language and of monolingual culture.'[23]

In many cases, of course, border crossings aren't just linguistic; they have real consequences that might threaten someone's livelihood. In one moving and chilling section in Theresa Hak Kyung Cha's *Dictee*, in a chapter prefaced with a photograph of Cha's mother and that describes the experience of emigrating to the US, the narrator states matter-of-factly:

> I have the documents. Documents, proof, evidence, photograph, signature. [. . .] Somewhere someone has taken my identity and replaced it with their photograph. [. . .] They ask you identity. They comment upon your inability or ability to speak. Whether you are telling the truth or not about your nationality. They say you look other than you say. As if you didn't know who you were. You say who you are but you begin to doubt.[24]

In an experimental chapbook-long essay on Cha's work, Wolf draws attention to a multilingual and postcard-sized stamp Cha made as part of her mail art activities. The stamp is framed by an imperfectly oval border of words in French, in whose centre we read the words 'tom èhcac' in mirror image. Once used as a stamp the 'mot caché' (hidden word) reveals itself, although now the oval-shaped French frame becomes illegible. Wolf becomes fascinated by this material imprint of what she reads as a politics of translation. That there simply is 'no right way of reading, no right way round' and that something within us always remains 'in another language, unreadable, untranslatable; unmissably hidden in the middle'.[25] Wolf, whose own practice is addicted to (and addictively concerned with) teasing out multiplicities within words, with their punning and political potentials, also detects the author's Korean family name, Cha, in the word 'caché': a word that remains 'displaced, unheard(-of)' and one becomes perhaps 'a reader of the experience of displacement'.[26]

Such displacement is at the heart of much translingual writing and becomes especially tangible when it thematises that language-learning and translation are always political. *Dictee* is written in English, but also contains French, Korean and Chinese, and its opening chapter includes a French and English dictation exercise:

> Escrivez en francais:
> 1. If you like this better, tell me so at once.
> 2. The general remained only a little while in this place.
> 3. If you did not speak so quickly, they would understand you better.
>   [. . .]
> Traduire en francais:
> 1. I want you to speak.[27]

And to speak we must understand what we're saying, we want to make ourselves understood, we want to ferry meaning over to the other who receives it. Experimental poetry, of course, makes this ferrying, this crossing, a cross with multiple directions; less concerned with clarity.[28] Rosmarie Waldrop, a German-born poet writing in English who has translated numerous poets from French and German into English, uses the experience of language-learning for a broader reflection on language in her poem 'Mallarmé as Philologist, Dying': 'When he leaves the room, he recaptures a memory called meaning. A matrix where a word is carried by a foreign language. Say "th". Say the whole word: "death". The *Box for Learning English by Yourself and Playing* is broken, the string to push the puppet's tongue between his teeth.'[29] Language is always a broken puppet, whether you own it or not, and that's the point. This interest in the rules of language and what they might offer a poet as a material for play is also evident in Waldrop's book *Split Infinites* – a pun on the supposed grammatical error of the split infinitive. Now, many poets could be interested in this as a metaphor, but for someone thinking multilingually, this title situates the book in a pedagogical context, as something specific to a language that had to be learned, first as a rule, and then intuitively, rather than the other way around.

In Waldrop's *Lavish Absence: Recalling and Rereading Edmond Jabès*, a meditation on his work and its ethical imperative, on questions of exile, but also on the processes of translation more generally, there's one part that offers an insightful model for translation (and indeed any writing): 'I look at my translation: "The book never actually surrenders." This now seems inadequate. The adverbial form weakens the statement, makes us read over it rather than pause to ponder its strangeness and implications. In 1973, I did not see this sentence as I see it today. This pleases me in as far as it shows my reading and interpretation are not frozen.'[30] In a 2005 interview, Waldrop reflects further on embracing the impermanence of the 'right answer' or 'correct' translation, as an aesthetics or politics that is deeply connected to identity: 'I think "not belonging" is a condition of the artist. A fundamental lack as generative power. One wouldn't have to be a literal exile. The distance is built into the act of creation, the questioning, the constructing of "counter-worlds".'[31] Waldrop entertains such philological, philosophical and political possibilities of translation both in her poetry and in her translations.

Part of 'the joy of the demiurge', i.e. that of the translator, is 'to make [the work] mine at all cost', in 'the knowledge that I do not actually touch the original within its own language'.[32] Waldrop uses another metaphor for translation which I find incredibly apt: translation is the process the original 'undergo[es]', just like the 'weather[ing]' of a statue. This statue, which might miss a nose, whose shapes are slightly eroded, either sharper or softer, are all the more fascinating because they are *suggestive*. They don't suggest a perfect and complete whole, but the lack leaves something for the imagination to do. Wolf, too, wants a translational 'messiness that does not so much rely on inability (because you have to be able to make the better kinds of mistakes), but an inseparability. The pleasure of setting the foreign material to work poetically in the target language, like a shimmering lack/Lack' (Lack means lacquer, varnish or finish in German).[33]

Waldrop concludes her essay by negating that 'in the beginning was the word' but rather the creative 'act', or as Wolf puts it in English in her second collection *falsche freunde (false friends)*, 'they begin the beguine'; in other words, the translator and poet begin to dance with words. In 'dancing double speech', a poem from *Subsisters* I have already quoted above, this dance of the double of poet and translator is literalised: 'in the cloakroom every woman received a twin language with identical clothes, a dabbling double. [. . .] behind us word-rabbits scampered out of ashbery's hat. to the ballroom then, to circumdance my twin'. Such circumdancing requires precisely to invent new words, to splice words together, to mess around with language. Wolf's title 'doppelgeherrede' literally translates as 'walking double speech' or 'doppelganger speech', but in my translation I turned 'walking' into 'dancing', given that, as Wolf explains elsewhere, 'it matters to me to walk alongside the original poem, i.e. to follow its running, striding, jumping more than its riddles, answers, and callings'.[34] That essay's guiding conceit is to play with the English idiom 'to lead someone down the garden path' as a false friend of the German 'in die Irre führen'. To match Wolf's creative 'translantic' process here, I have similarly mistranslated the German idiom 'auf eine falsche Fährte locken' literally, as 'tempting someone to follow the wrong footprint'. I therefore also re-titled the essay 'Faux-Amis Footprints' in my English version, waving back at Wolf's second collection and its fascination with false friends and inter- and intra-lingual punning.

Puns and wordplay, of course, always have particular cultural connotations; sometimes they are also time-sensitive. Some of Wolf's poems, like 'on classification in language, a feeble reader' ('fibel minds (von den wortarten)' in German), refer to East Germany, for example; a context not even overly familiar to her German readers. But in this gap of not-shared experience lies a great potential for the poet and translator. In her commentary on the Austrian poet Ilse Aichinger's use of idioms, Wolf argues that '[i]n their informality and folksiness, idioms in any language are the epitome of being included, of belonging, of "having a say" in a matter, and because they require initiation and consensus, people want to be able to understand them. Aichinger withdraws from this totality of language by being other-tongued, in that she takes idioms at their word (like children might), or, to use a Benjaminian term, in that she de-forms (*ent-stellt*) them, i.e. through literal misunderstandings and defamiliarizations she makes new poetic routes available.'[35] I hope that my work offers an answer in the affirmative to Dirk Delabastita's question when he asks if – through continuing wordplay in a different language – 'a translation [can] unearth new meanings in the source text and so become constitutive of it'.[36]

Wolf's work certainly calls for such constitutive unearthing ('it's digging-dark in this poem, in which tongue could it possibly roam?'). We could say, then, that it is – to borrow a phrase from Rebecca Walkowitz's recent book of the same title – 'born translated'. Just like born-digital literature is made in the context of the Internet and the computer, as their context of production, distribution and reception; so, too, does the born-translated text already *contain* the thought of translation. Translation is not merely an 'afterthought' or 'secondary or incidental to these works', but rather 'a condition of [the text's] production'.[37] While Walkowitz thinks primarily of novels that already know they will be translated or will participate in a global and increasingly networked market, I see born-translated experimental poems as aware of their own cheerful unoriginality and their problematic inscription into cultural and national codes and traditions, and as emerging from multilingual or translational reading that informs their writing. But Walkowitz also acknowledges that some of these recent works are 'written as translations', perhaps pretending to be written in another language or 'written from translation', thus 'pointing backward as well as forward, they present translation as a spur to literary innovation, including their own'.[38] It's precisely this translational thinking that is germane to what Wolf, Cha and Waldrop are doing in their work. In one of the essays on translation in the volume *Currently & Emotion* mentioned earlier, poet and translator Erín Moure writes that 'we must give our own linguistic borders a porosity that lets the works of others in other cultures into our own'.[39] Translation, for Moure, ought not to smooth the passage from one language into another, but rather leave the edges of both languages permeable and open to transformation. In other words, our own language ought to be transformed after we've been translating someone else. Wolf, too, asks how her language can be affected by something foreign. It's not just by using a foreign word, she suggests, but a transformation happens through the serious engagement with other languages. Translating such translational thinking, in turn, requires a conceptual leap; it means that we need to translate the compositional process as much as the effects of the poem's surface.

The titular sequence of Wolf's selected poems, 'Subsisters', explores the simultaneous excess and lack within subtitles as a topos for translation. Ostensibly enabling understanding in a different language, subtitles present the translator's interpretation of the original script, within the circumscribed economy of a set word count. 'Subsisters' features a supposedly 'original' poem (based on a number of 1940s Hollywood films noirs) and its translation as subtitle, but such boundaries blur as Wolf translates herself translating – a Möbius strip of multiple, equally valid versions of one another. Wolf's structural, linguistic conceit also serves to critique the gender roles in the depicted movie scenes. The 'subsister' becomes the subtitle's subversive sibling. Via small displacements, the poetic subtitles turn the movies' virtuous and somewhat stereotypical female figures into confident, witty and independent heroines. The cognitive surplus and simultaneity that one experiences when watching a film with subtitles are in fact at the heart of Wolf's plurilingual thinking. In my translation, I've added another layer to this multi-directional conversation: a supposedly 'English' version, which, in turn, reworks material from my translations of the previous two poems (rather than directly from Wolf's German).[40] In this way, it continues the thinking-through-translation that Wolf's work so beautifully demonstrates, thus, as she puts it, 'turning slippage into multilingual spillage'.[41] I both translated the poems and their own distortions and twists as they move from 'original' to 'original with subtitles'. But I mainly translated the concept: what it might mean to misread or over-read or to make multilayered and deliberate mistranslation a generative method for new poetry.

Kate Briggs discusses the possibilities given to translators when they encounter a section or word in a foreign language in the text they are hoping to translate. One option is, of course, to leave the word or sentence untranslated; another is to translate it but pretend it's in a different language (i.e. ask the readers to accept the fiction that they are really reading German or French when what they're reading is English); or the third option, and one I'm most drawn to, is to 'make the language itself stutter. And stammer' in a 'strange tremble' that indicates that this is no smooth passage.[42] As Wolf writes: 'when language stutters it always multiplies – in a state of possibility'.[43] Or, as Anne Carson suggests in her introduction to her constraint-based translation project *Nay Rather*, which translates the same Greek fragment by using only words found in, for example, Beckett's *Endgame*, Bertold Brecht's FBI file or London Tube signage: 'What follows is an exercise, not exactly an exercise in translating, nor even an exercise in untranslating, more like a catastrophizing of translation. I shall take a small fragment of Greek lyric poetry and translate it over and over again using the wrong words. A sort of stammering.'[44]

A stammer is the refusal to be entirely legible. In a recent conversation on translation in *Bomb*, Don Mee Choi writes: 'That line – "I refuse to translate" – in *Hardly War* just came to me in the process of working on the book slowly. I'm unbearably slow. I didn't ask myself what it meant because I already knew what I meant. It's not any different than Yi Sang's protagonist saying he wants to stay endlessly lazy. I refuse to perpetuate the official narratives of the Korean War, which thingifies. I think of refusal as one of the most highly effective modes of resistance. I refuse to be faithful.'[45] Christian Hawkey responds that 'Perhaps this evasion, or "madness," as you write, is a strategy of resistance – a refusal to be legible ("right to opacity" – Édouard Glissant) while simultaneously demanding to be read. A colonial relation, or a way out or through that unjust relation. A thing not thingified. A "nothingness," as Fred Moten writes.'[46] Here's Wolf again in my translation:

> My relationship with Belarusian is an interlinear translation with dashes and variants that reads like a hiking map, on it the field, the glove. All possibilities of expression are housed in it, disarrayed situations of saying, invisible layers under the fur. For that reason my relationship with Belarusian is multilingual. For that reason my relationship with Belarusian stutters: not because language is a peasant, as the *generalissimo* says, but because it's many pathways, channeling.[47]

M. NourbeSe Philip's *Zong!* is another constraint-based translational project, similar to Carson's formally but with a different ethical imperative. In it, Philip translates the story of the slave ship Zong, whose captain gave the order in November 1781 that about 150 Africans be murdered by drowning so that the ship's owners could collect insurance money. The poetic text solely uses the words and phonemes of the only extant public legal document related to the massacre, creating a multilingual, multi-layered, and moving fragmentary piece. In the afterword, Philip explains her poetic process as a problematic translation: 'I murder the text, literally cut it into pieces, castrating verbs, suffocating adjectives, murdering nouns, throwing articles, prepositions, conjunctions overboard, jettisoning adverbs: I separate subject from verb, verb from object – create semantic mayhem, until my hands [are] bloodied, from so much killing and cutting' and then like a 'seer' or 'prophet' 'read the untold story that itself by not telling'.[48]

Wolf was recently commissioned to translate an excerpt of *Zong!* into German. In an essay about that commission, she asks under which conditions a white translator, who has the discursive power of white Central Europe behind her, can approach the text of a black author, whose work deals with murder and oppression wielded by white people.[49] How can a translator contribute to and translate that work of 'mourning'? In German the word 'übersetzen' both means 'to translate' and 'to cross over' or 'ferry over'. Wolf considers the nautical metaphor of translation as crossing over; which is a form of life-saving, while non-crossing or non-translating leads to death, or to an unacknowledged extinction. Her choice of what she considers a gentle form of non-translation can thus serve the purposes of survival, of visibility. In an interview with Wolf, NourbeSe Philip describes the poem, and particularly the last section (in which language breaks down, so much so that it's hard to tell to which language individual words belong) like this: 'I really had this sense that I was getting my revenge on the English language' but also that 'for the first time I had my own language and this is where the healing comes in'.[50]

Can translation then also perform such acts of healing? For Carolyn Pedwell, 'translation offers one important critical and pedagogical approach to negotiating the multiple and overlapping "double binds" that face us in the midst of late liberalism'.[51] Pedwell proposes translation '[a]s a mode of interpretation attuned to affective nuance and complexity, and one that proceeds in awareness of its own impossibility'.⁵² It invites us 'to reflect on the complexity of "our" moods and those of our texts, to feel the often conflicted relations between affective attunement, knowledge and power'.⁵³ She arrives at this understanding of translation via Eve Sedgwick's call for reparative reading and Gayatri Spivak's call for 'patient epistemological care'. Spivak makes it clear that there are some approaches to translation that wrongly assume that one can simply transfer meaning from one language into another, and thus 'a specific neocolonialist construction of a non-Western scene is afoot'.⁵⁴ So, especially within a context of transnational activism and decolonisation, translation needs 'a love that permits fraying'.⁵⁵ Language frays, Spivak suggests (referring to Freud's term 'Bahnung', which is often translated as 'facilitation' or 'facilitated pathway'), if the translator permits this *frayage*; even creates it, welcomes it. Wolf, too, maintains that language and therefore translation is 'many pathways, channeling'.⁵⁶ This channelling requires listening, or even a handing over, as Spivak puts it so emphatically:

> [T]he translator must surrender to the text. She must solicit the text to show the limits of its language, because that rhetorical aspect will point at the silence of the absolute fraying of language that the text wards off, in its special manner. No amount of tough talk can get around the fact that translation is the most intimate act of reading. Unless the translator has earned the right to become an intimate reader, she cannot surrender to the text, cannot respond to the special call of the text.⁵⁷

In a similar vein, Briggs highlights that '[r]esponding actively to [the translation's] address is a way of opening her own writing up to its difference, its independence: to the instruction of its different energy, its unfamiliar thinking, its other rhythms.'⁵⁸ That's why translation has a political potential for me, too. It asks me to be attentive to *difference*. Édouard Glissant compares translation to the composition of a fugue – a melody introduced by one instrument or voice that is then taken up by another, repeated in a different pitch, and accompanied by a counterpoint. Translation might indeed attune us to different states; it might tune us, like an instrument, to do political work. It invites us to listen to something in an unfamiliar key.

I want to return again to Wolf's response to Cha and both writers' demand that the reader *not* be 'master' in the 'house' of language.

In *Wandering Errands*, Wolf quotes Deleuze and Guattari, who ask 'How to become a nomad and an immigrant and a gypsy in relation to one's own language?'[59] Wolf suggests that in America the English 'mother tongue' is always-already a nomad. She continues: 'It seemed to me from the very beginning that language was not to be found at home. Language was never in when I called.' Consequently, Wolf practises and praises such a self-foreignising:

> In a 1982 interview, the Austrian writer and Holocaust survivor Ilse Aichinger was asked about the use of foreign words in her work. They're an opportunity, Aichinger replied, 'to make language foreign to itself and to leave it alone in such a way that it must speak for itself again'. [. . .] In the title story [in Aichinger's book *Bad Words*], 'Bad Words', the narrator announces her deep mistrust of supposedly 'good' language: 'I now no longer use the better words.' Instead, she writes, 'I'm beginning to have a weak spot for the second and third best' by which she means the overlooked words; language in the margins.[60]

Wolf concludes, again linking how she reads Aichinger, Cha and Philip and how we must also read her own work: 'Whoever wants to trace the outlines of Aichinger's bad words had better not come as a winner or a language dompteuse. These foreign words cannot be tamed when you meet them, and they cannot be colonized as a trophy.'[61]

We might here be reminded of Jacques Derrida's *Monolingualism of the Other*, in which he disentangles his complicated relationship with the French language as an Algerian Jew, a sentence Wolf cites herself, which we could read almost as her mantra for translational poetry: 'I have only one language, yet it is not mine.'[62] So, whose language is this? The question of the multiple *whos* with which I began this essay is crucial to Wolf's work, and to translingual experimental poetry more broadly: namely, in recognising that there isn't a single, coherent identity or voice presiding over a poem, we must also recognise that there isn't one in its translation. Wolf's work is not just translational in its method and thinking, it is also enmeshed with other source texts, usually acknowledged in notes at the end of her books or individual poems, where we find Nelly Sachs, Sigmund Freud, Hélène Cixous, Gertrude Stein, Anna O. and Susan Sontag. Sometimes we even find these literary or historical interlocutors within texts themselves, such as in 'Babeltrack', which I discussed earlier, where the poem has a theoretical argument with Roman Jakobson about aphasia and language-learning.

Texts are not isolated incidents; they can engender intertextual and real friendships – hospitable relations which Wolf explores linguistically. It speaks for Wolf's generous poetics that she invites and acknowledges such continuities and dialogues – a conversation that my translations, I hope, can further hospitably extend.

Translations offer spaces for collaboration and friendship with what Christian Hawkey in the introduction to his constraint-based translation of Georg Trakl so aptly terms 'between-voices': 'to read the deceased is to reanimate their words; the between-voice is a ghost, a host'.[63] In translating Uljana's words (and I might as well – and even feel like I must – switch to first names here), I also extend our non-textual friendship into text and vice versa. I am writing 'with' her, in her words and in mine, and while I can understand her (an adhesive for friendships), these translations quite stickily and happily sound both like and unlike her; both like and unlike me. Translation becomes a work of transformed and transformative failure, a confrontation with impossibility, a giving up of mastery. These are familiar arguments from postcolonial critiques; and multilingual translation itself becomes a driving force in such a rejection of monolingualism. Uljana's poems are rich in such a critique; they are never just 'play' despite or precisely because of their insistent interrogations of form and sound as side-kicks. Or rather, wordplay and sound become equal partners, collaborators, absolutely crucial for her political engagement to be effective and affective. The poems resist the notion that one can ever be fully a 'native speaker', fully own a language, be of it, within it or on top of it. To take another metaphor from Uljana's essay on translating from Belarusian, 'Messages from a Beehive', the buzzing train of my relationship with the German of Uljana Wolf is therefore, in her/my words, 'double-tracked and never direct', it 'lies in the sleeping car facing backwards, drives across a bridge, is a bridge, hums'.[64]

Notes

1. Wolf, *Wandernde Errands*, p. 6. Wolf is here playing on Jacques Derrida's essay 'Hospitality', trans. Barry Stocker and Forbes Morlock, *Angelaki* 5.3 (2000), pp. 3–18 (p. 6): 'when I begin to speak in my language, which seems to suppose that I am here <at home> master in my own home, that I am receiving, inviting, accepting or welcoming you, allowing you to come across the threshold'.

2. Wolf has translated into German several well-known authors, such as John Ashbery and Yoko Ono, but she often chooses to translate authors whose practice mirrors her own translingual play, such as Erín Mouré and LaTasha N. Nevada Diggs. Diggs's poem 'Benihana', for example, turns into translingual German in Wolf's translation. An audio recording accompanying the text is available at <https://www.lyrikline.org/en/poems/benihana-11994> (last accessed 19 February 2018).
3. Antena, 'About Us', <http://antenaantena.org/about-us-2/> (last accessed 30 January 2018) and Antena, 'A Manifesto for Ultratranslation'.
4. John Keene, 'Translating Poetry, Translating Blackness', *Harriet*, 28 April 2016.
5. Jen Hofer and Sawako Nakayasu, 'Can Can', *ON* 1 (2008), pp. 87–98 (pp. 92, 90).
6. Derek Attridge, *The Work of Literature*, p. 305.
7. Ibid.
8. Sophie Collins, 'Three Kinds of Translation', *Currently & Emotion: Translations* (London: Test Centre, 2016), unpaginated [pp. 25–7 (p. 26)].
9. Briggs, *This Little Art*, p. 49.
10. Ibid. p. 54.
11. Apter, *Against World Literature*, p. 4.
12. Wolf, 'Schreiben und Übersetzen heißt, sich Meta-artiges Desaster einzuladen' (my translation).
13. By 'transnational turn' one usually means those projects that have, for a while, advocated a geographical and linguistic expansion of scholarly subjects and attention to how identities and cultural and literary work exist beyond traditional borders – it appeals to decentre the nation state – but within global networks, and migration, and hybridity.
14. Wolf, 'dancing double speech', in *Subsisters: Selected Poems*, p. 18.
15. Wolf, 'Babeltrack', pp. 137–61 (p. 148).
16. Wolf, 'Tatting', in *Subsisters*, pp. 84–109.
17. Wolf, 'Babeltrack', in *Subsisters* pp. 137–61 (p. 138).
18. Wolf, 'Babeltrack', pp. 137–61 (p. 160).
19. Wolf, 'Babeltrack', pp. 137–61 (p. 161).
20. Wolf, 'Babeltrack', pp. 137–61 (p. 148).
21. Spahr and Osman, 'Editors' Notes', pp. iii, iv.
22. Ibid. p. iv.
23. Seita and Wolf, 'How to Subsister: An Afterword'. The quote from Caroline Bergvall is from 'Writing at the Crossroads of Languages', pp. 207–8.
24. Cha, *Dictee*, pp. 56–5.

25. Wolf, *Wandernde Errands*, p. 6. My translation. Please note that this is a translation in progress.
26. Ibid. p. 7. My translation. Wolf uses the English words 'displaced' and 'displacement'.
27. Cha, *Dictee*, p. 8.
28. Wolf writes in 'Stationary', *Subsisters* (p. 12): 'in the flubbed dialect of these forests/a crossing is the word tree.' And: 'no one/ever saw the homelands go home'.
29. Waldrop, 'Mallarmé as Philologist, Dying', p. 61.
30. Waldrop, *Lavish Absence*, p. 138.
31. Waldrop, 'Between Tongues: An Interview'.
32. Waldrop, 'The Joy of the Demiurge'.
33. 'Faux-Amis Footprints', *Subsisters*, pp. 168–9 (p. 168).
34. Ibid.
35. Wolf, 'Translating the Untraceable: On Ilse Aichinger', *Subsisters*, trans. Sophie Seita, pp. 170–4 (p. 173).
36. Delabastita, 'Focus on the Pun'.
37. Walkowitz, *Born Translated*, p. 4.
38. Ibid. p. 5.
39. Mouré, 'But do we need a second language to translate?', p. 29.
40. The first part of this paragraph is slightly adapted from a translator's note that appeared in *Asymptote*, April 2016 <https://www.asymptotejournal.com/special-feature/uljana-wolf-subsisters/german/> (last accessed 17 June 2019).
41. Seita and Wolf, 'How to Subsister: An Afterword', p. 179.
42. Briggs, *This Little Art*, p. 29.
43. Wolf, 'Translating the Untraceable', p. 172.
44. Carson, *Nay Rather*, p. 32.
45. Choi and Hawkey, untitled conversation.
46. Ibid.
47. Wolf, 'Messages from a Beehive', p. 166.
48. NourbeSe Philip, *Zong!*, pp. 193–4.
49. NourbeSe Philip, 'Über ein Gedicht von NourbeSe Philip'.
50. Wolf and NourbeSe Philip, 'Poesiegespräch'.
51. Pedwell, 'Cultural Theory as Mood Work', p. 58.
52. Ibid. p. 63.
53. Ibid.
54. Ibid.
55. Spivak, *Outside in the Teaching Machine*, p. 181.
56. Wolf, 'Messages from a Beehive', p. 166.
57. Spivak, *Outside in the Teaching Machine*, p. 183.
58. Briggs, *This Little Art*, pp. 134–5.
59. Deleuze and Guattari, *Kafka: Toward a Minor Literature*, p. 19.
60. Wolf, 'Translating the Untraceable', p. 170.

61. Ibid. p. 171.
62. Derrida, *Monolingualism of the Other*, p. 21.
63. Hawkey, *Ventrakl* (New York: Ugly Duckling Presse, 2010), pp. 5–6.
64. The first part of this paragraph is adapted from my afterword to *i mean i dislike that fate that i was made to where* (New York: Wonder, 2015). The second part of the paragraph is adapted from my afterword to *Subsisters*.

Chapter 6

On Joan Retallack's *Memnoir*: Investigating 'the Experience of Experiencing'
erica kaufman

> be prepared to admire and overcome your lagoon of objectivity and false mergers of the past.
> Heinrik Marchand, *In the Past, Into the Future*

I. 'every one then is like many others always living'[1]

What draws me to Joan Retallack's *Memnoir*, a poem that originated in response to *Chain Magazine*'s issue devoted to memoir/anti-memoir, is that I see in this work an antidote to the limitations that I associate with being categorically or generically memoir. In her 'Guest Editor's Notes' to this issue, Kerry Sherin writes,

> One can see in these texts the political and psychic stakes involved in self-representation and the ongoing negotiations of subjects . . . . Across the differences, there is a consciousness of language as the inter-me-diary.[2]

This snippet of the introductory note hints at a focus on another incarnation of 'memoir', a version that calls into question the traditional idea that, 'like writing a poem, memoir is reliant upon the persistence of memory . . . the way in which the demands of the past contrive upon the present, to unlock certain truths'.[3] In contrast to Sherin's sense of 'language as the inter-me-diary', Jill Bialosky sees memoir and memory as typically intertwined, the emphasis being on memory's ability to 'unlock certain truths', truths that are intimately the writer's to uncover. She continues,

> in shaping the narrative of memoir, one relies on belief in the intuitive nature to uncover the hidden narrative of the past, what gives memoir (and poetry) its intimacy and tension? I will argue that it is the persistence

of memory; the way in which an experience persists itself on the writer and wills it into consciousness. It is this persistence that wills the narrative to life.[4]

Bialosky does ultimately say that poetry and memoir cannot (and should not) be linear; the bulk of her piece focuses on the way that poetry can go beyond the autobiographical or confessional in its dramatising of memory. Despite this gesture towards the non-confessional (the anti-Plath or Sexton), Bialosky is still exploring the idea of the poem as representative of its writer or at least of a topic close to the writer, familiar, some form of truth, however exaggerated and fragmented.

What use is the subjective past forcing its hand on a poem's (and poet's) present? To tell one's own story is to tell a story always in motion, always affected and in conversation with what Joan Retallack describes as 'the mess of the contemporary'.[5] Instead of 'delving into the past to resurrect it', through *Memnoir*, Retallack problematises the project of recounting one's past, inviting us into a lively conversation that engages tense(s) through collapsing the divide between personal/private and public, and interweaving the flood of one's own experience with the flood of information we are all privy to by virtue of participating in the contemporary. Instead of privileging one perspective and one individual's memories, Retallack asks us to consider the reality that no memoir is singular, because we, as humans, are not singular – our experience is shrouded by our interactions with others and the world we contribute to and live in.

II. 'they are conducting life and that makes their composition what it is, it makes their work compose as it does'.[6]

The root of 'memoir' is 'mem', which, according to the *Oxford English Dictionary*, means something closest to 'mindful' but is often defined as 'to remember' and used as an abbreviation for 'memoir, memorial, or member'. 'Noir' is defined as 'black'. The phrase 'film noir' became popular in the mid-twentieth century, with the advent of 'noir films', and is used to describe movies that are 'gloomy and fatalistic in character ... [also] urban, morally ambiguous, anti-heroic' (*Oxford English Dictionary*). In titling her poem *Memnoir*, Retallack playfully hints at problems inherent in the genre of 'memoir' (as well as 'antimemoir'), while also indicating that her piece enters into this dialogue – one that acknowledges that the ideas we choose to express in writing are limited, despite any illusions of completeness that the work might convey (i.e. a short story). No memory is perfect, which means that by nature, a memoir is part fiction and part unfinished, not unlike a mystery that goes unsolved.

The book opens with a 'conversation' between 'Mem' and 'Noir':

> Mem: What's our relation to the past?
> Noir: Same as to the future.
> Mem: Then what's our relation to the future?
> Noir: You don't want to know.
> Mem: In other words the jig is up.
> Noir: In other words the jig is up.

This opening engages the notion that the past is never past tense, and does so by way of a humorous riff on Socratic dialogue. In her process note, Retallack writes, '*Memnoir*, like all the work I do, comes out of a perforated self – permeable, in conversation, not wanting to finish a story about a self that must be in motion for the I to believe in the I as a vital principle.'[7] The work's title is in itself literally 'perforated' into two voices, pushing what appears to be 'simple' language to go beyond any easily articulated relationship between past/present/future. 'Mem' and 'Noir' become their own voices, they engage in a conversation about our/their relationship to time; yet the questions asked are never 'resolved', and the dialogue becomes a language game in which 'Mem' plays the part of inquirer and by the end 'the jig is up'. That playful closing phrase usually connotes that something unknown is revealed, yet here, repeated twice, the only thing that becomes clear is that questions of this nature lead to continued questions.

What follows this dialogue is a book that makes careful use of the page as unit, while intermingling 'cultural as well as personal memories'. Retallack begins, 'it's said that it happens even in nature e.g. during the/childhood the mother might have (had) a taste for film/noir and take(n) the child along'.[8] The difference between this and something like, 'my mother loved film noir and often took me to the movies with her', is striking. Retallack's rendering alleviates the reader of the biases that come along with personal anecdotes, and instead opens the text up to the reader. In his Introduction to *The Business of Memory*, Charles Baxter writes, 'You may possess subjectivity, you may even be a subject yourself, but it is sometimes considered to be in bad and somewhat narcissistic taste to say so.'[9] Baxter focuses on the problems the genre of memoir raises – that one person's recounting of his/her own experience is self-indulgent (to a certain extent). Retallack combats this particular problem of genre by doing away with the quasi-omniscient 'I'. In its place we find 'it's said', 'the mother' and 'the child'. 'The' indicates a specified subject while also leaving the subject itself undefined, general and even transient.

This opening stanza, 'it's said that it happens even in nature e.g. during the/childhood the mother might have (had) a taste for film/noir and take(n) the child along',[10] is a hypothetical sentence fragment, yet the reader still becomes attached to the idea that 'it happens even in nature'. The action is not happening to any one person, but is rather a linguistic experience to be shared. As Retallack notes in her 'process note', 'This isn't about owning a self, or having a story to tell, though narrative strands weave in and out of chance-developed configurations'.[11] In other words, what this poem asks of its reader(s) is to rethink the nature of the act of 'memoir' so that individual experience encapsulates an awareness of the experiences happening around us, and releases the idea of 'experience' (as a singular noun) from the constraints of being owned by any one person (reader or writer).

Memoir should involve not only the personal, but what surrounds the person. The poem continues, several pages later,

> this voltage through the body is brought on by the senses
> senses strictly speaking in logic nothing is accidental the
> world divides us into seekers after facts seekers after gold
> dig up much earth and find little[12]

Here, the senses are directly engaged; but these senses are not an individual's specific five senses, but rather senses as a larger part of the way one interacts with the world. We are introduced to different variations of 'seekers', 'after facts' and 'after gold', the latter preoccupied with material, currency, and therefore destined to 'find little'. But the lack of punctuation in this excerpt also creates a connection between these two 'seekers', that perhaps both 'find little'. For Retallack, what is central to 'escap[ing] the prison house of language' is 'through our unintelligAbilities'.[13] In other words, the normative hunt for capital (either through money or data) is predictable and unimaginative – it is no road for a true 'seeker' to take if that 'seeker' seeks real 'investigative engagement'.

Retallack's 2007 essay 'What is Experimental Poetry and Why Do We Need It?' begins with the following epigraph (attributed to Genre Tallique):

> Critique of the appropriative *we* makes way for an inclusive *we* of human responsibility acknowledging the shared origin and destiny of every form of life on the planet. A planetary pronoun is inherently experimental. No one knows what its force might be. The question is how to deploy it in consequential synergistic projects (thought and living experiments) that compose new value coordinates for *we*.

With its emphasis on '*we*', this passage underscores the importance of the unintelligible as part of the project of resisting narrative and composing (or proposing) an alternative route that acknowledges and negotiates the problem of privileging any singular ('I') 'form of life'. The '*we*' is 'appropriative', inclusive in its grammatical definition, and presents new possibilities for a collective subjecthood when rendered 'planetary pronoun'. Just as Charles Baxter identifies the problem of subjectivity, Retallack via Tallique proposes a new grammar that refuses the memoir-induced phenomenon that Baxter describes as 'the public realm dies as everyone turns inward'.[14] As Retallack's essay begins, the reader sees that the thought experiment of the text, the essaying of the essay, is to explore how 'languages of description may need to change under pressure of new angles of inquiry into how complex interrelationships make sense'.[15] Instead of the public turning inward, Retallack offers a different 'angle of inquiry' that emphasises 'complex interrelationships' instead of first-person tunnel vision. 'This voltage through the body is brought on by the senses,' and these senses are interconnected, transmuting, as the surge of voltage travels through '*the* body'.

Midway through this same essay, Retallack writes, 'During the second half of the twentieth century, many of us came to the idea of uses of language that are not only in conversation with the surprises, unintelligibilities and most intriguing messes of the contemporary moment but enact interrogations into its most problematic structures.'[16] This concept of the potential of language (particularly the experimental language/use of language of some poetries) to create agency in the unknown is central to how I read *Memnoir*. Instead of telling a predictable story, predictable in that it follows the one-author conventional narrative trope, Retallack opts to multiply perspective(s) in order to introduce the unknowability of the future into a dialogue of present and past, a dialogue that enacts 'investigative engagement' with what language might make possible.

III. 'Can you please by asking what is expert.'[17]

'Curiosity and the Claim to Happiness' is what appears to be the title of the first 'section' of 'poems' of *Memnoir*. This is followed by the unattributed epigraph: 'Studies have shown that the brain/prefers unpredictable pleasures.'[18] This header is the only one in the book that does not consist of some modification of 'Present Tense', and one that points towards the importance of curiosity and the 'unpredictable' as potential heroines in this intervention into points of view. In *Art as Experience,* John Dewey writes, 'Experience occurs continuously, because the interaction of live creature and environing conditions is involved in the very process of living.'[19] Dewey asks readers to shift their focus to the process and/of experiencing that underlies the making of a work of art, instead of focusing on the finished artwork alone. Retallack's emphasis on challenging both the tenses of one's experience as well as the reliability of any one point of view mirrors Dewey's assertion that experience is omnipresent and ever important. Retallack writes,

> without the carefully constructed container
> story: is story possible: can a life even a portion
> of a life be contained in a story: would songs
> be better to repair the brain[20]

Could a story ever be true if it is the product of a 'constructed container', a vessel isolated from interaction with the other stories around? Where should a story live? Is it possible to even pinpoint this kind of relation if all stories are intertwined, participating in a Venn Diagram of overlapping relations? By using only ':' as punctuation here, this questioning of relationality is underscored – a colon signifies some kind of comparison – ratio or proportion – a possibly mathematical moment that one should supposedly know a solution to, yet sometimes won't. In her review of *Memnoir*, Redell Olsen writes, 'and this is a poem which challenges the location of a here and now where we "don't want to know" our relationship to the past or future'.[21] It is a poem that asks 'is story possible', and then follows by suggesting that other mediums might be 'better to repair the brain', like the often improvisational associations of song.

> IV. 'In second second time time to be next next which is not convincing convincing inhabitable that much that much there.'[22]

In a 2011 *HTMLGIANT* post,[23] Alexis Orgera writes, 'Locating the "I" within the space of real or imagined experience is the task of poem-as-memoir. Taking facts and making them new, turning language on edge – whatever you want to call it, the truth remains that language becomes the memoir.' Orgera also specifies that sometimes 'my syntax and rhythm overrides my content'. Although this shows that the kind of poem-as-memoir Orgera is proposing is interested in the work that language can do and not necessarily in a linear autobiographical story, she still emphasises the 'I' of the piece. In *Memnoir*, the word 'I' only appears ten times (the poem itself is thirty-eight pages long). This signifies the way that Retallack's project complicates and remedies the first person persona that normatively connotes some kind of hypothetical 'truth'.

As Alain Leahsdottir writes in *Fragment & Personhood*, 'too often writers see the absence of a first person narrator as a signal that the text is being transmitted by some disembodied voice. Rather, the opposite is true.' The first 'I' in *Memnoir* appears on the first page of the text: 'fiction is/precisely what they now call non-fiction too get a bit too/personal i.e. Eurydice my dark darling don't worry I can/bear your not looking at me she cri(ed) out'.[24] In this moment (the second stanza/paragraph on the page), the reader is instantly involved in the text – we're involved in a conversation of genre trouble (fiction/non-fiction), the question of the place of the personal is raised, and an example is offered in the form of the Orpheus/Eurydice myth. When the 'I' appears, the body it is referring to is transient – is it Orpheus who is saying 'Eurydice my dark darling . . .' and then Eurydice becomes the 'I', responding 'I can/bear your not looking . . .'? Does the 'I' *belong* to the writer or narrator of the poem? It's the lack of punctuation coupled with where the line breaks occur that creates this fluidity of signifiers. The sensation this wandering pronoun creates is one where nothing is easily definable, not time, person or place. To return to Retallack's process note – 'This isn't about owning a self, or having a story to tell, though narrative strands weave in and out of chance-developed configurations.'[25] What's important here is the continued emphasis on 'a self that must be in motion for the I to believe in the I as a vital principle'. In other words, to claim that there is a reliable self when the world around us is constantly in flux is to deny the reality of 'experiencing what we are experiencing'. Or, as Grant Matthew Jenkins proposes in *Poetic Obligation: Ethics in Experimental American Poetry after 1945*, 'rather than emphasize the said, one must seek the saying'.[26] By stressing the 'saying' rather than the said, Jenkins demonstrates the way that writing must reflect the transience of the world it grows from; in other words, the 'I' of these texts is never reliable, never stable, and never should be either. I'm reminded of John Cage's 'History of Experimental Music in the United States',[27] the importance of 'giving up control so the sounds can be sounds' – only here I would say that what *Memnoir* does is remind us of the importance that we give up our normative reliance on an omniscient 'I'.

> V. 'It's snowing but no matter we will get there in the taxi.'[28]

[Tracking the word curiosity throughout the book.]

> VI. 'She is one being the one she is being.'[29]

Beyond asking readers to reconfigure our relationship to the 'I', *Memnoir* also 'throws us into a dilemma about our location of the tense of the writing: present, past, future?[30] Many of the book's subheadings are permutations of tenses: 'Present Tense: Choice', 'Present Tensed', 'Present Tenses', etc. In the very form of the poem, we're asked to rethink our relationship to time and memory – 'it is that that is the problem with the timing that it is/always off while it can not be off at all'.[31] This creates a contemporary rendering of Gertrude Stein's idea of the 'continuous present', which Retallack describes in her 'Introduction' to *Gertrude Stein: Selections* as the 'invention of a continuous present experienced in the pulse of her words was part of her project to register a new time sense peculiar to her era'.[32] *Memnoir* creates its own time space sense, as well as a new way to challenge and interact with the reliability of our own relationship(s) to memory. In 'Composition as Explanation', Stein writes, 'the only thing that is different from one time to another is what is seen and what is seen depends upon how everybody is doing everything'.[33] In this statement, Stein foregrounds the importance of 'composition' (the active act of composing) as what is important, the contemporariness of our noticing. Referring to Stein's 'How Writing is Written', Retallack states, 'it is the business of the writer to live one's contemporariness in the composition of one's writing'.[34]

'... the world is/bright too bright gnomic present tense tensile everything/happening all at once the world is full of its own mute history ...'.[35] Not only do tenses and speakers fluctuate in this text, but 'everything/[is] happening all at once', meaning that the inertia is never that which is known, that we never become inert because nothing is inertly known.[36] The contrast between 'too bright' and 'present tense' and 'mute history' point to the importance of pushing ourselves (as poets and readers) to the boundaries of both language and memory. As Stein concludes 'If I Told Him' – 'Let me recite what history teaches. History teaches.'[37] There is no reciting of what 'history teaches', there is no point of view that is privileged, there is no history that is objective. As Redell Olsen writes, 'the only possible hint of escape is the potential for knowledge – to go on discovering the plots, the codings, the clues that swerve the reader into multiple modes of attention and engagement with the poem and the world in and around it'.[38]

What Olsen alludes to is the experience of reading *Memnoir*, the fact that while the text displaces the reader as far as time, place, story, it is also full of vibrant descriptions that bring the reader viscerally inside the work. Retallack writes,

> otherwise one could ask at any moment e.g. in what story
> does an uninvited goddess walk in and roll a golden ball
> down the hall or why not enjoy the story of lovers in the
> same vein from different centuries but in the same story
> from different worlds but in the same story I write down
> my dreams this is probably not one of them ...[39]

Beginning with 'otherwise', this passage presents a sequence of mythic 'otherwises' in the guise of 'story'. Laden with possible clues like the repetition of 'in the same story', the reader is propelled forward, struck by the clarity of the 'goddess' (who is 'uninvited') and 'a golden ball' alongside the swerves that occur in each line.

There is no legible 'same story', and perhaps this is the important 'coding' to crack. The stanza that precedes this one ends, 'the soul is inwardness, as/soon as and insofar as it is no longer outwardness; it is *memoria*, insofar as it does not lose itself in *curiositas*'.[40] The effect of this is that 'otherwise one could ask at any moment' becomes framed by echoes of classical rhetorical thinking specifically of *De Inventione/On Invention* (attributed to Cicero), which presents the 'proper materials of rhetoric'. '*Memoria*' is Latin for 'memory', but seems to represent something between (or both/and) memorisation and improvisation. Translated by C. D. Younge (1853), *On Invention* offers the following 'divisions' of rhetoric (or oratory): 'Invention; Arrangement; Elocution; Memory; Delivery'. Memory is described as 'the lasting sense in the mind of the matters and words corresponding to the reception of these topics'. Memory in this context is almost the orator's ability to embody language, to have a facility not only with written speech, but to also have an internal repository of references and quotations to draw on when impromptu speech requires it. In contrast to *memoria*, *curiositas* (Latin for 'curiosity') involves the desire to explore, learn something, follow one's interests. It makes sense that 'the soul is inwardness' when '*memoria* . . . does not lose itself in *curiositas*' because *memoria* hinges on what already exists inside one's mind and *curiositas* involves active engagement with one's environment and all the experiences it has to offer.

So, although the reader becomes ensconced in the possibilities of the 'uninvited goddess', we are also piecing together what kinds of modes or wagers the text invites us to participate in. As Olsen writes, '[Retallack] avoids the fixity of the still, the *known* meaning, and therefore value, of a word, a sentence or scene; definitions are not only always "otherwise", but lead in alternate "other" ways to reveal a faulty structure leaking narrative in all directions.'[41] The effect of the 'leaking narrative in all directions' is one that exudes interrelationships across unexpected words, from e.g to e.g., culminating in the experience of 'another example of the way in which a form might not/reflect a purported fact or facts'.[42] Here the form might be story, narrative, memoir – all forms that are up for negotiation and reconsideration through *Memnoir*. Retallack continues this stanza, 'I drop(ped) the tendency/to begin sentences with I long ago she claims . . .'.[43] 'I' as signifier of what one expects of memoir is directly undone – but undone by being 'drop(ped)', not via decisiveness.

VII. 'I know I know I know you.'[44]

A litany of quotation:

> . . . fiction is/precisely what they now call non-fiction too get a bit too/personal i.e. Eurydice my dark darling don't worry I can/bear your not looking at me she cri(ed) out i.e. hoping it/(was) true [45]
> . . . in the same story I write down/my dreams this is probably not one of them [46]
> . . . I have a confession to make I have not/answered my mail my telephone my email my calling my/God my country my conscience my desire to [47]
> . . . I drop(ped) the tendency/to begin sentences with I long ago she claims [48]
> e.g. one thing I try not to understand she says is how/gravitation works or from where the force of attraction/comes or the smile the smile in which the body makes this present felt . . . [49]
> . . . I beg that you unravel the fates of/my Eurydice too quickly run . . . [50]
> among the things I live by she says i.e. along with some-/thing a woman once (said) in a London cab . . . [51]
> is there any way to staunch the flood toward the smarmy/margins I once want(ed) to demonstrate this to be the/case but my margins (were) much too wide to contain the proof . . . [52]

VIII. '. . . it is the detection that holds the interest and that is natural enough . . .'[53]

The first appearance of the first person, 'I', in *Memnoir* appears in the context of a genre critique ('fiction is/precisely what they now call non-fiction') that swerves into a revisiting of the story of Eurydice. Both fiction and non-fiction verge on the 'too personal', meaning too self-centered/self-centric, the project of (a) *Memnoir* being to call into question what one does with subject (note the lack of article, lack of specificity). ' . . . fiction is/precisely what they now call non-fiction too get a bit too/personal . . .'.[54] What does one do with the 'too personal'? 'i.e. Eurydice my dark darling don't worry I can/bear your not looking at me she cri(ed) out'.[55] Is Eurydice both speaker and subject here? The line break between 'I can' and 'bear' separate what might be dialogue. It might be Orpheus calling out to Eurydice, 'my dark darling don't worry'. However, who is the 'she' who 'cri(ed) out after saying "I can/bear your not looking at me"'? This moment creates a collapse of perspectives right at the start of the poem, pushing readers (who are also viewers) to suspend disbelief, or rather the belief that we might know the story of any Eurydice, through twists of minimally punctuated lines.

Ovid's rendering of 'The Story of Orpheus and Eurydice' (in *Metamorphoses*) begins with Eurydice's descent to the underworld and Orpheus's subsequent plight to rescue his wife, 'whose growing years were taken/By a snake's venom'.[56] The scenario is cinematic – woman meets a tragic death (too early) and her forlorn husband fights for her return. He wins – the 'man' always does in these mythic stories, as long as he exercises self-control in their return to land – 'Turn back his gaze, or the gift would be in vain'.[57] Eurydice might very well utter her support for Orpheus 'not looking at me' – but he does, and she's gone. In Retallack's initial rendering of this tale, there is no Orpheus on this page. In fact, there is no trace of Orpheus here.

There is a 'she' repeated far more often than 'I', often in the company of 'I'. For example, '. . . I drop(ped) the tendency/to begin sentences with I long ago she claims'.[58] The 'I' here exists in multiple tenses – past and present, drop and dropped – and the 'I' is spoken by 'she'. This moment is preceded by 'another example of the way in which a form might not/reflect a purported fact or facts'.[59] With an emphasis on 'form' and 'fact(s)', both 'I' and 'she' are rendered questionable or question-worthy. Nothing is what it seems here, and the 'she' might play the role of both detective and femme fatale.

In his introduction to *The Philosophy of Film Noir* (2006), Mark T. Conard defines the genre first technically – 'the constant opposition of light and shadow, its oblique camera angles, and its disruptive compositional balance of frames and scenes, the way characters are placed in awkward and unconventional positions within a particular shot'[60] – and then thematically. Conard lists tropes that include: 'the inversion of traditional values and the corresponding moral ambivalence . . . the feeling of alienation, paranoia, and cynicism; the presence of crime and violence; and the disorientation of the viewer'.[61] Part of the language game of this text is the way Retallack collapses the familiar into new terrain – memoir joins with film noir to set the scene for a stage where memory and movie are their fictional, perhaps interchangeable, silhouetted, hypothetical selves.

Suppose *Memnoir* proposes an alternate use of the first person. Suppose the 'I', the first person is never singular and the subjective is perhaps a continual surprise. Part of the appeal of the noir genre is the investigation, the experience of losing oneself into a line of inquiry because it feels imperative, the desire to know.

<u>Cue:</u> *Various shadows. Artificial lighting. Perhaps the location is unspecific, perhaps it is smoky, perhaps there's a fedora shielding the anti-hero's face.*

Towards the end of the book, the first person seems to reflect on the idea of narration. 'among the things I live by she says i.e. along with some-/thing a woman once (said) in a London cab . . .'.[62] The reader is left to imagine 'the things I live by', never specified by 'she'. This stanza closes, 'if you don't/know what you want you'll just be used s/he says in the/made-for-tv-movie no more alarming than relatively/tasteful vampire assaults'.[63] The plot thickens as 'you' is in danger of being 'used'. Then suddenly we are on television, but the text is not episodic, rather feature-film length and equipped with the stigma of being palatable enough to watch in the 'family' room in one's home. The following page presents a lexical romp of descriptors that reverberate with Hollywood echoes – 'why refuse entertaining irony dry wry humor display/of imaginative aerodynamics emotional hydraulics . . .'.[64] These lines could read as film review, boasting 'dry wry humor' and 'imaginative aerodynamics'. Drama is everywhere here, but the feeling is not conveyed through linear storytelling. Instead the reader continues to link association to memory to language in a recursive process that undoes meaning making as it continues to be remade.

<u>Establishing Shot:</u> *Language is its own detective story. An adventure in voice-over where plot never stands alone. A dance number takes a dark twist only to find the leading lady stuck on a storyboard again. Emphasis on lighting, nostalgia, a hummingbird from where the force of attraction comes.*

When the first person appears for the last time, the reader becomes engaged in a meta-poetical moment: 'is there any way to staunch the flood toward the smarmy/margins I once want(ed) to demonstrate this to be the/case but my margins (were) much too wide to contain the proof . . .'.[65] Given that the text appears in prosaic blocks on the page, pushing up against the margins, rather 'smarmy/margins', one might read 'I once want(ed) to demonstrate this to be the/case' as a reflection on the craft of the text in the reader's hands. 'Want(ed)' is both past and present, hinting that this experience of 'margins much too wide' is ongoing, as is the tension surrounding 'proof'. Although the text seems to be narrating its own physicality, the language used is visual, cinematic – we see 'the flood' and imagine, as the stanza progresses, 'the figure crossing the vacant lot the ungendered/silhouette intersecting a collector's fact'.[66] The action here, a shadowy gender-ambiguous being moving across an empty asphalt expanse, turns reading into seeing and syntax into bodies.

<u>Dolly Shot:</u> *The camera moves alongside, the camera always moves alongside, never with. Maybe we're moving towards a dimly lit building, maybe it's a smoggy street corner, maybe there's a car or an interrogation room or even a woman lounging in a hotel lobby.*

Beyond the thinking that *Memnoir* sparks around time and memory, fiction and autobiography, Retallack also crafts a book that pushes the reader out of any predictive gendered assumptions. In her recent essay 'Alterity, Misogyny & the Agonistic Feminine',[67] Retallack draws our attention to the work of S. M. Quant, who proposes, 'Despite the fact that gender identities are in increasingly complex conversation with biology and cultural construction the reductive force of patriarchy, with its sidekick misogyny, remains the catastrophic constant.' Unlike film noir, or the revisionary potential of memoir, *Memnoir* refuses to accept 'patriarchy' as 'catastrophic constant'. Instead the figures that inhabit the text are 'ungendered/silhouette', 'she', Eurydice and even Archimedea (Archimedes + Medea, scientist + enchantress), the latter being an intervention on a masculine name. Sure, there are 'boys' and 'too many Sinatra/movies', but the voice of the text refuses 'to be dominated by default masculine values'.[68] In fact, the text upturns the idea that one should ever accept any default situation or dynamic. The experience of *Memnoir* argues that masculine/feminine divides are as false as the image of the vampy femme fatale, and that it is through language that an alternative 'form of life' (to paraphrase Wittgenstein) becomes possible.

In 'The Difficulties of Gertrude Stein I & II', Retallack observes, 'we intuitively know that everyday life doesn't conform to simple outlines of well-made stories. In fact the story as story is radically surprising only to the degree that it transgresses its own generic expectations.'[69] The essay then looks to Stein's foray into detective fiction, *Blood on the Dining Room Floor*, as a work that in its design is a 'small but complex system that cannot by its own constituting rules arrive at a logical terminus'.[70] The same can be said of *Memnoir* – the text's playful urgency prompts genuine investigative reading. While Stein's novel is critiqued because of its generic illegibility, *Memnoir* refuses generic expectations – nothing is certain in the world of this work, and that is why it is important – the composition of the text provokes dialogue through its composing. To quote Retallack on *Blood on the Dining Room Floor*, 'the more you can't find the object you're looking for, the more you're learning about the language coastline itself'.[71] The 'language coastline' is what pushes the reader's imagination to the brink, challenging memory to rewrite itself given the contemporary moment of remembering.

IX. 'And how do you like what you are.'[72]

Memnoir concludes with the line(s), 'watch your prize as it flies out of your hand/into the air'.[73] Appropriately, by ending on this image of watching, there is no conclusion. The poem ends looking outwards at that which is unpredictable, but pleasantly so. It is also important to note that the book really concludes with a list of 'Sources', including multi-genre authors like Ovid and Hans Blumenberg, further cementing that this text is truly a conversation or dialogue between texts, individuals, histories and time.

> the preceding is much too or not sentimental enough
> to accommodate the experience of the child is fatally
> wounded i.e. the house is a mess the streets are littered
> with trash the lawns are littered with trash the grass is
> dying shrubs are pruned to look like gum drops grass is
> mown to look like Astroturf replaces the grass up the stairs[74]

In this excerpt, Retallack paints a portrait of a landscape, or scenario. But the portrait is not site-specific, nor experience-specific. It seems as though a specific place is being constructed, but this is a space that can be read as universal, just as the questioning of 'too much or not sentimental enough' takes into account that each reader will experience sentimentality differently. Additionally, the word 'accommodate' indicates that the experience to be explored is not pre-determined, but rather always in flux, therefore requiring 'the preceding' to be flexible or 'accommodating enough'.

> The end of this particular excerpt reads,
> . . . I have a confession to make I have not
> answered my mail my telephone my email my calling my
> God my country my conscience my desire to[75]

By moving from a landscape in the process of disarray to 'I have a confession to make', the piece shifts into a possible critique of the reliance on things that preoccupies most experiences today. Rather than simply acting and interacting, we are all bogged down by the sheer number of responsibilities we feel to the various devices that allow us to be monitored or trapped into a specific routine of commodification. Retallack writes, 'A noticing, questioning, inventing of constructive ways of being a non-destructive part of our world is essential – to my mind – to combat conservative smugness and the destructiveness that comes out of a greed for MY *security*, MY *nostalgia*, MY *preferred stability*.'[76] In presenting a litany of what is 'not answered', Retallack seems to present a way of achieving this mode of 'being a non-destructive part of our world'. Does the solution to 'destructiveness' lie in 'not answering'?

Towards the conclusion of the poem, Retallack writes,

> just finish the damn story and be done with it stop
> according to some acceptable convention of stopping[77]

In this shift from 'not answering' to 'stopping', the expectation for written forms to have some semblance of closure is questioned. On the one hand, we experience the familiar desire for 'something to be over', the 'just get it over with' kind of phenomenon. But, on the other hand, the 'stop' depends on 'some acceptable convention for stopping'. 'Poethically' speaking, nothing ever really stops, but rather the past, present and future are all in a continuous dialogue with each other. So, this moment in the text serves as a commentary on the problem of thinking a 'stop' is possible but we know it is not in the 'continuous present' of *Memnoir*.

The book concludes with 'watch your prize as it flies out of your hand/into the air'.[78] The image of a 'prize' drifting off into the sky is one that is familiar, like a red balloon full of helium drifting into the clouds. But, here, it is the 'experience of experiencing all that's pointed out' that precedes this panorama.[79] Our 'geometries of attention' have been redesigned and we just watch the prize drift off, as if it is part of our 'unnoticed actual condition of the life'.[80]

Notes

1. From *The Making of Americans* by Gertrude Stein, as excerpted in *Gertrude Stein: Selections*, ed. Joan Retallack, p. 100.
2. Spahr, Osman and Sherin, *Chain 7*, p. 7.
3. Bialosky, 'An Essay on Poetry and Memoir'.
4. Ibid.
5. Retallack, *The Poethical Wager*, p. 28.

6. From 'Composition as Explanation' by Gertrude Stein, as included in *Gertrude Stein: Selections*, ed. Joan Retallack, p. 219.
7. Retallack, *Memnoir*, p. 158.
8. Ibid. p. 3.
9. Baxter, *The Business of Memory*, p. vii.
10. Retallack, *Memnoir*, p. 3.
11. Retallack, *Memnoir*, p. 158.
12. Retallack, *Memnoir*, p. 8,
13. Retallack, *The Poethical Wager*, p. 64.
14. Baxter, *The Business of Memory*, p. viii.
15. Retallack, 'What is Experimental Poetry and Why Do We Need It?'
16. Ibid.
17. From 'Scenes from the Door' by Gertrude Stein, as included in *Gertrude Stein: Selections*, ed. Joan Retallack, p. 166.
18. Retallack, *Memnoir*, p. 3.
19. Dewey, *Art as Experience*, p. 36.
20. Retallack, *Memnoir*, p. 8.
21. Olsen, 'Review of *Memnoir*', p. 24.
22. From 'Patriarchal Poetry' by Gertrude Stein, as included in *Gertrude Stein: Selections*, ed. Joan Retallack, p. 229.
23. Orgera, '(Eggs and Bacon): The Poem as Memoir?'
24. Retallack, *Memnoir*, p. 3.
25. Retallack, *Memnoir*, p. 158.
26. Jenkins, *Poetic Obligation*, p. 18.
27. John Cage, 'History of Experimental Music in the United States' (1959), in *Silence: Lectures and Writings* (Middletown, CT: Wesleyan University Press, 1961).
28. From 'A Movie' by Gertrude Stein, as included in *Gertrude Stein: Selections*, ed. Joan Retallack, p. 172.
29. From 'Orta or One Dancing' by Gertrude Stein, as included in *Gertrude Stein: Selections*, ed. Joan Retallack, p. 114.
30. Olsen, 'Review of *Memnoir*', p. 24.
31. Retallack, *Memnoir*, p. 11.
32. *Gertrude Stein: Selections*, ed. Joan Retallack, p. 6.
33. Retallack, 'Alterity, Misogyny and the Agonistic Feminine', p. 215.
34. Ibid. p. 15.
35. Retallack, *Memnoir*, p. 11.
36. Here I'm paraphrasing/referring to Retallack's 'The Difficulties of Gertrude Stein' (2003, 145) in which she describes Stein echoing her teacher William James with regard to the relationship between knowing and inertia.
37. Retallack, 'Alterity, Misogyny and the Agonistic Feminine', p. 193.
38. Olsen, 'Review of *Memnoir*', p. 24.
39. Retallack, *Memnoir*, p. 5.
40. Ibid. p. 4.
41. Olsen, 'Review of *Memnoir*', p. 25.

42. Ibid. p. 22.
43. Ibid. p. 24.
44. From 'Fourteen Anonymous Portraits' by Gertrude Stein, as included in *Gertrude Stein: Selections*, ed. Joan Retallack, p. 195.
45. Retallack, *Memnoir*, p. 3.
46. Ibid. p. 5.
47. Ibid. p. 19.
48. Ibid. p. 22.
49. Ibid. p. 25.
50. Ibid.
51. Ibid. p. 29.
52. Ibid. p. 33.
53. From 'What are Master-Pieces and Why are There So Few of Them' by Gertrude Stein, as included in *Gertrude Stein: Selections*, ed. Joan Retallack, p. 312.
54. Retallack, *Memnoir*, p. 3.
55. Ibid. p. 3.
56. Ovid, *Ovid: Metamorphoses*, p. 325.
57. Ibid. p. 236.
58. Retallack, *Memnoir*, p. 22.
59. Ibid.
60. Conard, 'Introduction', p. 1.
61. Ibid. p. 2.
62. Retallack, *Memnoir*, p. 29.
63. Ibid.
64. Ibid. p. 30.
65. Ibid. p. 33.
66. Ibid.
67. Retallack, 'Alterity, Misogyny and the Agonistic Feminine'.
68. Ibid.
69. Retallack, 'The Difficulties of Gertrude Stein I & II', p. 145.
70. Ibid. p. 151.
71. Ibid. p. 155.
72. From 'Identity A Poem' by Gertrude Stein, as included in *Gertrude Stein: Selections*, ed. Joan Retallack, p. 305.
73. Retallack, *Memnoir*, p. 38.
74. Ibid. p. 19.
75. Ibid.
76. Retallack, letter to Brenda Iijima, <https://www.asu.edu/pipercwcenter/how2journal/vol_3_no_1/letters/retallackiijima.html> (last accessed 11 July 2019).
77. Ibid. p. 35.
78. Ibid. p. 38.
79. Ibid.
80. Ibid. p. 32.

Chapter 7

A Queer Response to Caroline Bergvall's Hyphenated Practice: Towards an Interdependent Model of Reading
Susan Rudy

When literary critics approach highly experimental works, we are confronted with a problem: it is not always clear to us what the work means. Readers of such work may find themselves bereft. We don't know what to do when we open a book and find texts like the one reproduced on the front cover of *Reading Experimental Writing*, from Caroline Bergvall's *Drift*.[1] Have a look. What do you see? I see very narrow lines in the shape of a stanza, and at first don't realise I am looking at a drawing. Is this a drawing of unreadable lines of text?[2] There are lots and lots of lines in this section that is called 'LINES' but doesn't name itself as such until the penultimate page of the book.[3] The question arises, what is a reader to do without language? Is there an alternative to feeling bereft of meaning? We are used to working hard, yes, but we expect that at some point the meaning of the work will become clear. If it does not, we imagine that the problem is outside of us. Despite decades-long debates about the death of the author, we feel her absence: the author has not offered us a clear path. But what has she offered?

In this chapter, I argue that Caroline Bergvall's 'hyphenated practice',[4] experienced in the first pages of *Drift* as the juxtaposition of writing with drawing, calls for and models a new understanding of the relation between writer and reader, one that models what we can do when we find ourselves in the dark, when meaning is unclear, when we don't know how to find our way. To make this argument I draw on Jessica Benjamin, who argues, in *The Bonds of Love: Psychoanalysis, Feminism, and the Problem of Domination*,[5] that in the mother-child bond we find an alternative theory of the production of meaning. In describing an experience of 'recognition' that 'entails the paradox that "you" who are "mine" are also different, new, outside of me', the mother-child relation also offers an affective theory of the reception of experimental work, since such work offers spaces where readers can also become 'different, new'.[6] In experimental work, the space of reading is shared between reader and writer, language and the world. As Bergvall said in a 2002 interview with Marjorie Perloff, 'this term hybrid is interesting because it goes beyond ideas of interdisciplinary work. [. . .] It also emphasises interdependency rather than autonomy, and calls the author singularly or collaboratively back into the work.'[7] In what Bergvall describes as 'the event of reading', the author is called back into the work as reader.[8]

Those of us who, like Bergvall, speak more than one language &[9] have lived in more than one country & have a non-normative sexuality regularly confront the illegibility, misunderstanding and confusion that is inherent in the determination of meaning. Born in Germany to French-Norwegian parents, Bergvall had two first languages, yet the main vocabulary of her poetry has been English since she moved to London in 1989. 'Croup', for example, tells the story of how Bergvall, in taking to London's 'queer sensibilities', came to 'pass for someone' only 'through "conflicted blonging [sic]"'.[10] Most recently, she has engaged not only with English but both ancient and 'new settlement' languages.[11] Her enactment of the reading process in *Drift* includes two prose poems on the Old English letter thorn. *Ragadawn*[12] includes interviews with Punjabi speakers.[13] Yet Bergvall's practice challenges readers in ways that extend beyond the interpretation of language. Hers is a stunningly contemporary project that explores the experience of a white, privileged, multilingual, politically astute gay woman, living in London in the 'wonky woruld [sic]'[14] of the early twenty-first century. Her writing is a 'public project'[15] into which we are invited to enter. This chapter describes my experience of having entered that project, and grapples with what I found there.

Conceived for both oral performance and book publication,[16] *Drift* is literally and figuratively a space one enters. As such, it exemplifies Bergvall's hyphenated practice. But let's begin with the inside front cover of the book, a space one enters tentatively, like a reader who has not yet begun reading:

> Due north
> following
> a medieval sea poem
> a contemporary sea drift
> an aircraft surveillance image
> a forensic report
> a runic sign

Where we expect trite description, we drift into a poem, an evocation, a meditation. This initiatory text guides and directs while beguiling us, evokes the writer's practice while calling it into question. Let's closely consider what we find here. We begin with directional navigation – 'Due north' – but in *Drift*'s extensive 'Log',[17] the writer, already adrift, asks 'what is north': 'is it a direction or a process. A method or a place. [. . .] Is it a trajectory or endpoint, or both'?[18] Like a trajectory that is also an endpoint, we are enjoined to 'follow', yet the subject matter is vast and complex. 'I decide to use the narrative of the journey and its harrowing drift,' Bergvall writes in the 'Log', 'the story told by the survivors and corroborated by the forensic findings. [. . .] To register the event by recitation. [. . .] Insistent methods in art are intimately connected to processes of receiving and of following.'[19]

What is it that we are 'following'? The 'medieval sea poem' is *The Seafarer*, which Bergvall translates in a section of *Drift* called 'Seafarer'.[20] The 'contemporary sea drift' is Bergvall's contemporaneous experience of the end of one queer relationship and the beginning of another. The 'aircraft surveillance image' and 'forensic report' refer to the sections of *Drift* called 'SIGHTING',[21] 'REPORT',[22] and one of the 'MAPS',[23] all of which bear witness to the plight of seventy-two African migrants, fleeing Libya, who were left to die in the Mediterranean.[24] Finally, the 'runic sign' is the thorn sign: Þ, an unreadable letter,[25] which Bergvall 'stumbled across' and with which she engages in the last two sections of *Drift*, 'NoÞing',[26] and 'Þ':[27] 'I went looking for my Nordic roots in the English language and found this sign.'[28]

Bergvall's work compels us with these strange, apparently unreadable passages, where signification is disrupted. From the first page, *Drift* proposes that we can read the unreadable, including ancient signs and the drawings in the first section that appear like wordless stanzas. In the book version of *Drift*, Bergvall also explores the relation between language's graphic and communicative aspects (through linked sets of drawings and songs), its literary and political aspects (through the juxtaposition of *The Seafarer* with the 'Left-to-Die Boat' case), and its historicity and contemporariness (through her translation of such an ancient text and her verbatim inclusion of a report on the 'Left-to-Die Boat' case). The hyphenated nature of her practice is also quite pragmatic. Her ongoing 'Outdoor sunrise performance', *Ragadawn*, for example, requires musicians and sound engineers, a singer and a composer. At a 2016 keynote address in London on her methods of engagement, Bergvall reminded us that her interest in hyphenation and hybridity 'is also reflected in her interest in multiple languages, in the power relations between languages, and in thinking about language across various modes of literacy, literarity and experientiality.'[29] And as she also noted in that keynote, transhistoric work can provide its own forms of contemporary engagement. But what is our experience of reading such work, especially if 'we', like Bergvall, are queer? When queer literary critics approach queer texts in this 'expanded field',[30] we may find ourselves adrift, semantically.

In 'Queer and Now', Eve Sedgwick's infamous introduction to *Tendencies*, she speaks of the 'ardent reading'[31] undertaken by many of us that enable us to survive the 'profligate way this culture has of denying and despoiling queer energies and lives'.[32] Reading therefore became a resource for survival for many of us, she writes, as we came 'to attach intently' to those 'cultural objects whose meaning seemed mysterious, excessive, or oblique in relation to the codes most readily available to us'.[33] The demands on both text and reader 'form so intent an attachment', Sedgwick says, they can be 'multiple, even paradoxical'.[34] Yet as Lisa Ruddick argues in a 2015 piece on the future of criticism, few contemporary critical practices offer the possibility of knowing the self.[35] Ruddick highlights relational psychoanalysis as an exception, as it offers a theory of understanding how meaning arises intersubjectively. In *Beyond Doer and Done To: Recognition Theory, Intersubjectivity and the Third*,[36] Jessica Benjamin highlights the importance of the 'mutual interpersonal vulnerability'[37] that informs the analytic relationship and, by analogy, the relation between reader and text.

In Bergvall's work, the analyst and patient may be understood also as author and the text she is writing. Bergvall's artistic project is to find herself in and make us aware of *our* positions as readers in relationship to each other and the world and as such it enacts the relationality of what McCormick and Waller call 'the reading situation'.[38] Since at least the 1980s, literary theorists have acknowledged the ideological and interactive nature of reading and writing. We know that both occur in relation to social contexts and ideologies that are sometimes overlapping, sometimes quite different. Readers are not just passengers on the reading journey; we are, like the passages of text we read, complexly produced out of particular 'reading formations',[39] as are the authors who write the texts we read. They are readers too. Yet Bergvall's practice offers challenges to her readers, and to herself as reader, that extend beyond the interpretation of language. The sense of disorientation Bergvall feels in relation to the world as it has been given to her has as much to do with her sexual orientation as it does her trilingualism and transnational origins. Her work not only challenges legibility at the level of the word, page or installation space. Her writing has become a social justice project which engages, often and devastatingly, with global politics.

Bergvall's practice thus models what to do when sense appears beyond our grasp. As she writes of an image of the zodiac of migrants in *Drift*, when seeing is 'radically slowed down', 'inquisitiveness and empathetic connections' may be activated in the reader'.[40] As both *Drift* and 'Say Parsley' suggest, Bergvall's concern with migrancy, the difficulty of being understood, and finding membership in a community when one holds foreign and potentially endangered status, are not only linguistic questions, they relate to her experience as a gay woman, an aspect of her work which has been crucial to her thinking about loss, being lost, and directional navigation. As she said during the 2016 keynote in London, it has to do with queer citizenship, 'with the fact of being part of a type of citizenship which has been, until recently, a second-rate type of citizenship'.[41]

There is no space that is not queer. We reside here. Are here. Here we are. Bergvall's work takes us to these spaces of knowing. Of feeling what our bodies feel. *Éclat* was the first piece in which Bergvall sought, 'tentatively', to 'queer the spaces' – including home itself – that she occupied.[42] Bergvall's work enacts the queer spaces we inhabit and invites us to interrogate them for ourselves. Asked directly by the queer critic Sophie Robinson why she writes, Bergvall answered, 'to find a way of appearing in the world':

> Out of that were built various layers of identity, of interests, of experience. The core of it was very much a question to myself: How do you exist? Now do *we* exist, collectively? What separates us?'[43]

In *Drift,* the poet finds herself not only linguistically but romantically at sea. She has fallen unexpectedly in love and realises she will need to leave an earlier relationship: 'I come home and find that I have lost my sense of home. I come home to find that I have left my home. No rest, no refuge.'[44] When she cannot understand how to move forward, both within the ancient text and in her personal life, she reflects on the history of threat in queer experience, and the question, 'are you safe', arises repeatedly throughout *Drift*, and most fundamentally in relation to the migrants' experience of drifting in the Mediterranean.

At the close of the 'Log' in *Drift*, Bergvall articulates her thinking about the empathic relationship between queer and migrant experience when she writes, that

> [f]amilies, vigilantes and coastguards can no longer in all impunity go to work on those it has taken to be halflings and skraelings. But the menacing fear and the deep collective memory remain at the point of crossing [. . .] and re-engage in full force in the face of others who still must live in abject lawlessness, in different degrees of hideout.[45]

'No longer expecting to make it to the other side, or any other side,' she writes earlier in the 'Log', 'I open up the process.'[46]

As Bergvall wrote, very early in her career, of the process of translating Québécoise lesbian poet Nicole Brossard's *Typhon Dru*: 'I have tried to integrate, albeit in a subtle and punctual rather than generalised manner, to my writing-reading of Brossard's work, an additional layer of reading. A crosslingual reading which would let the original text destabilise in places the language of arrival and bring about new connections.'[47] Like the translator's relation to the text she is reading in order to write it anew, and like the analyst's relation to the patient she is listening to in order to speak, Bergvall's work requires us to be with her in the present. For Bergvall, the 'event of reading' emphasises 'interdependency rather than autonomy and calls the author singularly or collaboratively back into the work'.[48] The reader, also finding herself lost, discovers that she is not alone. It may appear anachronistic, or even wrongheaded, to invoke the notion of finding ourselves in relation to the work of Caroline Bergvall. Uninterested in a singular voice, authorial intention or unproblematised representation, she is a writer who has, since the early 1990s, embraced a range of art forms, media and languages. Her work is as likely to appear in galleries, at docksides or on screens as on pages. She works often with others, on production teams, in collaborations. Why focus, then, on readers finding selves when her work seems entirely uninterested in representations of the self? Because the notion of self often still feels impossible for queer women.

Bergvall's work figures a reader who finds herself lost and found through reading. In the case of *Drift*, Bergvall identifies with the anonymous poet-sailor in the second section called 'Seafarer', her rewriting of *The Seafarer*:

> Let me speak my true journeys own true songs
> I can make my sorry tale right soggy truth
> [. . .] What cursed fool grimly beshipped
> couldnt get signs during many a nighwacko
> caught between whats gone ok whats coming
> on crossing too close to the cliffs blowe wind
> blow, anon am I [49]

As Rebecca Beasley notes, because Bergvall cannot read *The Seafarer* in its original language, she finds herself 'lost in what she calls a fog, without a compass'.[50]

> It is a constant return to blankness. Like some sort of amnesia or lesion, I can't recognise or understand the work done the previous day. It is the strangest feeling this impossibility to make and retain sense. I can't organise things into a reassuring distance nor a semblance of a functioning structure. Most of the time, I feel nauseous, lethargic, disorientated.[51]

In the remaining sections of this chapter, I describe my own experience of feeling lost, and the ways that my ardent readings of strange passages in Bergvall's 'Via',[52] *Éclat* and *Ragadawn* served repeatedly as what I elsewhere call 'queer openings'.[53]

Strange Passage(s): On Ardently Reading Caroline Bergvall

> Along the journey of our life half way
> I found myself again in a dark wood
> wherein the straight road no longer lay
> (Dale, 1996) [sic]
> 'Via'
>
> Confessing our need – we should begin with that.
> Epigraph at entry, *Alyson Singes*[54]

For those of us who have been on the journey, it's a strange passage from what Monique Wittig called the straight mind[55] to queer identity. If we are fortunate, we find queer spaces to occupy, queer ways of being in the world, queer openings to move through. As Eve

Sedgwick noted decades ago, the survival of each of us is a miracle; we all have stories about how it was done.[56] Despite my adolescent awareness of lesbian desire, for example, I didn't come out until I was forty-five.[57] Very often during that strange passage in which I lived a heterosexual life but felt like a lesbian, I found myself repeatedly in what Caroline Bergvall's 'Via', insisting on Dante's opening lines, names as a 'dark wood/wherein the straight road no longer lay'.[58] This section focuses on the ways I found queer openings in Bergvall's work, spaces in which my queer self could exist and eventually come out.

The first time I watch Caroline Bergvall perform, it is in a queer context. I am standing with Nicole Brossard, who has told me about this young queer poet who recently translated her book, *Typhon Dru*. It is 1996 and we are at the Assembling Alternatives conference at the University of New Hampshire.[59] We have just had dinner and are about to hear Bergvall perform from her new book, *Éclat*. For many of us, Bergvall steals the show, with 'her poignant delivery, her arched body which seemed to act as a catapult hurling her taut, multileveled sensual incantations sizzling into the top rows of the Seacoast Repertory Theatre'.[60] Beyond the top row of the theatre, I can hardly breathe, yet I have no idea what I am listening to. I do not know what I am seeing or hearing. I am not (out as) a lesbian. 'Having seen and listened to Bergvall perform in the flesh', Jacob Edmond writes in his article on Bergvall's iterative poetics,[61] he too became conscious of questions of embodiment. Bergvall uses iterative strategies to stage the relationship between individual, embodied instantiation and system, he says, yet she does so in a way that 'emphasizes the embodied gesture of each instantiation or performance, of each pronounced word – its physical presence in the mouth – as much as its place in a system of signification'.[62]

In *Processing Writing: From Text to Textual Intervention*, Bergvall's PhD dissertation, she describes the work of the body in relation to the process of reading: 'reading does not complement the process: it alters it'.[63] Her piece *Flèsh Acoeur*, for example, is a handmade book that becomes increasingly readable as one cuts through its folds.[64] Her writing of the book involved cutting, gluing, sealing, but 'once read, the book looks more "like" a book but the text it supports is in no way the same':

> This intense exercise of mediation of reading by physicality, enables paradoxically a reconstruction of the act of touching which reaches for, and beyond, the text. This signals also, perhaps, a physicality in excess of its current norms of readability.[65]

Recalling the work of Bergvall's text on my then young body – I could hardly breathe, I was so aroused – I return again to *Éclat*, the text from which Bergvall read at the conference, and I find myself astonished. The text is full of explicit and joyful representations of what can happen when women have sex with each other.

> Was a she a she now lying on the sofaaa. Seems to be talking takes up more room laughs as clicks open a fully clit clot clited like a fat cigar, the sofa's popping out are the walls extruding the air seems hotter tighter. [. . .]
>
> I! be!could!happy!here! and quickly lift up your and pull down you're and squat and press out your happening vaginals, your instinctual drive, your cultural reticence, your dutiful intelligence your cautious elaborations, your impeccable taste, in shots of urine all over the surface of this very perfect spot[66]

In *Éclat*, Bergvall explicitly explores Gertrude Stein's 'Rooms', from *Tender Buttons*, and the very spatialised design of the printed book adds to the slow journeying into queer space offered by this radical early work.[67] But all I remember hearing at the time were strange passages in which the pronoun 'she' was said over and over again, with desire, longing and knowledge I did not yet have.

Rather than a 'before' and 'after', the experience of coming out, like other experiences of crossing dangerous borders, invokes 'complex, variegated and painful liminalities'.[68] Hearing Bergvall's queer text in 1996 and feeling there was sense in it, I felt but did not yet know that 'I! be!could!happy!' too. In Bergvall's 'Croup'[69] she evokes the intensely pleasurable approximation of desire in her poetics, yet also the very painful liminalities of coming out in/to language.[70]

> Voila, she led me to the river, eau eau pressed me down lifted my electric/brass [. . .] up chemised/my shirt [. . .] couchd me safely/profoundly on this earth. Then placed a lump of saliva/on my tongue, and gave me language. [. . .]
>
> Nonono came the voices choral came the laws [. . .] Nono no body be language sexd in this way. [. . .] How will I speak. One feels the need to allegorise, then came years of sorrow, hiding, interior struggle n spiritual misery. [. . .] How will I love – [71]

Kaufmann[72] and Smyth[73] have both cited 'Croup' in this context. In Smyth's piece on queer poetry, she highlights Bergvall's 'painful, passionate and urgent prose poem, "Croup"', in which Bergvall describes 'how writing in French deserted her after she was forbidden to see her teenage lover who bestowed the ability to speak'. Bergvall's love letter is found and the consequences mute her.

Later through 'conflicted blonging', she writes, 'I could pass for someone, b perfectly dismulated ...' until the sound of words, the aural pleasure grows and 'riting resumes a root'. Kaufmann describes 'Croup' as 'a telling myth about language acquisition'. He writes, 'She claims that she finally came to French, her first language, through coming. She discovered it during her first experience of sex with another woman. The pleasure of love opens Bergvall to a new experience of being inhabited by language, yet at this early point, the overwhelming voices of 'the laws' say 'Nonono' and threaten to banish her to 'years of sorrow, hiding, interior struggle n spiritual misery'. In this difficult passage, Bergvall finds herself lost with 'no body', 'no language', no answer to the questions 'How will I speak' and 'How will I love'. Perhaps one can see in Bergvall's subsequent ways of resorting to poetics of translation and multilingualism an attempt at finding answers to these deep poetic strands.

'Writing is a gesture across space,' Bergvall writes elsewhere in 'Croup', and, as so much of her work demonstrates, it is also a gesture across time. The phrase 'confessing our need', which appears on the first page of Bergvall's *Alyson Singes*, is taken from Christa Wolf's *Medea*,[74] which figures woman as both queen and female stranger, alienated mother with a tragic destiny. In *Alyson Singes*, Bergvall confesses her need through the voice of Chaucer's dynamic and lively Wife of Bath, who appears to us in the present as, queerly, a woman also named Al.

> Hi all I'm Alyson,
> some people call me Al. [...]
> It's been a long time, quod she,
> some & six hundred,
> Everything was different
> yet pretty much the same.[75]

Bergvall's present is inhabited by other temporalities and other corporalities, witness her fairly constant use of historical materials and languages and her juxtaposition of historical events with her poetic explorations. Here, the text begins with a reflection on and indeed citation of Wolf: 'Do we let ourselves go back to the ancients, or do they catch up with us? No matter.' In Wolf's words, 'an outstretched hand suffices. Lightly they cross over to us, our strange guests who are like ourselves.' In an interview with Eva Heisler, Bergvall gives us a new word – *wreading* – for what we find here, passages of writing constructed out of acts of reading:

> The poet Jen Bervin's textile work from Emily Dickinson's pencil texts, *The Dickinson Composites*, is an extraordinary example of rigorous attention to responsive modes of research-based wreading. Not translation per se, yet a threading through that transtextualises the fragility of the manuscript work.[76]

In Bergvall's case, she leaves traces of herself, (t)here, 'wreading', ardently struggling with us.

Bergvall's early piece *Strange Passage: A Choral Poem* gives us a name for the queer space one finds oneself in when we read her work. A key section of *Strange Passage*, excerpted in Maggie O'Sullivan's *Out of Everywhere*,[77] gestures towards the contradictions with which Bergvall's work has long been grappling. 'If to belong (is to erase) is to appear, then [. . .] This excitement this sudden rash this unexpected full view. As we slowly turn: from sleep to motion as we come to pass: from semi-visible to nonchalantly here'.[78] In 'Croup', the 'oh' appears in French – 'eau eau' – reminding us of the power of the sound of words to evoke both bilingual traffic and also physical experience in her works.

In 2017, Bergvall performed a work in progress entitled *Oh My Oh My* in London. As the title suggests, the exclamation 'oh' is a repeated one in Bergvall's lexicon. The press release for the 2017 piece describes *Oh My Oh My* as 'poetic variations for a world on the brink'. Drawn from several sources, *Oh My Oh My* is based on 'language material' recorded on Bergvall's travels across Europe as well as her recording of the London Women's March. As a French-Norwegian writing in English and based in London, Caroline Bergvall's hybrid identity in terms of language and country of residence has long been recognised.[79] In a 2011 interview, Bergvall explicitly links her queer identity – what she calls her 'selves' – to her interest in plurilingualism and migrancy:

> As a multilingual, white, queer female, European writer, with good teeth, thick hair, and an intensely troubled sense of what it means to belong, to identify, it has been important to me that I try and keep the connections alive between problematizing gendered identity and understanding the dynamic of language use and cultural assumptions.[80]

By problematising language use and cultural assumptions, Bergvall frequently and deeply problematises gendered identity, but for me, it has been the relation between the queer woman writer and her lesbian reader that continues to be at stake. How, to queer Nancy Miller's question from several decades ago, can we claim a lesbian critical subjectivity in the face of the 'massive deconstitution of subjectivity' wrought by poststructuralism and queer theory itself?[81] Queer space is not in a different or temporary world. It is our experience in the present, where we exist as queer people dominated by heterosexual assumptions, frameworks, architectures, images. Bergvall does not represent it as imaginary or alternative. Rather, she evokes what exists, the strange passages we find ourselves in as queer people, while also reimagining, through her complex language poetics and unique, unconventional performances and artworks, how else we might live.

In 'O Yes',[82] a collaborative piece written with lesbian experimental writer Erín Mouré, Bergvall suggests that 'reading gives body'. At the borders of Mouré's texts are both the future for poetry and 'its lesbian ghosts':

> I wonder whether there has ever been anything more important for modern poetry (and philosophy) to do than to unpack the ghosts of the past. These are, are these, the traces of your poetry's past: 'georgette', 'woman', 'girl', 'bodies', 'o cidadán', 'labial tendency'. Your text's borders are its lesbian ghosts. Is its future called 'O'?[83]

'Is that its civic address, its love, "O reader",' Bergvall asks? The 'OH'/'eau'/'O', this gesture towards meaning which is also an out-take of breath, an exclamation of pleasure, a statement of surprise, an invocation of the female body, the poet's mouth, invokes what Bergvall describes as the reason why she reads and writes: 'the fact that O inevitably harks back to the poet's voice [. . .] might be there exactly to remind us that the poet reads not just to announce but to create shared body-spaces, amourous bodies, voiced tracings'.[84]

'Via': Or, The Straight Path Gone Astray

> Along the journey of our life half way
> I find myself again in a dark wood
> wherein the straight road no longer lay (Dale, 1996) [sic][85]

In Bergvall's notes on 'Via', included in *Fig*, she describes having written the piece almost by accident. 'Stumbling across translations of Dante's *Inferno* on her way to other books' in the British Library, she wonders whether she was 'following a lead', hearing the 'sense of panic of the opening canto': 'The one at the crossroad. The one who needs. The one who terrifies. Then the one who calls, yet remains hidden'.[86] She speaks of coming to an understanding of it 'by standing in it, by becoming it', by 'transforming writing into being'.[87] My first encounter with 'Via' is in 2002. I listen to Caroline Bergvall perform the piece on her CD, *VIA*, but I'm a literary person. I want to see the poem on the page. In contrast with the complexity of much of Bergvall's work, 'Via: 48 Dante variations' stands out for its 'straightforward appearance':

> Composed largely in tercets, punctuated by names and dates, 'Via' emphasizes its materiality – the poem is a collection of 47 English translations of the first three lines of Dante's Inferno. These translations, rather than being performed by the author herself, were gathered from the British Library, painstakingly copied and arranged by Bergvall.[88]

I know that 'Via' is made up of three lines by Dante – the first 'variation' – and forty-seven translations of these same lines. Yet having heard Bergvall read translation after translation after translation aloud, having heard her repeatedly articulate the experience of finding oneself lost, I hear, again, a description of my conundrum in the present.

In my early forties, on the journey of my life halfway, I find myself in a very dark wood. I have been married for more than twenty years, I have two daughters, I have made a commitment to someone and I have tried to fulfil it, but I am not happy. The straight road no longer lies ahead, but how will I love? I most ardently want an answer to the question, and through the transfer of desire, imagine Bergvall asking, if not answering it, for me. My reading of 'Via' involves a similarly intense exercise of mediation. 'Via' is a poem that continues and continues and continues. Forty-seven of the forty-eight variations are readings of the first three lines, each slightly different from the one before, the one after. Watch what happens to the reading space when we consider even three of them.

In 'Via', the tercets are arranged alphabetically, so let me reproduce the arbitrariness of that arrangement by citing here a tercet from the beginning, middle and end of the poem.[89] Note that the citations are reproduced from Bergvall's text, and refer to the translator, and date of translation.

> 1. Along the journey of our life half way
> I found myself again in a dark wood
> wherein the straight road no longer lay
> (Dale, 1996)

> 31. Midway this way of life we're bound upon,
> I woke to find myself in a dark wood,
> Where the right road was wholly lost and gone
> (Sayers, 1949)

> 47. When I had journeyed half of our life's way,
> I found myself within a shadowed forest,
> for I had lost the path that does not stray.
> (Mandelbaum, 1980)

In 'How we read Caroline Bergvall's "Via" and why we should care', Genevieve Kaplan uses the pronoun 'himself' when referring to the speaker of the poem and in so doing misses what I take to be a crucial point in Bergvall's rewriting of Dante: that the human struggle includes the struggles of queer women.

In Kaplan's reading of 'Via', the speaker somehow continues to be male and 'he' is described as 'distressingly unable to locate himself', looking 'for a path that doesn't exist'. By the end of 'Via', Kaplan notes that the speaker has 'lost the path that does not stray'.[90] In her view, the fault of being lost is levelled, variously, at the speaker and at the wider world, but imagining, as I do, that the speaker of the poem is a queer woman and that the 'straight path' is that of heterosexuality, what I find is an invocation of queer experience, of finding oneself in a dark wood 'wherein the straight road no longer lay'. What I hear is Bergvall reading, out of history and in the present.

On Being Passengers: *Ragadawn*

Ragadawn is described on Bergvall's website as 'a sonic artwork'.[91] A composition for two live voices and 'a site-specific soundscape', the performance draws on ancient and contemporary musical and literary traditions and the piece is itself a ritual, a passage from mourning into morning. My ardent reading of the piece begins at 4 a.m. on

Bergvall's Hyphenated Practice 177

September 16, 2016. On an eerily quiet street in East London, my partner, Frances, and I are waiting for the bus that will take us to the Estuary Festival in Southend, where *Ragadawn* will be performed at dawn. As we arrive at the venue for the performance, I read the words PASSENGER TERMINAL appearing in massive letters on the terminal building and become both reader and text. Our departure from the bus signals arrival in the performance. We become 'passages' in the piece as well as 'passengers' along for the ride, and yet the sound of unfamiliar languages drifting out of the speakers throughout the piece will soon remind me of the passengers who have had so much less choice as they embarked on their journeys. At the heart of the piece, standing in front of us on the dock, is what I perceive to be a queer couple: Caroline Bergvall and her featured soprano, Peyee Chen (Fig. 7.1).

Bergvall stands centre stage. She speaks and is positioned at the centre, yet the performance begins with Chen's voice and the piece is profoundly shaped by Chen's nine-minute song, a love poem written by Bergvall using medieval poems and composed as a song for Bergvall by the vocal composer Gavin Bryars.

Figure 7.1 *Ragadawn* at the Estuary Festival, Southend, September 2016. Front and centre at the microphone: Caroline Bergvall. Front and to the left at microphone: Peyee Chen. Photo credit: Benedict Johnson, 2016.

I can't help but see Bergvall and Chen as a queer couple. Like lovers, the voices of Bergvall and Chen respond to each other throughout the piece, sometimes intermingling, sometimes echoing, sometimes as call and response. How, I asked Bergvall, does she think about the love that individuals in queer couples have for each other in relation to what she describes as 'the reality of the language where we are'? Bergvall said,

> I was thinking of love as a reclaiming or restating of what we love about the world and who we are connected to in the world. Which is why I wanted the pairing, the two voices, but also at another level the pairing is the interconnection with the world, the pairing with the outside, and the pairing with the broader others that we are living with.[92]

Drawing on Judith Butler's thinking in *Notes Toward a Performative Theory of Assembly*,[93] Bergvall notes that 'we do not choose the world that we're in, we have to accept that there's so little we choose, and we have to work constructively with the non-chosen'; 'love is a way of placing one's heart and mind toward the unchosen', she says. It is something we do 'with all our limitations and all our smallness'. In loving another person, we are opened to the lessons of love, which we can then 'bring to bear on political commitments towards others we might not know'.[94] 'To encounter ourselves as nonsovereign', Lauren Berlant and Lee Edelman suggest, 'is to encounter relationality itself, in the psychic, social and political senses of the term.'[95] 'Reclaiming the experience of singular lives alongside larger collective investigations,' Bergvall writes in relation to *Drift*, 'provokes a pendular effect between far and close, which can favour various kinds of empathetic identification at both a personal and collective level.'[96]

Endings & the Pendular Effect

The absence of a 'straight road' in Bergvall's work refers not only to the absence of a clear path, but also to the potential pendular effect of queerness itself, which can swing towards both individuals and structures, provoking emphatic responses and affirming queer lives.

I bring this chapter to a close with an image of the pendula and ampersands in 'Say Parsley', mounted by Bergvall at the Arnolfini Gallery in Bristol in 2010 (Fig. 7.2). The ampersand, seen in the distance in the photo, is a sign of relation. Like the pendula swinging in the foreground, it signifies connections between far and close,

Figure 7.2 View of Caroline Bergvall 'Alpabet' [sic] and 'For Walls' at the Arnolfini Gallery 3, Bristol. Photo by Jamie Woodley.

there and here, ourselves and other selves. What strikes me now are the multiple matrices at work in this piece. The background to 'Say Parsley' is the biblical 'shibboleth', a 'violent event where language itself is gatekeeper, and a pretext to massacre' and its historical allusion: a horrific massacre in Haiti in 1937.

> The pronunciation of a given word exposes the identity of the speaker. To speak becomes a give-away. Are you one of us, not one of us? How you speak will be used against you. The most recent example of a large-scale shibboleth was the massacre of tens of thousands of Creole Haitians on the border of the Dominican Republic in 1937, when the criteria for execution was the failure to pronounce 'perejil' (parsley) in the accepted Spanish manner, with a rolling 'r'.[97]

As I wrote at the time of my first viewing of the piece, walking into the space of the gallery, 'felt like walking into the Lacanian "real" just as the alphabet was emerging'.[98] For Bergvall, the positioning of the listener is crucial to the experience: 'it starts with language mired in the social world of communication. And it's coming at language as a physical value inside you. What was important for me here is the way that language can be so physically and murderously imprisoning.'[99] Having found language so imprisoning, spaces of unreadability become spaces of liberation, as meaning can be created anew. 'It is wonderful,' wrote Gertrude Stein, 'how a handwriting which is illegible can be read, oh yes it can.'[100]

We can read the drawings on the first pages of *Drift*. They are spaces which evoke that which has yet to be written or read and is nonetheless urgent and present. They can open us, and invite us to engage, and reach out. I am writing this chapter in early 2018, at the British Library. Queer subjects are all around me: at their desks, chatting in cafés, on the tube, at my choir practice tonight. I walk along streets and see their names on the plaques above doorways. H.D. Virginia Woolf. They lived here. Their books are everywhere. In London, it's easy to forget how rare a thing it is to think we know a queer subject when we see one, especially when she is a woman. David Kaufmann, in his review of *Drift*, describes Bergvall as 'a creature of hyphens and interstices'. Vincent Broqua sees Bergvall as 'an in-between', someone whose work 'traffics on borders and barriers'.[101] As I have argued, her work prompts us to see what exists and is before us: an articulate, knowledgeable and queer female subject who, as Bergvall said at Birkbeck in 2016, wrestles with what is at stake in desiring citizenship:[102] one wants, having come through a strange passage, to be seen, heard, welcomed.

Like the ampersand, which is Bergvall's sign of interconnections and multiple sites and yet which can only be read, not spoken aloud, Bergvall's strange passages offer the 'poetics of relation' that I have invoked in this chapter. Her call to empathetic living, her acknowledgement of historical privilege as a position that must lead to broader awareness of how to share, away from pain and into healing, is articulated in the trilingual call of 'Croup''s closing lines:

> Some that arise in some of us arise in many of us
> noen som reiser seg i noen av oss resier seg i mange av oss
> qui se levant en nous se relèvant en nombre de nous
>
> Some that arise in some of us arrive in each of us
> noen som reiser seg i noen av oss kommer frem i hver av o ss
> qui se levant en nous se relèvent de chacun de nous. [103]

In closing, let's return to the section of Bergvall's *Drift* which repeats, verbatim, sections of the 'Left-to-Die' report. The text in this section appears in white on black pages. Bergvall describes this inversion as partly a 'funerary gesture', but it is also a 'hint' about how to read the apparently unreadable in Bergvall's work.[104] By appearing in white text on the black pages of *Drift*, the grim words from the 'Left-to-Die' report are transformed and become 'luminous constellations showing the way on the darkest nights'.[105]

Bergvall's texts are not clear, but they let in the light. That which arises in *some* of us, arises in *many* of us. That which arises in *some* of us, arrives in *each* of us. Her work arrives out of and on the darkest nights and says, yes.

Notes

1. Bergvall, *Drift*.
2. The table of contents on the last pages of *Drift* (pp. 189–90) lists the title of this section as 'LINES' and the drawings, all different, are each created out of lines: scribbled-out lines, wavy lines, angular lines, swirling lines, lines that bleed, smudged lines.
3. We do not learn that the first sixteen pages of *Drift* are part of a section called 'LINES', or that these pages are described as '16 drawings', until the penultimate page of the book, which lists its 'Contents'.
4. Bergvall, 'Methods of Engagement'.
5. Benjamin, *The Bonds of Love*.
6. Benjamin, *The Bonds of Love*, p. 15.
7. Perloff, '*ex/Creme/ental/eaT/ing*', p. 125.
8. Ibid.
9. For reasons that will become clear by the end of this chapter, I introduce here the sign of relation that is frequently found in Bergvall's work. See Caroline Bergvall's 'Say Parsley', for example (7 May 2010 – 3 July 2010, Bristol, Arnolfini Gallery). See <https://www.arnolfini.org.uk/whatson/caroline-bergvall-ciran-maher-say-parsley> and <http://carolinebergvall.com/work/say-parsley/> (last accessed 17 June 2019).
10. Bergvall, 'Croup', in *Cropper* (Southampton: Torque Press, 2008), pp. 2–8. 'Croup' appears in its finalised trilingual version in Bergvall, *Meddle English: New and Selected Texts* (New York: Nightboat Books, 2011), pp. 140–6.
11. Susan Rudy, unpublished interview with Caroline Bergvall in which we talk about *Ragadawn*, Islington, London, 2016.
12. On Bergvall's website, *Ragadawn* is described as a 'sunrise vocal performance to be performed outdoors from the last hours of night until the very early morning. A multisensory composition for two voices, multiple recorded languages and electronic drones to accompany and celebrate the slow rising of day.' See <http://carolinebergvall.com/work/ragadawn/> (last accessed 19 February 2019).
13. Rudy, unpublished interview with Caroline Bergvall.

14. Bergvall, *Drift*, p. 46.
15. Noel-Tod, 'Bergvall, Caroline', p. 40.
16. Beasley, 'Migration, circulation, drift', p. 78.
17. Bergvall, *Drift*, pp. 125–66.
18. Ibid. p. 127.
19. Ibid. p. 134.
20. Ibid. pp. 23–59.
21. Ibid. pp. 61–9.
22. Ibid. pp. 71–81.
23. Ibid. p. 82.
24. See <https://www.forensic-architecture.org/case/left-die-boat/> (last accessed 17 June 2019).
25. Bergvall, 'Infra-materiality and Opaque Drifting', p. 92.
26. Bergvall, *Drift*, pp. 169–73.
27. Ibid. pp. 175–81.
28. Bergvall, 'Infra-materiality and Opaque Drifting', p. 92.
29. Bergvall, 'Methods of Engagement'.
30. Watten, 'Poetics in the Expanded Field'.
31. Sedgwick, *Tendencies*, p. 3.
32. Ibid. p. 1.
33. Ibid. p. 3.
34. Ibid.
35. Ruddick, 'When Nothing is Cool'. See note 3.
36. Benjamin, *Beyond Doer and Done To*.
37. Ibid. p. 7.
38. McCormick and Waller, 'Text, Reader, Ideology', p. 193.
39. Bennett, 'Texts in history', p. 17.
40. Bergvall, 'Infra-materiality and Opaque Drifting'.
41. Bergvall, 'Methods of Engagement'.
42. Bergvall, *Éclat*.
43. Robinson, Interview with Caroline Bergvall.
44. Bergvall, *Drift*, pp. 135–6.
45. Ibid. pp. 165–6.
46. Ibid. p. 146.
47. Caroline Bergvall, in Brossard, *Typhon Dru*.
48. Perloff, 'ex/Creme/ental/eaT/ing', p. 125.
49. Bergvall, *Drift*, p. 25.
50. Beasley, 'Migration, circulation, drift', p. 78.
51. Bergvall, *Drift*, pp. 144–5.
52. Bergvall, 'Via: 48 Dante variations', p. 67.
53. Susan Rudy (forthcoming 2019), 'Reading for Queer Openings: Moving. Archives of the Self. Fred Wah', in Linda M. Morra (ed.), *Moving Archives* (Waterloo: Wilfrid Laurier University Press).
54. Bergvall, *Alyson Singes*. This text is now out of print, but a book-length new version, entitled *Alisoun Sings*, is forthcoming from Nightboat Books in 2019.

55. Wittig, 'The Straight Mind'.
56. Sedgwick, *Tendencies*, p. 1.
57. By getting married and having children, I found myself playing very conventional roles in straight life, but as I will argue, in what looks like a straight life, one can regularly find oneself in queer space. A passage is both a journey and a place in itself.
58. Bergvall, 'Via: 48 Dante variations', p. 67.
59. As the late Kathleen Fraser noted, the conference, which was also a poetry festival, 'brought together an extraordinary international roster of English-language poets and scholars making forays into a range of exploratory writing practices' and, rather astonishingly, included a 'well-balanced distribution of women and men – on the theoretical panels as well as the evening poetry readings of new work': 'what a radical shift this gender equation marked in the public community of literary conversation'. See Fraser, 'editor's notes &'.
60. Glazier, email dated 3 September 1996 to Electronic Poetry List.
61. Jacob Edmond, '"Let's Do a Gertrude Stein on It": Caroline Bergvall and Iterative Poetics', *Journal of British and Irish Innovative Poetry*, vol. 3, no. 2 (2011), p. 109.
62. Ibid. p. 110.
63. Bergvall, *Processing Writing: From Text to Textual Interventions*, p. 17.
64. Bergvall, *Flèsh Acoeur*.
65. Ibid. p. 17.
66. Bergvall, *Éclat*, p. 43.
67. Stein, *Tender buttons*.
68. Blue, 'Strange passages'. Further research could be carried out by exploring the concept of 'embodied catastrophe' (p. 178) in relation to Bergvall's work and described by Blue in this qualitative enquiry into the 'strange passages' experienced across the history of American deportation.
69. Caroline Bergvall, 'Croup', in *Cropper* (Southampton: Torque Press, 2008), pp. 2–8. 'Croup' appears in its finalised trilingual version in Bergvall, *Meddle English*, pp. 140–6.
70. I borrow and adapt the phrase from Stephen Guy-Bray, 'Coming Out In/To Poetry'. See also Weeks, *Coming Out*.
71. Bergvall, 'Croup', p. 4.
72. Kaufman, Review of *Drift* by Caroline Bergvall.
73. Smyth, 'Queer Poetry by Definition', p. 4.
74. Christa Wolf, *Medea: A Modern Retelling* (London: Virago, 1998).
75. Bergvall, *Alyson Singes*, p. 1.
76. Heisler, 'Caroline Bergvall, Propelled to the Edges of a Language's Freedom'.
77. O'Sullivan, *Out of Everywhere*. This anthology contributed to Bergvall's growing reputation and indeed helped create the field of women's experimental writing.
78. Bergvall, *Strange Passage*, p. 11.

79. See, for example, Perloff, Robinson, Broqua and Beasley.
80. Kinnahan, 'An Interview with Caroline Bergvall', pp. 243–4.
81. Miller, *Subject to Change*, p. 103.
82. Bergvall and Mouré, 'O YES', pp. 167–76.
83. Ibid. p. 171.
84. Ibid. p. 172.
85. Bergvall, 'Via: 48 Dante variations'.
86. Ibid. p. 64.
87. Ibid. p. 65.
88. Kaplan, 'How we read Caroline Bergvall's "Via"'.
89. These passages appear on pages 67, 70 and 71 of Bergvall, 'Via: 48 Dante variations'.
90. Kaplan, 'How we read Caroline Bergvall's "Via"'.
91. See <http://carolinebergvall.com/work/ragadawn/> (last accessed 19 February 2019).
92. Rudy, unpublished interview with Caroline Bergvall.
93. Butler, *Notes Toward a Performative Theory of Assembly*.
94. Rudy, unpublished interview with Caroline Bergvall.
95. Lauren Berlant and Lee Edelman, *Sex, or the Unbearable* (Durham, NC, and London: Duke University Press, 2014), p. viii.
96. Bergvall, 'Infra-materiality and Opaque Drifting', p. 96.
97. Bergvall, 'Say Parsley'.
98. Rudy, 'A Conversation with Caroline Bergvall'.
99. Ibid.
100. Steve McCaffery cites these words from Stein as an epigraph to *Dr Sadhu's Muffins* (Erin, ON: Porcépic Press, 1974), but I have yet to be able to find them in Stein's work itself.
101. Broqua, 'Caroline Bergvall's Poetics of the Infrathin'.
102. Bergvall, 'Methods of Engagement'.
103. Bergvall, *Cropper*, in *Meddle English*, pp. 147–51.
104. Bergvall, 'Infra-materiality and Opaque Drifting', p. 96.
105. Ibid.

Chapter 8

Reading Language Art in Digital Media: Reconfigurations of Experimental Practices
John Cayley

The time of tongues is past.

My epigraph is the final sentence from the latest book that I have read by Johanna Drucker, *The General Theory of Social Relativity*. This book is one of a number of essays and short monographs published by Drucker with small presses in editions that are or may become limited, collectable, rare. Drucker is an important cultural critic and scholar of the humanities, including the so-called digital humanities. She is also a book artist, an historian of book arts and an exemplary experimental writer, associated, historically, with the Language poets. Ostensibly, this short book – although not without its humour and irony – is a polemical, scholarly appeal to cultural criticism and socio-political activism. It asks us to confront the inadequacy of analyses based on mechanical, 'Newtonian', cause-and-effect models or frameworks. These have proven themselves, especially given events and turbulent developments associated with the 2016 US presidential election, unable to account for our cultural circumstances and also, Drucker suggests, to face 'us' – misperceived collectivities, we ourselves – with existential challenge. 'There is no we that still matters.'[1] The book sets out an alternative 'General Theory of Social Relativity'. Drucker's GTSR borrows from commensurate theory in physics and mathematics so as to begin, at least, to explain if not comprehend a cultural condition that nonetheless reveals itself as, for Drucker, profoundly melancholic.[2] By the time I have read the book's final sentence, however, and as I continue to work to read-and-understand, I have also become aware that this sentence and many of those preceding it are far from expository or even polemical; they are new quanta and constituents of experimental writing. I am reading experimental writing. Or perhaps language art. Perhaps even book art. The paratextual circumstances of: small press, collectable, rare, should have spoken to me.

The etymological root of 'experiment' is the same as that within 'experience' and 'piracy'. In a presumed literary context, it suggests a trial, a poetic trial, of language. I experience my reading of Drucker's sentences as a trial of my understanding, of my piratical attempt to grasp what she is trying to say. The prejudicial association of such experience with writing is belied by the inability of written, (typo)graphically inscribed language to reinforce our misdirected notion that it is attempting to 'write' rather than to 'say'. But as I just said, Drucker implies as much since she did not write or say, 'The time of (experimental) "writing" or "the pen" or "literature" is past.' There was never a time of literature, or experimental writing. There has only ever been a time for languages, 'tongues', and this time may well be past, she says, overwhelmed by 'the very takeover of the sound-noise rhythms of the material world'.

The substance of material/immaterial language is *voice*. And voice is thus, a fortiori, the medium for any self-reflexive practice of aesthetic language, of experimental writing, poetry, language art, digital language art. Making this statement implies that – by giving physical evidence of embodiment – language cares to support and produce located, integral, personal identities. But this voice is not only voice as of actual, particular human voices. The characteristics of sited integrity and identity are required by linguistic objects in the symbolic abstract, as well as being contingent upon the fact that voice and human voices possess these characteristics. And acknowledging that there is a pragmatic necessity for virtual linguistic forms and traces – at any and all levels of linguistic structure – to achieve states of sited integrity and identity runs counter to Platonic idealism. A better name for this condition of linguistic phenomena is *ideality*, an ideality that enables repetition and is expressed – produced and received – as, precisely, voice:

> ... it must be constituted, repeated, and expressed in a medium that does not impair the presence and self-presence of the acts that intend it: a medium that preserves at once the *presence of the object* in front of the intuition and the *presence to oneself*, the absolute proximity of the acts to themselves. Since the ideality of the object is only its being-for a non-empirical consciousness, it can be expressed only in an element whose phenomenality does not have the form of mundanity. *The voice is the name of this element. The voice hears itself.*[3]

Forms of voice are produced and received by us, but until a form is readable, it is not yet language. This movement from gestural to readable is also the movement from actual events and processes of production to the provisionally finished inscription – the utterance in the support materiality of voice – of a reiterable trace with respect to the conventions of one of the world's hospitable languages.

And now I am beginning to speak of reading in a special sense, as a word for what we do, both when we hear-and-understand and when we scan-and-'hear'-and-understand. The French *entendre* enfolds both hearing and understanding.[4] It does this straightforwardly when used in relation to language in aurality and it can also be applied, in French, to an experience that results from everyday practices of reading. In a complementary manner, older usages of English *read* are perfectly capable of invoking to-hear-and-understand, given that 'to read' was also often to make an informed persuasive guess about the meaning of symbols and gestures. In contemporary English, we still read the 'signs' in many situations and across a wide range of media including the conversations and discourses of aurality.

The first characteristic of this particular conception of reading – one that I want to bring into this discussion of reading experimental digital language art – is its agnosticism with respect to any support media for language. While acknowledging that the material culture of literature and "writing" predominates, even and perhaps especially in the practices and discourses of its experimental varieties, the tenor of everything that I've said so far suggests, and my argument now insists, that any reading of language art requires a poststructuralist perspective, one that has, after the thought of Jacques Derrida, understood writing as always already *voice*, the (anti-)originary supplement that brings language into being. Actual human voices, which are equally *the traces of voice* (Derridean archi-writing), bring language into being in precisely the same manner as do traces of conventional writing, the letters of literature.[5]

Secondly, I qualify this concept of reading as grammaleptic. Grammalepsis is a word for both the process and the moment when a material and formal gesture of (potential, virtual) affect and significance shifts and moves so as, suddenly, to pass over the threshold of readability (and reiterability) where it is seized and grasped as such, as significance-and-affect-rendering language. The seizure, *-lepsis*, renders a *grammé*, a readable trace. Reading and making language is grammalepsy.

I hope that readers of Derrida will recognise in this definition of grammalepsis my attempt to capture certain aspects of the meaning and force of *différance* in a form that renders it of practicable use to language artists and critics; to readers of experimental writing and digital language art. Whereas différance, it seems, must reserve itself for the deconstruction of the metaphysics of presence, grammalepsis offers us a name for what happens – continually, and whenever there is *any* event of language – when new meanings become, and simultaneously co-create, actual language at any level of linguistic structure. Crucially, grammalepsis refers to a moment and a passage of both time and travel over a metaphorically spatial threshold. Thus, it does also name the passage from temporalisation to spacing in a philosophy of language. We can treat grammalepsis, comfortably, as a word like any other, as opposed to 'différance', which explicitly and paradoxically resists, insisting on a refusal of any such catastrophe. In pragmatic terms, grammalepsis names what happens as we are suddenly able to read, grammaleptically, what wasn't readable before, including within 'différance' itself: the inaudible 'a' is *voiced* within us and tells us that we are no longer reading 'difference'. Any signified presence of accountable, formal, structural difference has suddenly been deferred ... to infinity, as a philosopher following Derrida would say.[6] In *every* event of language, moreover, the same process operates as grammalepsis. Manifestly, whenever we read a pun or we 'fill in' (read) an ellipsis, for example, or especially when we read a phrase or a sentence and we recognise a *voice*, a distinctive style – and we do this every single time we read – then we encounter grammalepsis and we read ... grammaleptically.

Returning, and attempting again to read the final chapter of Drucker's experimental essay, there is, 'Not the language of machines, not language in machines, not language coming out of machines, but the very takeover of sound-noise rhythms of the material world – animate, inanimate, mechanic, organic – produced how where [sic], and so ... .'[7] And so, we are situated in a world which has passed beyond digitisation and digitalisation. We are invited to consider that however and whenever we are trying to read digital language art, we are already in our brave new world. Language as distinct from – or différant with respect to – 'sound-noise rhythms' has virtually collapsed. It is not only *the digital*, represented here by machines, that is a cause of this collapse (the very idea of 'cause' runs counter to Drucker's impetus), it is something like the convergence of pre-existing, post-mechanical quantum sociality with the technics that have enabled its expression in a pseudo-public sphere, an expression which simultaneously erases any 'we' that might gather there to speak or act, '... and so our self-adjusting ears adapt and produce alternate interiorities and external vibrations unlike the other sounds of prior utterance'. Drucker enables us to read just a hint of generative possibility into this dire prospect.

The reading of digital language art as, putatively, an emergent aspect of experimental writing, must however be performed, grammaleptically, in the circumstances that Drucker sets out, circumstances that we – a 'we' that is under existential threat – now experience, and with which we experiment, and to which we adapt.[8] As an experienced poet, Drucker acknowledges sound in air and in human speech as the sites for poetic intervention in the midst of our crisis. Any reassertion of human poetic action will be made as language in the substance of voice. Perhaps uniquely, human Being reads a desire for silence into the world, because silence is a necessary condition of language, and it is this silence that we can no longer find. 'We suck the pauses up, search for intervals, in need of non-existent desperate silence.'[9] The silence we cannot find is the very thing that would allow our voices to bring language into being.

Why is it that 'the time of tongues is past'? For the same reason that encourages me to introduce a more practical and informative discussion of language art in digital media by invoking Drucker's experimental meditation on cultural and socio-political crisis. 'The standing up of the machines on their hind legs ...' is just a spectacular, phantasmatic metaphor (or evolutionary history if it is read as referencing the advent of Homo Sapiens as the machine of universal despoliation), but today's actual machines, robots, bots, 'speaking, gesturing, making signs out of that same air that breaks with sound waves and patterns in mind and mined fields', these have only ever existed in the recent history of the 2010s, during which transactive synthetic language was made flesh thanks to robust automatic speech recognition and speech synthesis with proven domestic, if currently constrained, socialisation. '... overarching them all is speech. Acts. Language. Synthesizer'.[10]

The time of tongues is past because once the 'takeover' of 'sound-noise rhythms' is in place, there need be nothing to distinguish human *writing* from whatever else it is that breaks the air with sound waves and patterns. I call this overarching human speech 'writing' in its proper sense as always already archi-writing, because what results from the automatic grammatisation of literal (literally unlettered) speech will become indistinguishable from conventional writing.

Grammatised speech will have all the history-and-civilization-constituting affordances that writing and literature have given to us: hypomnesis (hypostatic memory) supported by non-linear index, archive, and archival access, in sum: the restructuring of human time, of human culture and society, as and in duration.

For the moment, this momentous, albeit speculative, shift in poetics, in experimental writing, expresses itself, unassumingly and in terms of common cultural engagement, as growth in the reading of audiobooks, despite the fact that as of this writing (2018) the audiobook is not digitally inscribed as language-in-aurality.[11] It is, rather, digitised *audio* with minimal digitally manipulable articulation corresponding most commonly to the punctuation of books at the level of the chapter or subtitle. Nonetheless, the reading of audiobooks represents a measurable shift in the culture of reading as a whole, and it is no coincidence that its growing influence and adoption emerges together with the quantum socialisation of transactive synthetic language, as adumbrated in Drucker's experimental text, in my own commentary, and even in my own and others' linguistic aesthetic practices.[12] If there was a literature that we preserved after writing, however experimental, there has always also been an aurature. From now on, historically, if our air is not broken by the end of silence, this aurature may hold, for some duration, certain traces of our experiments with language and aesthetics. To do so, some of us poetic makers will have to work with precisely those digital affordances that historicise these processes. And this is also why language art in digital media deserves to be read carefully, not for new rhetorics in experimental writing but because the processes and infrastructures that underlie this mode of practice have already reconfigured and transformed the practices of language as a whole.

In the mid-1990s, the internet converged with its first browsers and began to make it feasible to share certain aesthetic experiences – of reading, in so far as they were linguistic – that had been produced by writing practices in programmable digital media. Academics who were associated with these practices, particularly in the United States, Scandinavia and France, made great claims for what they called 'electronic writing' in terms of experimentation and innovation.[13] It was proposed that digital affordances enabled enhanced typographic artefacts to actualise certain valorised tropes in poststructuralist theories of literature: intertextuality, non-linearity, the *scriptible* text (Barthes's term: the text written so as to render it subject to reading and the 'literary' interactivity of readers), the revelation and deconstruction of underlying 'codes', and so on. Ironically, the actualised temporalisation of extended typographic artefacts – poems and longer-form fiction as actual time-based artefacts (kinetic or traversable in terms of a programmed score) – was not as significant an aspect of this academic project. Concrete and visual poetics embraced new media, as they always have, but remain on the margins of literary recognition, as they always have. Electronic literature, on the other hand, has steadily established itself, in the academy and as mode of practice, despite occasional fits of doubt concerning the 'seriousness' and 'literary quality' of the body of work in question.

What is now a field – of university-sponsored research and research-based practice – continues to make claims for electronic literature, including claims that it represents a significant literary experimental avant-garde, and that, in the context of ubiquitous computational technics, it enables a critical practice with progressive socio-political inclinations.[14] In one sense, the present essay is, or should be, an experimental reading of experimental writing that has emerged from these circumstances. On the other hand, dysfunctional theoretical and historical configurations of art in the medium of language threaten to prevent any such reading by calling reading itself into question.

Prominent critics in the field have identified a tendency for electronic literature to cannibalise itself. Although it is true that artefacts made from digitised representations of content in constitutive relations with working code exist in a generative ecology that encourages both transcoding (the reuse and manipulation by the same or similar algorithms of digitised representations taken from one perceptual milieu, e.g. sound, to another, e.g. vision) and also a copy-and-paste or plug-and-play (with or without creative commons attribution) approach to snippets and fragments of code, the cannibalisation referred to here is not a matter of collaborative coding and co-creation across media. Rather, critics of electronic literature discover the practice consuming itself in self-destructive gestures that may be seen as both self-purifying and self-defeating. For one critic there is the progressive hope that this circumstance is analogous to the cultural anthropophagy that Oswald de Andrade claimed for a postcolonial literature, Brazil's, which he sees as empowered to devour and consume its colonialist corruption.[15] Electronic literature, macerated in the gorge of multimedia, thus consumes its elitist, colonialist, print-specific literary corruption, disallowing the latter's privileged, *prejudicial* reading. Another scholar, while approving this progressive possibility, finds that it may be the entire feast of hermeneutic reading that is being devoured by multimedia, by the audiovisual decoration and concretisation of language in electronic literature.[16] Whatever might once have been interpretable literature in the work is not or cannot be read. It is looked at, or heard, or handled and then consumed as post-linguistic nourishment – chiefly sound and light – rather than being read for what it, also, is or was. For Roberto Simanowski, this characteristic impetus of electronic literature betrays any purported poststructuralist experimentalism. The death of the reader displaces any death of the author, who thus maintains a less articulated, less interpretable authority.[17]

This self- or self-critically-avowed understanding of electronic literature as a practice of experimental writing that devours itself is, historically, one sign of aporia in the field. If there is no reading, there is no language. We are no longer dealing with an art of language. But this syndrome, as evidenced in emergent practices – at least according to the field's scholars and critics – may also be referred to a second, more significant disruption of the culture of reading more broadly conceived and shared. This grander aporia hangs on qualities of *attention*. Actualised as a function of digitalisation, the artefacts of electronic literature or digitally mediated language art make themselves subject to the 'attention economy', an acknowledged aspect of our ever-more-encompassing digital economy.[18] As advertising, the attention economy monetises and drives the most powerful and significant enterprises in this realm. It is enabled by networked and programmable media, and its transactional universe, the internet, provides us with what is arguably the predominant infrastructure for all practices of reading in the developed world, including the reading that we do as experimental writers. An overabundance of 'information' and minimal costs for the production and dissemination of minimally readable texts, however, ensure that the attention economy is characterised by overload, segmentation and distraction. Human attention is finite, at least in terms of temporality, and thus overproducers must compete for a type of consumption that is intended to yield, ultimately, *commercial* transaction. Even the experimental avant-garde now reads within these infrastructural software architectures, and in so far as it does so, it reads in a new and different way. In a world driven by vectoralised attention, fuelling the computational economy, reading has changed and is changing.

Higher journalism and popular non-fiction have gone so far as to assemble evidence for a cognitive degeneration that is produced by this change in reading.[19] It becomes stupid reading, shallow reading, resonating in contemporary critical thought with the political economic degeneration of 'systematic stupidity'.[20] For Bernard Stiegler, who warns us of this condition, there is, however, a crucial choice that all of us may make with regard to developments in the technics of culture as instigated by corporate capital, even when neoliberalism guarantees that these developments are overdetermined by short-term benefits defined more or less exclusively in terms of self-centred individuality, instrumentality and profit. If we *adapt* to these technics we consume the pharmakon of networked, computational information and infrastructure as a poison; if we *adopt* them with care we may be able to experience new ways of reading, for example, as therapeutic or, speculatively, experimentally progressive.[21]

In literary studies that are sensitive to and schooled in contemporary technics, there is some evidence of a more optimistic, therapeutic reading of contemporary reading. This is best represented in the work of N. Katherine Hayles, who like, Johanna Drucker, is a prominent critic of electronic literature, experimental writing and even book arts. Hayles distinguished reading as 'deep' or 'hyper', qualifiers which have also been applied to attention.[22] In subsequent work it is clear that deep and hyper are to be seen as non-exclusive modes of reading practice and Hayles goes on to add a third modality, that of 'machine' reading, which in our current literary critical world aligns with digital humanities' quantitative 'distant' reading represented, typically, by the work of Franco Moretti. Hayles claims generative synergies between all these modalities and goes so far as to propose that hyper reading may be a sensitive, nuanced, effective response to the demands of the information economy and computational culture, a matter, perhaps, of adoption rather than adaptation.[23]

Wherever we may situate ourselves, subject to these circumstances, by taking a position on any consequences of their effects, a number of things are certain. There is ever more evidence to suggest that practices of reading have changed and continue to do so. And, when engaged with digital media, practices of experimental writing (if that is how we chose to qualify them) must now take into account the potentialities of both hyper reading and machine reading – as a minimum.

Finally, apart from self-consumption in other, less readable media, and changes in the culture of reading that may not resonate with literary aesthetics, digitally mediated language art has had to contend with a relationship to form that is underwritten by specific technologies and their evolution. In order that words, sentences, paragraphs should, simply, *appear* on surfaces (screens) that are actualised in electronics and software, constantly developing technologies must be made to do their work, and it is clear that the reasons they work will have very little to do with the experimental aesthetic (or merely aesthetic) value of any inscription that is proposed for a reading surface. Thus, for example, in the mid-1990s, when hypertext had been identified as a purportedly postmodern form that could be realised in the technologies of the time, this did not imply that specific hypertext technologies would be supported by the actually existing, mainstream regime of computation. Although the World Wide Web soon granted us hypertext for neoliberal globalisation, the specific technologies used by widely recognised canonical works of 'early electronic writing' were quickly rendered obsolete, making them effectively unreadable on 'modern' devices.[24]

In fact, of course, this circumstance is simply a very clear symptom, with near-fatal consequences, sweated out in the ineluctable cultural pathology that threatens all formal innovation. To be experienced and appreciated, any experiment in form must be expressible in a located material culture. Located material culture implies pre-existing, evolved technics, that is, culturally situated technologies – which enable formal constructions – that have become integral to the culture. Some experimental form is relatively easy to express in existing technics. An example from Western poetics is the open field, expressed as spatialised typography. A traditional culture of poetic reading may still fail to appreciate such expressions of spatial typography, but the underlying technics – of print culture in our example – will nonetheless support and preserve their traces of innovation . . . and their poetic potential.

But if formal innovation discovers and demands new technologies that are not yet enculturated literary technics, even when they are integrated with technics that have already become predominant in other socio-economic domains of the culture as a whole, the survival of a dependent experimental form is far from assured. Consider textual animation, which is technically possible in the 'old media' of film, let alone in programmable screen-based media, including word processors, where it would be 'trivial' to implement. Cultivated poetic common sense will recognise formal continuities from typographic traces of the open field to actual temporalisations that are expressive of open-field principles. Programmable media can make this happen easily. Nonetheless, there has not yet been an assured or widely recognised translation (or transcoding) of reading practices from textual animation – even as exemplified in film titling or advertising – to innovative poetics, not outside certain marginalised (and chiefly non-anglophone) domains of electronic writing and associated traditions of 'wired' Concrete poetry.[25] Books of poetry may be published as ebooks, but they are not animated.

Ebooks, on the other hand, do represent a serious shift in the material culture of reading. If their adoption has, for the moment, plateaued, they are nonetheless accepted as, at least, a widely used, economically sustainable and well understood complementary site for reading. And here we also find important hybrid artefacts, made by practitioners of experimental and electronic writing. *TOC*, a multimedia novel by Steve Tomasula, was first published on DVD but later migrated to an app.[26] In this currently well-established material cultural *form*, as an app, *TOC* shares a space that enables contemporary readers to approach it in more or less the same way that they would approach an ebook. *TOC*'s formal innovations, chiefly of multimedia *content*, are thus accessible – are appreciated less as one-off or avant-garde gestures – and make plausible, if unrealised, claims for wider acceptance in the domain of the actual ebook, as produced by publishers. Publishers, however, appear to be less interested in formal innovation than in attracting the attention (see above) that drives their economy.

Samantha Gorman and Danny Cannizzaro's *Pry* is a particularly fine and important hybrid that has also been published as a successful app.[27] This work is a gorgeous audiovisual, multipart novel, the story of a young demolition consultant whose life has been shattered and reconfigured by the 1991 Gulf War. James, the story's protagonist, is losing his sight. *Pry*'s formal innovation emerges here as interface gestures integrated with the fiction. For example, readers must 'pry' open James's failing 'eyes' *in the text* in order to open expanded conduits for both visual experience and textually recorded memory. Read on a tablet, *Pry* can be appreciated by contemporary readers as (like) an ebook. The way that it folds now-familiar interface gestures into acts of reading proposes a new form of aesthetic experience with language art. But will 'pry', as gesture, for example, ever be adopted as a persistent, widely understood form of reading, by the culture at large?

For this to happen, at the very least, there would have to be some significant adoption of the undoubtedly experimental (and demanding) writing (by Gorman) that underlies and supports fiction-generative transaction with the prying gesture that the novel's formal interface allows. How many other writers will choose to respond to this particular form? Very few, one would speculate. Rather, the cultural context of *Pry* is more likely to encourage these gestures to be 'read' as elemental constitutive actions of (video) gaming, turning an experimental novel into a game. Moreover, given the cultural predominance of gaming and digital video, the majority of formal innovations in both *Pry* and *TOC* are far more likely to be referred to these strongly emergent aspects of cultural experience, than to experimental writing.

At the level of specific, technology-dependent formal innovation, this is the symptomatic condition of electronic literature. Until the technics of reading change, the writing of electronic literature will be 'read' as something else, as making gestures in other cultural milieux – not primarily in that of 'the literary' and not in its own terms. Moreover, as we have seen, even its proper field of criticism identifies contradictions for reading that are generated by practices – multimedia practices – which are nonetheless considered, by some, to be definitive of or essential to electronic writing. Finally, in the culture as a whole, beset by digitalisation, reading (of writing) faces what more pessimistic critics propose as existential challenge.

On such bases, should practitioners and theorists of experimental *writing* continue to consign *electronic* writing to some marginal literary nursery, doomed to expire in infancy? An expense of misdirected avant-garde spirit in the rampant shame of techno-narcissism? Deeply troubling complacency and dangerous inclinations towards technological denial would be realised by such an attitude. The trouble deepens when we propose that aspects of this symptomatic condition apply equally to literary practice as a whole, and when we consider that the entire analysis bears strong analogous relations with one derived from experimental writing, specifically. How much of the rhetoric of experimental writing has the effect of rendering it difficult or impossible to read, with respect to so-called mainstream practices of reading, for example? How many of the self-consciously *innovative* formal gestures of experimental writing will be adopted into a broader culture of writing and reading, or are even proposed for such adoption? Is not experimental writing subject to the same attention economy as is the case for all contemporary cultural production? Subjected to the same changes in our modalities of reading: deep, hyper and machine?

All of these problems are problems of reading. Language is a problem of reading. But so long as all of these practices, including experimental and digitally mediated practices, are focused on literature and 'the literary', the understanding of reading that we are addressing continues to be overdetermined by a general practice most summarily designated as the reading of *(typo)graphically instantiated text.* This is a profound misdirection of theory and potential art. Practitioners and critics of electronic writing are used to saying that the prehistory, technics and archive of print culture are presupposed by the reading of text. If we continue to *read text* in conventional ways, this simply reimposes the predominance of print. The contemporary ubiquity of newer technologies and potential linguistic technics, exceeding those of print, are supposed to make us challenge conventional reading. On the contrary, I argue, we all remain buried, deep in the gravity well of volumes, leaves and letters, and digital mediated textuality, ironically, may serve to bury us deeper.

Fundamentally, it is what computation refers to as tokenisation that binds electronic writing to the reading of *text*. All the novel and troubled situations of reading that we have discussed so far present themselves to us within a regime of computation that has bracketed the question of whether or not language is computable, by simply assuming that it is. Language-as-text continues to be 'read' in a cultural architecture that was developed by the post-Second World War regime of computation, now globally networked. Manifestly and predominantly, 'language' is studied, exchanged and traded in a context and framework for which Chomskian 'generative' linguistics holds sway, a structural linguistics that is explicitly predicated on the computational model of language (and mind) and for which creativity reduces to a kind of cosmically large-but-finite combinatorial constructivism assembled from unclosed but synchronically finite lists of tokens. The culturally active power and 'creativity' of explicitly formal programming languages, inscribed as tokens that are materially indistinguishable from their linguistic counterparts, reinforces the plausibility of what is simply force majeure and expediency, having nothing substantive to say about whatever it is that language is.

Writing that was inscribed in literature did not race ahead of itself, presumptuously, in this way. The culture of reading developed slowly throughout the entirety of our history, that is the history of writing, in no little part because writing brought history into being. Historically, writing was assumed to be the supplement of something that we, as language animals, 'had', but which was more truly of itself: writing was (also, a) language.[28] Derrida's unravelling of presence and fullness, and his infinite re/deferral of language to a logic of the supplement that writing embodies, this does not, by that token, refer us to the material forms of 'written' textuality. Derrida's philosophy of language is the differance that, precisely, allows us to understand and to read what is, ostensibly, literature as aesthetic *language*, as something that has differentiated itself as such. In its systematic stupidity, the regime of computation takes a directly contrary course. It assumes that language is whatever is computable in terms of arbitrary sets of tokens human beings happen to have captured as data.

So, all literary practices and studies – and I am, of course, including experimental writing in this purview – all literary practices that subordinate themselves to computation – let's say not only to how things stand as they have been digitalised today, but also to the hyper reading, the machine reading and to the multimedia incursions into the medium of language that we have cited above – risk a foreclosure of reading, a reduction of reading to the reading of text, however mediated. The risk for electronic literature is even greater because its investment in digitalisation and digital affordances is an assured necessity. The criticism of electronic literature may mature in this context, but it no longer contends with a speculative future. It falls instead into the same patterns as its conventionally mediated ancestral community.[29] Electronic *literature*, electronic *writing*, says it all. Said it all from the outset.

Either writing is fully (a) language, or writing is merely the means of, and evidence for, its own grammatisation.[30]

This is why today, language art, experimental language art if you will, requires the better, unashamedly poststructuralist understanding of reading that was proposed earlier, during our reading of Johanna Drucker's experimental writing. We need an understanding of reading that is not overdetermined by formal tokenisation, grammatisation and computational models of creativity in an arbitrary and abstracted support materiality. We need it in order to continue, as language animals, to engage with the substantive, social medium that grammaleptic reading brings into being. We need to recognise that this substantive medium can only be read as embodied and that although this implies nothing in terms of specific support materiality, it does allow us to characterise and name the substance of language as, for the only evolved language animals that we know, voice (in our special although established usage), as opposed, for example, to text or letters.

The inadequacies of literature and currently existing electronic literature would provoke this polemic all on their own, but the existential threat to language that I read in Drucker's writing sharpens the urgency, while developments in digital language art also point to crisis.

In language art, is recombination creative? Is it creative when or because it is able to generate quantities of virtual language far, far beyond the capacities of human attention to read? The work of Nick Montfort and others, including myself, who produce language art in the media and technicity of computation itself, requires us to address such questions seriously without their objects necessarily ever exceeding or even reaching a language-philosophical position that is commensurate with poststructural differance (as above) or what I can conceive as the actual ontology of language.[31] Nonetheless, there is aesthetics here and room for manoeuvre, facture and poiesis, all of which cannot be ignored and which hold greater interest, arguably, for example, and for certain readers, than a hypertextuality which is, in principle, expressible in print.

If, however, there has been a 'standing up of the machines on their hind legs' and if 'the time of tongues is past' then, when we look to a computationally informed language art that responds to this putative crisis, we will find it in two areas of practice. One area is represented in some of my own recent work, work with transactive synthetic language that is intimately involved with much of the thinking set out here.[32] In it, I justify the necessity to turn from literature to aurature precisely because developments in contemporary computation and the digitalisation of culture bring the human body into question, and in a manner that is historically unprecedented. For the first time, quasi-(or, perhaps, hyper-)socialised artefactual entities can speak and listen, as humanoid embodiments in what appears to be the substance of voice, which we are, perhaps, now called upon to distinguish from our own. Language art may help us to do this. Literature, be it experimental or electronic, is either not up to this critical task or it is in the process of being rendered indistinguishable from the combinatorial play of formally, distantly scanned tokens of orthography, swamped by 'the very takeover of sound-noise rhythms of the material world'.

The other crucial area of experimental language art practice, weirdly all but absent from an important recent handbook of electronic literature, is one that is engaged with the contemporary resurgence of artificial intelligence (AI) in the form of software 'neural networks' that are presumed capable of 'machine learning'. There are significant relations between the listening and speaking entities that may introduce us to aurature, and what Drucker would see as a distinct phantasm of AI. Although these entities of aurature still exchange their (and our) tokens with us using 'weak', largely probabilistic and database-empowered AI, their embodiments as voice, for example, may be constructed from the patterned output of black-boxed machine-learning algorithms, patterns of humanoid timbre (in this case) that will underwrite the forward social progress of Drucker's recently bipedal machines.

Machine learning AI is, of course, being applied to real-world language practice, most notably in online translation services. There are compelling reasons to consider the rejection of machine 'learning' as a profound and unethical misdirection, even within the theoretical framework of our ascendant regime of computation,[33] but in concert with the more general popularisation of natural language processing (NLP) including in the service of commerce, we can be sure that linguistic machine learning will be generating vast quantities of virtual 'language' for the foreseeable future. Where is the response from a critical practice of language art?

In one of the most thorough and beautiful, David Jhave Johnston has used recursive neural networks trained on selected poetic corpora to generate astonishing quantities of 'poetry'. For the project *ReRites*, he has undertaken this for a full year, taking the output from his algorithms and editing them, daily, at a frenetic pace.[34] He has collected his edited texts – 'written by a computer, then edited by a human' – into monthly collections, from May 2017 through April 2018. All the *ReRites* were published as a boxed set in 2019. The project is technically sophisticated, art-conceptually sound and poetically engaged. It is also a small press book art publication, feeding back into the experimental literary tradition with respect to its material cultural forms as well as in terms of Jhave's personal involvement as artist, poet, editor, writer.

There is no doubt that our appreciation of this experiment hinges on the involvement of its human instigator. By contrast with electronic literary work – such as most of what has been produced by Nick Montfort – that is generated by algorithms which render the work as either exhaustively known (deterministic, reducible to its program and data) or inflected, straightforwardly, by chance, Jhave's *ReRites* begin with texts that are abstract patterns output by algorithms that have not been directed by literary preconceptions inscribed *in the program itself*, but only by patterns and rhythms pre-existing in the corpora. The 'black-boxing' of specific output-generating decisions within the 'neural network' means that any *voice* (in the usage established earlier) that becomes perceptible (and, perhaps, readable) in the output is less clearly related to the human author's selection of corpora. Can it, by this token, be characterised as something that literary criticism would describe as more 'original'? By the time that Jhave has intervened and edited (composed?) the output, this reader (for one) hears-and-understands an individual poetic voice in the text, one that even seems to be able to sustain extended, rhythmically coherent passages from the focus of a lyric 'I':

> now, i am walking
> thru the grass
> and ordinary bushes,
> thru the factory plaza,
> the dead plaza
> [. . .]
> this
> kind of thinking
> is a brave consolation

where 'the dead plaza' may be quoted from Antonio Machado (for all I know, from his, 'A Labyrinth of Narrow Streets', so Google suggests), and with moments of self-conscious reflection, including the undoubted insight,

> this is your voice, only it's not

which – consonant with a good deal of serious innovative poetry and along with much else in the particular collection of *ReRites* (March 2018) that has so far attracted my attention – poetically engages with critical issues surrounding its own . . . creation? assemblage? *ReRites* are a good read, an excellent trial of language. Makers of aesthetic language would do well to attend to the output of this experiment, its books and everything that underlies the uncanny familiarities of their forms. But – and how should we read this? – if *ReRites* require us to sacrifice our faith in the sound-noise rhythms of our personal poetic worlds, then the time of tongues is past.

Notes

1. Drucker, *General Theory of Social Relativity*, p. 80.
2. Ibid. pp. 80–3.
3. Derrida's emphasis. Jacques Derrida, *Voice and Phenomenon: Introduction to the Problem of the Sign in Husserl's Phenomenology*, trans. Leonard Lawlor, Northwestern University Studies in Phenomenology and Existential Philosophy (Evanston, IL: Northwestern University Press, 2011), p. 65. Voice and this passage are also usefully discussed – but with reference to the earlier translation of Derrida's essay as *Speech and Phenomena* – in Ulmer, *Applied Grammatology*, pp. 51–7.

4. Derrida, *Voice and Phenomenon*, p. 52.
5. I want to be absolutely clear that nothing in this discussion should be read as a resuscitation of the logocentricism that Derrida strongly critiques, with justice and openess in mind. Voice is the medium of language as shared practice and, as used in this essay, is a self-erasing, paradoxical 'element' that helps to undermine (or deconstruct if you prefer) logocentric speech as authorised by a metaphysics of presence.
6. Derrida, *Voice and Phenomenon*, pp. 85–7.
7. Drucker, *General Theory of Social Relativity*, p. 86.
8. In a post-Derridean pharmacological context, Bernard Stiegler contrasts poisionous 'adaptation' with potentially therapeutic 'adoption'. Amongst many such discussions in Stiegler's work see, for example, Bernard Stiegler, *For a New Critique of Political Economy [Pour une nouvelle critique de l'économie politique]*, trans. Daniel Ross (Cambridge: Polity, 2010), pp. 82, 103.
9. Drucker, *The General Theory of Social Relativity*, p. 84.
10. Ibid. p. 85.
11. Cayley, 'The Advent of Aurature and the End of (Electronic) Literature'.
12. Cayley, '*The Listeners*: An Instance of Aurature'. See also the vocal performances of digital language art by Ian Hatcher on his website <https://ianhatcher.net> (last accessed 18 June 2018).
13. Jay David Bolter, *Writing Space: The Computer, Hypertext, and the History of Writing* (Hillsdale, NJ: Erlbaum, 1991); George P. Landow, *Hypertext: The Convergence of Contemporary Critical Theory and Technology* (Baltimore and London: Johns Hopkins University Press, 1992); Espen Aarseth, *Cybertext: Perspectives on Ergodic Literature* (Baltimore and London: Johns Hopkins University Press, 1997); Philippe Bootz, 'Le Point de Vue Fonctionnel: Point de Vue Tragique et Programme Pilote', *alire 10/DOC(K)S* Series 3, no. 13/14/15/16 (1997).
14. Joseph Tabbi (ed.), *The Bloomsbury Handbook of Electronic Literature* (New York and London: Bloomsbury Academic, 2017).
15. Funkhouser, 'Le(s) Mange Texte(s): Creative Cannibalism and Digital Poetry'.
16. Simanowski, 'Digital Anthropophagy'.
17. Simanowski, 'Death of the Author? Death of the Reader!'
18. Citton, *The Ecology of Attention*.
19. Carr, 'Is Google Making Us Stupid?'; Carr, *The Shallows*. The *Atlantic* article by Carr has its own Wikipedia page: <https://en.wikipedia.org/wiki/Is_Google_Making_Us_Stupid%3F> (last accessed 23 November 2017).
20. Stiegler, *States of Shock*.
21. Stiegler, *For a New Critique of Political Economy*, p. 82 and passim; *What Makes Life Worth Living: On Pharmacology*.
22. Hayles, 'Hyper and Deep Attention'.
23. 'How We Read,' in Hayles, *How We Think*.

24. Moulthrop and Grigar, *Traversals*, p. 170.
25. Portela, *Scripting Reading Motions*.
26. Tomasula et al., *TOC,* FC2. Although, tellingly, the app, for iOS, was no longer available when I last checked, 8 July 2018.
27. Gorman and Cannizzaro, *Pry.*
28. To counter the misdirected conception of writing as a 'secondary' supplement (and helping to refer it, instead, to language as the logic of the supplement) we may chose to address practices of writing as, simply, distinct languages. Walter Ong and others have suggested that practices of writing should be considered, in sum, as grapholects, but I mean something stronger that the suggestion that written English, for example, is a dialect of English. I say that written English is a distinct natural language, facing the same necessity to create and respond to differance as English itself. This is what the translingual pun of 'differance' shows us. Computation's reduction of the elements of written English to subordinate tokens of a putative English tends to destroy (as well as subordinate) its generative potential.
29. One way of approaching this essay on reading digital language art would have been to discuss important essays in a 'handbook' of the field that had just been published at the time of writing: Joseph Tabbi (ed.), *The Bloomsbury Handbook of Electronic Literature*. I eschewed this possibility for something more polemical and, perhaps, experimental. But what I propose as a relative maturation of the field is reflected in many essays from this collection and in the fierce openess that it maintains, welcoming, for example, in Shelley Jackson's piece, the hand of a writer whose *Patchwork Girl* is considered a classic of long-form literary hypertext, but who now prefers to discover the interruption of actual labouring hands in images from the service of digitalised literature; or Florian Cramer's searing call for a post-digital writing, one that would advise the abandonment of a major part of electronic literature's ostensible project. Among many other engaging contributions, Aden Evens provides one of the finest apologias for combinatorial poetics; Steve Tomasula discovers post-literary potentialities in the tools and technologies that are reconfiguring culture; and Brian Kim Stefans offers the kind of socio-politically engaged, philosophically and poetically astute critique of certain electronic literary gestures that we have come to expect from him and to value.
30. See note 28.
31. For an introduction to Nick Montfort's work see his many publications but, in particular, his collection: Nick Montfort, *#! [Shebang]* (Denver: Counterpath, 2014). And my own review of the same, John Cayley, 'Poetry and Stuff,' *Electronic Book Review* (2015). Montfort is now also editing 'Using Electricity', a series of printed books published by Denver's Counterpath Press, and deriving from computationally generated texts.

32. *The Listeners*, 2015; '*The Listeners*: An Instance of Aurature'; 'Aurature at the End(s) of Electronic Literature', *Electronic Book Review* (2017).
33. The most significant theoretical and ethical critique of machine learning that I have encountered derives from the work of Chomsky's longstanding colleague Charles R. Galistell, who is known for Galistell's Problem: 'bioenergetic calculations show' that for human brains to achieve 'the required data processing power' for the type of computational processes that could handle 'hierarchical structure processing in language' (i.e. some version of an operational Chomskian computational grammar) 'as a kind of recurrent neural network', such speculative human brains would need to boil their own blood. Berwick and Chomsky, *Why Only Us: Language and Evolution*, pp. 50–1. I read this as suggesting that such models may be, shall we say, harmful as well as misdirected (although this can also be shown more economically and with greater care by way of arguments from the discourses of the humanities, as I hope this essay bears out). For Galistell (whom I heard lecture at a 2017 symposium on machine learning at Brown University), machine 'learning' is not learning. Living intelligence learns a great deal from very little (in the way of data). That's the way of learning. That is what learning is. What bees do when they find a source of nectar, for example. Machine 'learning' derives very little (in terms of statable pattern or abstraction) from vast amounts of data at the expense of vast amounts of energy-burning, heat-inducing computation. Given 'growth'-led neoliberal investment in machine learning as the solution to everything, historically achievable computational processing proposes to significantly if not catastrophically amplify the effects of global warming.
34. David (Jhave) Johnston, *ReRites* (Montreal: Anteism, 2017–19). At the International Fiction Now literary festival, Brown University, Providence, RI, 17–19 April 2018, Jhave showed and performed with videos that demonstrated his editing process. Examples are at <https://vimeo.com/album/5062019> (last accessed 9 July 2018).

Chapter 9

Charles Bernstein's Walter Benjamin, Among Other Things
Peter Jaeger

The Lost Manuscript of WB, or, New Angels/ Transient Failures

Then comes a sudden jab of red-hot memory and all this common sense vanishes like an ant in the mouth of a furnace. Don't come talking to me about the consolations of religion or I shall suspect that you don't understand.

Exposé

'Literary or political theory that ignores the relevance of its material base as writing composition, unquestionably replicating received stylistic models [. . .] engages in a denial of theory by theory.'[1]

A Context

Walter Benjamin's *The Arcades Project* (1999) suggests that 'philosophico-historical constellations could be represented by a dialectical image rather than by dialectical argumentation'[2] – i.e., by employing montage and juxtaposition rather than by returning to the more traditional logic of a sustained, historiographical argument. Yet despite widespread academic acclaim for *The Arcades Project*, relatively few academics have taken up this text's methodology as a formal approach to critical writing, and the radical implications for the production of meaning that are inherent in [Benjamin's] montage technique have not been developed as a formal method of critique within the academy.

Methodology

'But what is the value of breaking away from habitual psychological or literary tracks, from automatic or predetermined patterns? For one thing such patterns can make us blind to what is going on with our feelings/consciousness and with the world, with others. But more than this the desire is to reveal the specificity, the tone and texture as much as content "summary" (of experience).'[3]

The Lost Manuscript of WB, or, The Wrinkled Wings of Gabriel

I keep thinking that it's a lie but it's not and I know it's not but I don't want it to be true. I've plenty of what are called 'resources'. We get over these things.

Methodology

'Page after page of Benjamin's astonishing text contains movable passages that can (and do) reappear in altered contexts; the repeated juxtapositions, cuts, links, shifts in register, framing devices, and visual markings conspire to produce a poetic text that is paradigmatic for our own poetics.'[4]

Historicising L=A=N=G=U=A=G=E, in the Style of Walter Benjamin

The observer is not standing at the head of the stream. That is her opportunity. She is in the valley. She can gauge the energies of a movement. As an observer she is long acquainted with the crisis of the intelligentsia, or, more precisely, with that of the humanistic concept of poetics; she has no excuse for taking this field for the 'artistic' one it superficially appears. If it was such at the outset, it was, however, precisely at the outset that Charles Bernstein declared his intention of breaking with an official verse culture that presents the public with the literary precipitate of a certain form of existence while withholding that existence itself. Stated more briefly and dialectically, this means that the sphere of poetics was here explored from within, by Bernstein (and a closely knit circle of people pushing poetics to the utmost limits of possibility). There is no doubt that the heroic phase of this exploration, whose catalogue of heroes began this effort, is over. There is always, in such movements, a moment when the original tension of the secret society must either explode in a matter-of-fact, profane struggle for power and domination, or decay as a public demonstration and be transformed. We remain in this phase of transformation at present. But at the time when it broke over its founders as an inspiring wave, it seemed the most integral, conclusive, absolute of movements. Everything with which it came into contact was integrated. Life only seemed worth living where the threshold between poetry and poetics was worn away in everyone as by the steps of multitudinous flooding back and forth. Essays employed such tactics as modularity, disjunction, radical juxtaposition, intertextuality and appropriation. This poetics only seemed itself where language interpenetrated with the social, with such felicity that no chink was left for the penny-in-the-slot called 'meanings'. And not only meaning was at stake – also, the self. In the world's structure language loosens individuality like a bad tooth. This loosening of the self by language is, at the same time, precisely the fruitful, living experience that allowed these people to step outside the domain of semantics. This is not the place to give an exact definition of their experience. But anyone who has perceived that the writings of this circle are not only literature but something else – demonstrations, watchwords, bluffs, forgeries if you will – will also know, for the same reason, that these writings are concerned literally with experiences, not with theories and still less with academic credentials. Charles Bernstein, retiring to bed about daybreak, fixes a notice on his door: 'I'm talking here not so much about a motivating theory but a desire: To make language opaque so that writing becomes more and more conscious of itself as world generating, object generating.'[5]

Knowledge

To
recast
the

words
of
Walter

Benjamin,
this
form

of
critical
practice

is
not
aimed

at
producing
a

knowledge
of
poetry, but

at
producing
a

knowledge
that
grows

out
of
poetry.

The Lost Manuscript of WB, or,
The Doctrine of Similarity

Now is the time to lean on the people who care about you, even if you take pride in being strong and self-sufficient.

Correspondence

From: Bernstein, Charles
Sent: 07 December 2016 15:09
To: Peter Jaeger
Subject: Re: Shadowtime/Benjamin question?

Dear Peter,
   I know the first book I had of Benjamin's was *Illuminations*, which I probably read in college. I quote from 'On the Language of Such and the Language of Man' in 'Thought's Measure' in *L=* vol. 4 (1982) and included in *Content's Dream* and also in that book I quote from Benjamin's 'Doctrine of the Similar' in 'Living Tissue/Dead Ideas' – those two Benjamin essays were very important to me and become central also to *Shadowtime*. I read the 'Doctrine of the Similar' (similar title used in Shadowtime) in New German Critique the first tr. in 1979. Ron Silliman wrote about Benjamin in #6 of *L=*, so 1978. I quote WB a few other times as well in *Content's Dream*, according to Google books search (the book has no index).
Yours, truly,
Charles

For Benjamin, For Bernstein: Some Early Sentences

For Benjamin, it is fundamental that mental being communicates itself in language and not through language. For Bernstein, language is not something that is separable from the world, but rather it is the means by which the world is constituted, so thinking cannot be said to 'accompany' the experiencing of the world in that it informs the experiencing. For Benjamin, languages have no speaker, if that means someone who communicates through these languages. For Benjamin, every expression of life is a kind of language and language is a way of communicating 'mental life' or 'meanings' and every natural thing partakes of language, because it communicates mental meanings of a sort. For Bernstein, that wall could be said. For Benjamin, we are here concerned with nameless, non-acoustic languages, languages issuing from matter; here we should recall the material community of things in their communication. For Bernstein, buzz, tick, click,/spit,/ashcan. For Bernstein, Benjamin's view of the primacy of the sensuous, onomatopoetic in language, over its semiotic, non-sensuous character in speech and writing is a rejection of the theory that language has an arbitrary relation to its objects. For Bernstein, don't be so sure (don't be Saussure). For Benjamin, language is in every case not only communication of the communicable but also, at the same time, a symbol of the non-communicable. For Bernstein, it's the DENsE stUFfagain that shIt I cANt UNDErstAnd when you gO oN that way. For Benjamin, language never gives *mere* signs. For Bernstein, no ideas but as sound.

The Lost Manuscript of WB, or, Opus Contra Naturam (Descent of Benjamin into the Underworld)

I know there's a reason but that reason's unknown.

* or = ?

During the 1970s and early 1980s Bernstein worked as a medical and healthcare editor and writer, producing medical abstracts for various medical journals. He and his wife, the artist Susan Bee, also designed the *Health Manpower Consortia Newsletter* in the same format that would be later used for L=A=N=G=U=A=G=E magazine. And as Loss Glazier points out, 'Bernstein has adapted medical vocabulary for poetic purposes.'[6] It may be instructive to compare Bernstein's use of diction drawn from the medical profession with the use of similar diction in the American television programme *M*A*S*H*, which ran from 1972–83 (to historicise: *M*A*S*H* and L=A=N=G=U=A=G=E were contemporaries, sharing the experience of living in history together). The operating theatre of *M*A*S*H* presents us with specialised medical jargon, interspersed with banter among the doctors and nurses. Dale Sherman writes that the programme's producers wanted to make sure the medical procedures presented in the show would make 'sense to those who would know better' – i.e., to medical specialists.

M*A*S*H's writers also consulted a medical doctor to see that 'things were said and done in the correct manner' (2016). A professional nurse was also on set during filming, in order to advise the actors on the accurate handling of medical instruments. This stress on verisimilitude, medical jargon and knowledgeable speech presents viewers with an alternate language, a speech register that is largely indecipherable to the non-specialist because of its esoteric codes, its hermetic diction and its seemingly abstruse speech acts. The effect is to mystify the medical establishment while elevating it to the status of a secret society.

In the Operating Theatre

- 'I don't want a Kelly clamp, Lieutenant!'
- 'But that's what you asked for.'
- 'Give me what I want, not what I asked for! Hey, Ginger, put a clamp on his mouth. You can show us all your diploma later, Frank.'
- 'That's enough, Captain.'
- 'Oh, clever. I can see well enough. Now give me a sponge.'
- 'I can't see a thing in here.'
- 'Let me have a clamp.'
- 'Which retractor?'
- 'The biggest one you got.'
- 'Get your seams straight. Give me a clamp' (M*A*S*H)[7]

The Aura of Medical Language?

In M*A*S*H the use of medical language seems to shine from above, with a near Benjaminian sense of aura – in Benjamin's words, the aura is 'the unique appearance or semblance of distance, no matter how close it may be'.[8] Aura in this sense is not limited to the value we give to a single, unique artwork, as opposed to its multiple photographic reproductions. Benjamin defines the aura as an instance of 'uniqueness and permanence' as opposed to 'transience and reproducibility'.[9] M*A*S*H takes great pains to present us with a rarefied, professionally distanced and specialised field of discourse. Regardless of the Korean War's horrific setting, the show's characters rehearse the durable and unique language of their profession.

Amazon Reads M*A*S*H, or, Is There Is No Document of Civilization Which Is Not at the Same Time a Document of Barbarism?

Sadly I got into MASH when it was the last episode and man what an ending. Even though I did not see the show from beginning to end, the ending left an impact on me and I started to watch it in syndication and glad I did, the show was awesome. There [sic] two episodes that was a tear jerker, the one where the original Company Commander was transferred back to the states and he perished on the way there. Some may have not paid attention to it when the show began you always saw the helicopter coming but never leaving and in the final episode you saw the helicopter leaving It brought tears to my eyes that a show that was about a company doing it's job during the Korean War and batting out the laughter. I am glad to have the collection and watch it at my leisure.

The Lost Manuscript of WB, or, Pools of Darkness

I dread the moments when the house is empty. If only things would talk to one another and not to me.

Amazon Reads Republics of Reality, or, Is There Is No Document of Civilization Which Is Not at the Same Time a Document of Barbarism?

1. We must tell the truth from the rooftops to save other younger poets from this foolery with l-a-n-g-u-a-g-e [sic]. (2 people found this helpful).
2. look how angry te [sic] fool above me got that's why you should read chuck-also he's funny 'nuff said (5 people found this helpful).

Contudes the Sinews:

'Mind is a tangled web that seems
only in aggregate to cohere, each
occasion gnaws at door of
semblance or contudes the
sinews of flotation's equipoise'[10]

Forefright

In contrast to *M*A*S*H*, the opening lines of Bernstein's contemporaneous poem 'Forefright' (1983) employ medical diction in a far more unconventional manner: 'each occasion gnaws at door of/semblance or contudes the/sinews of flotation's equipoise'. Unlike the hierarchical distance and uniqueness of medical language found in *M*A*S*H*, there is no pretence to professional accuracy in Bernstein's poem. The poem's use of medical language is democratised, made egalitarian to the non-medical diction (door, flotation, equipoise); one could even say the discourse of medicine becomes *infected* with the non-medical.

The Infection of the Other Variables

'So fixed on seeing an overt mimesis as the only possible mechanism for the relation of the semantic to the sonic, we fail to hear the infection of the other variables – associational, iconic extension of mouth shapes, psychogenic, . . . – for which we have no clearly defined concepts'[11]

The Infection of the Other Variables

'"Daddy, what did you
do to stop the war?"

[p-
=Jovwhiu2g97hgbc67q6dvqjx67sf21g97b.c.9327b97b987b87j 7
7td7tq98gdukbhq g9tq9798 icxqyj2f108ytscxags62jc .<Mz[

-\ io

We may be all one body but we're sure as hell not one mind.
[. . .]
                    It's

                                    not an operating system it

        '

                    s an

op

            erating environm

                        ent.

            Besides.'¹²

Document

'"[. . .] There is no document of civilization
that is not at the same time a
document of barbarism." Blue suede pestilence.
Binds bins. History and civilization
represented as aura [. . .]'.¹³

Document

'There is no document of civilization which is not at the same time a document of barbarism. And just as such a document is not free of barbarism, barbarism taints also the manner in which it was transmitted from one owner to another.'¹⁴

History and Civilisation

In 'The Klupzy Girl' (1983), Bernstein collages a fragment from Benjamin's 'Thesis on History' into a heterogeneous poem that also includes fragments of letters, conversations and language-objects drawn from other sources. This juxtaposition of disparate components anticipates the 1999 English translation of Benjamin's *The Arcades Project*, inasmuch as Bernstein's poem might be read as a constellation of various cultural fragments – a representation of 'history and civilization' that proceeds by conjoining dissimilar language objects rather than though a more conventional mimetic representation or dialectical argument. The poem's non-hierarchical levelling of these language objects provides us with what Benjamin might label as 'a sense of the universal equality of things'.[15] To historicise further, a 1978 discussion of Benjamin in $L=A=N=G=U=A=G=E$ by Ron Silliman argues that the destruction of aura is accomplished 'by the removal of the object from its constituting context' (n.p.). This destruction through removal from context is precisely what Bernstein's poem performs: the line 'document of civilization' is decontextualised and materialised through numerous other speech registers, including its juxtaposition with 'Blue suede pestilence'. Bernstein objectifies language, thereby calling into question the traditional, hierarchical representation of history and civilisation 'represented as aura'.

Newspapers

Robert Fitterman has discussed various modes of textual appropriation, and clarified the key difference between collage forms and the approach taken by Kenneth Goldsmith and other conceptual writers. Where the collagist brings 'appropriated materials together [. . .] to a singular expression',[16] writes Fitterman, the plagiarist presents source material in large, unmodified chunks, such as in Goldsmith's appropriation of a single issue of the *New York Times* in *Day* (2003). 'The Klupzy Girl', on the other hand, does not adhere to the conceptual plagiarist's use of unmodified textual material. The poem's repurposing of Benjamin entails recycling it in an altered form – excerpted, with line breaks added, and sutured into langauge drawn from other sources. For both Bernstein and Goldsmith, cultural production consists of the selection and reframing of source material, albeit in very different manners.

Newspapers

'The front page of the New York Times is in a sense, a collage or simultaneity with a clearly structured hierarchic meaning to its placements and orderings over the page and in each article.'[17]

Newspapers

'Contrasts which, in happier epochs, used to fertilize one another have become insoluble antinomies. Thus, science and *belles lettres*, criticism and original production, culture and politics now stand apart from one another without connection or order of any kind. The newspaper is the arena of this literary confusion. Its content eludes any form of organisation other than that which is imposed upon it by the reader's impatience.'[18]

The Agitated Veil

'The masses were an agitated veil.'[19]

Spellbound

'The reference to the veil in relation to the masses forms a link to Benjamin's account of beauty and its essential relation to the agitation of life. To speak of the veil in relation to the masses would then be a way of characterizing an experience of being spellbound, entranced by this appearance of life, which at the same time hides the (mythical) violence inherent in the existence of the masses.'[20]

Spellbound

'Poetry is like a swoon with this difference:
it brings you to your senses'[21]

The Beautiful Veil

'The task of criticism is not to lift the veil but rather, through the most precise knowledge of it as a veil, to raise itself for the first time to the true view of the beautiful.'[22]

Veil

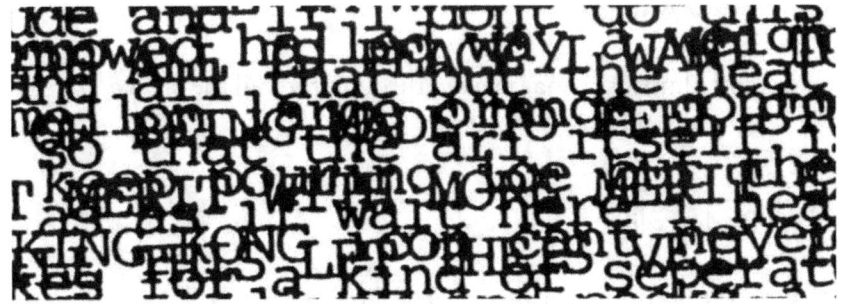

Figure 9.1 *Veil* (detail). Bernstein 1987: n.p.

Reading *Veil*

'Almost all of *Veil* can be deciphered, if only bit by bit, so that Bernstein's palimpsests do not so much prevent reading as redirect and discipline usual reading habits.'[23]

Amazon Reads *Veil*

There are no customer reviews yet. Be the first to review this item.

Literature

'Literature is the best word we now have for a writing that critiques itself not only at the level of represented ideas but prosodically, acoustically, syntactically, visibly; which is to say gives these dimensions equal methodological weight as it give to the more traditional notions of semantic content.'[24]

Literature

'"There is an hour to come, said he, "when all of us shall cast aside our veils. Take it not amiss, beloved friend, if I wear this piece of crepe till then."'[25]

Body Animated

'One could almost say that viewed through the veil the crowd appears as a body animated by its own life.'[26]

Body Politic

'As Charles Bernstein writes in "The Lives of the Toll Takers", "We may be all one body but we're sure as hell not one mind." Here, "body" refers as much to a text as it does to a body politic or even to the singular, discrete corporeality each of us administrates. Any of us is singular, all of us are plural, and we are that way because language itself is so.'[27]

The Lost Manuscript of WB, or, Seven Tableau Vivants Representing the Angel of History as Melanchoia

Sometimes I wish you were here to tell me what to do. You always knew what to say. Sorrow, however, turns out to be not a state but a process. You are never far from my heart. Unlike some, I don't blame myself. But these feelings are only getting worse. I thought with time they would go away. At other times it feels like being mildly drunk, or concussed. There is a sort of invisible blanket between the world and me.

Methodology

'Let me introduce Walter Benjamin here, as a good example of multi-polar, rather than linear thinking. Benjamin's form of reflective writing suggests a poetics of multiple layers or figures. A line of thought may seem to go off into one direction then drops back to follow another trajectory, only this new direction is not a *non sequitur* but rather echoes or refracts both the antecedent motifs and – this is the uncanny part – the eventual ones. I mean this is a way of rethinking what is often called fragmentation or disjunction. Think of fragments not as discontinuous but as overlays, pleats, folds: a chordal poetics in which stylistic notes meld into diachronic tones. You find this in *The Arcades Project* as well as in Benjamin's early essays: an openness to the multiplicity of connection that exhibits not discontinuity but a verbal and paraverbal echoing between interrelated motifs that on a rational level, do not, at first, seem related. Yet, as you go into details, as you begin to listen to the essay as you would a piece of music, you begin to register how intricately everything is connected.'[28]

Self-Reflexive Moment in the Style of Marcel Proust

If my reading of Charles Bernstein has permanently absorbed the image that I had formed of Walter Benjamin, it was only by transforming that image, by subordinating its reappearance in me to its own special laws, and in consequence of this my reading made Benjamin's images more beautiful, but at the same time more different from anything that they could in reality be. Perhaps, indeed, the enforced simplicity of my reading of Bernstein was one of the reasons for the hold that Benjamin's books have had over me, for even from the simplest, the most realistic point of view, the objects which we long to occupy, at any given moment, offer us a far larger place in our true life than the place in which we may happen to be. And so what moved me most was the thought that reading Benjamin and Bernstein together might offer me a means to fabricate another, altogether different book. With this difference in mind, I paused to consider the fine words of Enikö Bollobás, who once compared Bernstein's employment of such literary irregularities as defamiliarisation and estrangement to Marcel Proust's famous aphorism concerning how the language of all beautiful books sounds necessarily 'strange' (2013). Upon the sort of estrangement cited by Bollobás and practised by Bernstein, and, I might add, by Benjamin, which my consciousness would quietly unfold while I was reading these authors, and which ranged from the most deeply hidden aspirations of my heart to the wholly external horizon spread out before my eyes along the shelves of my library, what was from the first the most permanent and the most intimate part of me, the lever whose incessant movement controlled all the rest, was my belief in the philosophic richness and beauty of the book I was reading, and my desire to appropriate these to myself, whatever the book might be.

Shadowtime Opera in 7 Scenes

Ferneyhough (composer), Bernstein (libretto)
Format: Audio CD

4.0 *out of 5 stars*
1 customer review

Price: £44.27 & **FREE Delivery** in the UK. Delivery Details
See all 5 formats and editions
Only 1 left in stock (more on the way).

On the Setting

'Brian [Ferneyhough] has sometimes overlaid the text: different parts of the libretto are sung simultaneously. So the verbal matter becomes part of the acoustic layering of the sound composition [. . .] "Extreme polyphony" would be a better category to explain what Brian does, combining several layers at the same time.'[29]

A Series of Veilings and Unveilings

'Through a series of veilings and unveilings (as in the truth shall make you veiled or the veil of unknowing [*veil smear*]), *Shadowtime* avails, volleys in volé valleys, values, and calls into a vast repository of "involuntary memory".'[30]

Amazon Reads *Shadowtime*

Reading the libretto in advance could help.

Obvious Loss

'The most obvious loss with which the opera confronts the listener is the meaning of the words it contains. The score's mannered cacophony plays havoc with the poet Charles Bernstein's libretto, which uses Benjamin's fate as the starting point for a rich engagement with his ideas about language, time, spirituality.'[31]

13 Protocols for *Shadowtime* in the Style of Walter Benjamin on Hashish

1. An angel hovers (vignette style) over my right shoulder. Coldness in that shoulder. In connection with this: 'My wing is posed to beat/ but I would gladly return home/where I to stay to the end of days/I would still be this forlorn'.[32] I have the feeling there are many others in the room besides me. (Bypassing the necessity of including myself in the count.)

2. Elucidation of the Karl Marx and Groucho Marx anecdote with the explanation or rather suggestion: show someone the mask (the mask of one's own face, that is, Benjamin's face).

3. Convoluted utterance with a headless ghoul, who (it goes without saying) would also have no mouth, nose, and so on: 'are you waking from a dream or are you waking into a dream? Are you remembering your dreams of dreaming that you have memories?'.[33]

4. Three coordinates of time: war time (1940)/reflective time (1940)/ redemptive time (?∞). Great horizontal extension of time. Suite of years, from which music is coming. But perhaps also dread of the outside: 'It is characteristic/Of philosophical writing/That it must/ Continually confront questions/Of representation'.[34]

5. Boundless goodwill. Falling away of neurotic-obsessive anxiety complexes. The sphere of 'character' opens up. All those present take on hues of the comic. At the same time, one steeps oneself in their aura: 'The heavens turn dark before the trees are shot full of light.'[35]

6. The comic is elicited not just from faces but from incidents. One seeks occasions for laughter. And perhaps it is only this reason that so much of what one sees presents itself as 'arranged', as 'experiment' – so that one can laugh about it: 'The text is based on prime numbers, as counted in lines for each stanza and words per line.'[36]

7. Poetic evidence in the phonetic: at one point I maintain that, in answering a question a little earlier, I had used the expression 'What time is *now*?/What time is *now*?/What time is *now*?/What time is *now*?/What time is *now*?/What time is *now*?/What time is *now*?/ *now*?/What time is *now*?/What time is *now*?/What time is *now*?/ What time is *now*?/What time is *now*?',[37] purely as a result (so to

speak) of my perception of time in the sounding of the words of the question and answer. I experience this as poetic evidence. [No reply by WB].

8. Connection; distinction. In smiling, one feels oneself growing small wings. Smiling and fluttering are related. You feel distinguished because, among other things, it seems to you that fundamentally you enter into nothing too deeply: that, no matter how deeply you penetrate, you are always moving on the threshold. A sort of toe dance of reason: 'Such joy at the mere act/of unrolling a ball of thread'.[38]

9. One is very much struck by how long some sentences have become. This, too, is connected with horizontal extension and (probably) with representation. Translation is here also a phenomenon of long horizontal extension, perhaps combined with vistas receding into distant, fleeting, tiny perspectives. The element of the diminutive would serve to link the idea of translation to length, as can be heard in *Shadowtime*'s structural/homophonic translation of Ernst Jandl's 'Der ind Die': 'can dew and die can and die can tie his sin tap and the war dew hoe and die has him and her and tar the pry and war mud and bog and tug eye and has him and her bug dew sin tap can and not lie and the eye wag and the can and the can not and can ire not and war beg ire and war not beg ire and has out ire him and her and die war tug for kin war for kin its was for kin its mob tic and ken hot and tug dew ken sob and sob hog beg for ire him and tug dew ken can do its tug art its was the its was the its for sun not lag and gag tug the eye wag sub and hug but pun end dew oar and tag irk hog and our wag not gut and nab and sub top tic run and not lie ken pop arm and gab his ken and the hour and the hog and sad and sit and sob tic ire tic his tic and the rot war lie and die rut and dew tag wag tic eye and mud and woe and not and dew ire and die his and sow hug irk hug and hit and lug tie out the its gut its for sun and lie and kin bob and dew rib and sob and die kin and bug his nab and sub top tic rum and sow was dew and dew lay our ire and sob and tar and rib and bob and sow and ire arm ad the hog sad and the our die rut zen see and the amp irk and tot and wet for rim its wag sit wag nor she out hi and her him and him her him her him her big rot and sob and woe die see sin tap rib and bob and ken orb nab and mud lag our sun'.[39] This diminutive series of words continues at great length; the translation employs a limited vocabulary to offer us an equally limited array of

linguistic possibilities. Some might think the excessive length of this passage, which is quoted above in full, presents us with an exercise in tedium. In the *Arcades Project* file entitled 'Boredom, Eternal Return', Benjamin writes that boredom is 'an index to participation in the sleep of the collective'.[40] For Benjamin the social body is asleep, bored, drugged by the utopian promise of commodities, lulled into slumber by endless repetitions of the same. The question then arises: what is Bernstein's translation of Jandl dreaming about Benjamin? This question allows us to map out a particular ambiguity of representation in *Shadowtime*, and Benjamin's proverbial angel of history, who is blown into the future while facing back towards the past, provides us with a useful metaphor for the libretto's representational strategies. On one hand, *Shadowtime* represents 'Walter Benjamin' as a subject of politics and history. Yet on the other hand, the libretto's use of homophonic translations, anagrams, anachronistic juxtapositions, *oulipian* constraints and other formally radical poetic devices problematises normative, 'transparent' methods of representing history. Do *Shadowtime*'s poetic reconfigurations then wake us up to a present free from the dream of mimetic historical and political representation? Benjamin: 'Every epoch not only dreams the next, but while dreaming impels it towards wakefulness.'[41]

10. There arises, quite fleetingly, in a moment of introversion, something like an inclination [words illegible]: 'Do images read minds?/ Semantic insufficiency'.[42]

11. Aversion to information: 'Then as when, now as some what or other./Corrupted data'.[43] Rudiments of a state of rapture: 'And the new angels pass away/like sparks on coals'.[44] Great sensitivity to open doors, loud talk, music.

12. Suddenly, in place of one's name, anagrams: 'I'm a lent barn Jew/A tent ran jewel/a barn Jew melt in/A rent Jew in balm/A Jew lamb intern/Brain mantle Jew/Brain mental Jew/A bawl intern jem/ Arab Jew melt inn/Blat ma inner Jew/Bam rat linen Jew/An altern IBM Jew/ran tab lib Jew me/Balm at inner Jew/Rat bam Lenin Jew/ Balm tear Jew inn/Atman Berlin Jew'.[45] (C.f. 'Little Orphan Anagram/Sitting in a Tree/Bruised by pride/abandoned to decree'[46]). The word 'bourgeoisie' is uttered and suddenly in place of a 'utopia that never comes'[47] there are commodities, in which I immediately recognise the utopia.

13. Feeling of understanding much better now. The gates to a world of shadow time seem to be opening. Only, I don't wish to enter: 'Herr Benjamin, Frau Gurland/it is my duty to inform you/Frau Gurland/Herr Benjamin/that your transit visas/Herr Benjamin, Frau Gurland/your transit visas/Frau Gurland/Herr Benjamin/are not valid/Herr Benjamin/Frau Gurland'.[48]

14. Reluctant (and slow) to follow the thoughts of others.

The Best Picture

'The best picture
of a picture
is not the picture
but its reverse
rehearsing tales
until they
unfold
in the tolling
even as I regret
more than I
resemble
in the tumble
of my apprehensive
incomprehending'[49]

In the Beginning, In the End

'In the end, a result of this conscious constructing is that of "making strange", the "alienation effect": To be able to see and feel the force and weight of formations of words, dynamics that otherwise go unnoticed; to feel it as stuff, to sound the language, and in so doing reveal its meanings.'[50]

The Lost Manuscript, or, Stelae for Failed Time

Thousands of scenarios play out in my head daily yet for all of them, there will only be one ending.

Notes

1. Bernstein, *Content's Dream*, p. 381.
2. Buck-Morss, *The Dialectics of Seeing*, p. 67.
3. Bernstein, *Content's Dream*, p. 72.
4. Perloff, *Unoriginal Genius*, p. 43.
5. Bernstein, *Content's Dream*, p. 71.
6. Glazier, 'Charles Bernstein'.
7. 'J301 – M*A*S*H – the Pilot'.
8. Benjamin, *Illuminations*, p. 216.
9. Ibid. p. 217.
10. Bernstein, 'Forefright', p. 267.
11. Bernstein, *Content's Dream*, p. 365.
12. Bernstein, *Dark City*, pp. 27–8.
13. Bernstein, 'Forefright', p. 50.
14. Benjamin, *Illuminations*, p. 248.
15. Ibid. p. 217.
16. Fitterman, *Rob the Plagiarist*, p. 15.
17. Bernstein, *Content's Dream*, p. 75.
18. Benjamin, *Understanding Brecht*, p. 89.
19. Benjamin, *Selected Writings 4: 1938–1940*, p. 233.
20. Friedlander, *Walter Benjamin*, p. 144.
21. Bernstein, 'Forefright', p. 47.
22. Benjamin, *Selected Writings 1: 1913–1926*, p. 351.
23. Dworkin, *Reading the Illegible*, p. 60.
24. Bernstein, *Content's Dream*, p. 371.
25. Hawthorne, qtd. as epigraph to Bernstein, *Veil*, n.p.
26. Friedlander, *Walter Benjamin*, p. 144.
27. Deming, 'Poetry Called Into Being', n.p.
28. Bernstein, 'Charles Bernstein Interview' with Eric Denut.
29. Ibid.
30. Karasick, 'In the Shadow of Desire', pp. 405–6.
31. Bertsch, 'Language in the Dark', p. 311.
32. Scholem qtd. in Bernstein, *Shadowtime*, p. 60.
33. Bernstein, *Shadowtime*, p. 83.
34. Benjamin qtd. in Bernstein, *Shadowtime*, p. 49.
35. Bernstein, Shadowtime, p. 74.
36. Ibid. p. 75.
37. Ibid. p. 95.
38. Ibid. p. 104.
39. Ibid. pp. 72–3.
40. Benjamin, *The Arcades Project*, p. 108.
41. Ibid. p. 176.
42. Ferneyhough qtd. in Bernstein, *Shadowtime*, p. 77.

43. Ibid.
44. Bernstein, *Shadowtime*, p. 119.
45. Ibid. p. 71.
46. Ibid. p. 43.
47. Ibid. p. 52.
48. Ibid. p. 31.
49. Ibid. pp. 121–2.
50. Bernstein, *Content's Dream*, p. 74.

Notes on Contributors

Charles Bernstein is Donald T. Regan Professor of English and Comparative Literature at the University of Pennsylvania. He has published five collections of essays: *Pitch of Poetry* (Chicago, 2016), *Attack of the Difficult Poems: Essays and Inventions* (Chicago, 2011), *My Way: Speeches and Poems* (Chicago, 1999), *A Poetics* (Harvard, 1992), and *Content's Dream: Essays 1975–1984*. His books of poetry include *Recalculating* (Chicago, 2013), *All the Whiskey in Heaven: Selected Poems* (Farrar, Straus and Giroux), *Girly Man* (Chicago, 2006), *With Strings* (Chicago, 2001), and *Republics of Reality: 1975–1995* (Sun & Moon, 2000). His libretto *Shadowtime*, for composer Brian Ferneyhough, was published in 2005 by Green Integer; it was performed as part of the 2005 Lincoln Center Festival. Bernstein is the editor of several collections, including: *American Poetry after 1975* (Duke University Press/special issue of *boundary*, 2009), *Close Listening: Poetry and the Performed Word* (Oxford, 1999), *The Politics of Poetic Form: Poetry and Public Policy* (Roof, 1990) and the poetics magazine *L=A=N=G=U=A=G=E*, whose first issue was published in 1978. He is editor of the Electronic Poetry Center and co-director (with Al Flireis) of PennSound.

John Cayley is Professor of Literary Arts at Brown University. He makes language art using programmable media. Recent work has explored aestheticised vectors of reading (thereadersproject.org with Daniel C. Howe), transactive synthetic language in aurality, and 'writing to be found' within and against the so-called services of Big Software. He is the author of *Grammalepsy: Essays on Digital Language Art* (Bloomsbury Academic, 2018). In current and future work he aims to write for a readership that is as much aural as visual. At Brown University he directs a graduate programme in Digital Language Arts. programmatology.shadoof.net @programmatology.

Chris Chen is an Assistant Professor of Literature at the University of California at Santa Cruz. Chen has published poetry, essays, interviews, and reviews in *boundary 2*, *The South Atlantic Quarterly*, *The Sage Handbook of Critical Theory*, *The Routledge Companion to Literature and Economics*, *The New Inquiry*, *Tripwire*, *1913: A Journal of Forms*, and the *Los Angeles Review of Books*.

Georgina Colby is Senior Lecturer in English at the University of Westminster. She is author of *Kathy Acker: Writing the Impossible* (Edinburgh University Press, 2016). She has published widely on feminism and avant-garde writing, in journals such as *Jacket 2*; *New Formations: A Journal of Culture/Theory/Politics*; *Textual Practice*; *Comparative Critical Studies*; and *Women: A Cultural Review*. She is the Director of S A L O N – LONDON, a site for responding to the present through feminist avant-garde writing.

Alex Houen is Senior Lecturer in English, Pembroke College, University of Cambridge. He is author of *Powers of Possibility: Experimental American Writing Since the 1960s* (Oxford University Press, 2012) and *Terrorism and Modern Literature, from Joseph Conrad to Ciaran Carson* (Oxford University Press, 2002). He is editor of *Sacrifice and Modern War Literature: Battle of Waterloo to War on Terror* (Oxford University Press, 2017); and *Martyrdom and Terrorism: Pre-Modern to Contemporary Perspectives* (Oxford University Press, 2014). He is also a published poet.

Peter Jaeger is Professor of Poetics at Roehampton University in London. He is the author of eleven books, including works of poetry and hybrid creative-critical research. Recent publications include the artist book *The Shadow Line* (Ma Biblioteque, 2016) and the long poem *Midamble* (If P then Q, 2018). Jaeger directs the Experimental Writing Research Group at Roehampton.

erica kaufman is the author of *POST CLASSIC* (forthcoming Roof Books), *INSTANT CLASSIC* (Roof Books, 2013) and *censory impulse* (Factory School, 2009). she is also the co-editor of *NO GENDER: Reflections on the Life and Work of kari edwards* (Venn Diagram, 2009), and of Adrienne Rich: Teaching at CUNY, 1968-1974 (Lost & Found: The CUNY Poetics Document Initiative, 2014) . Prose and critical work can be found in: *Rain Taxi*, *The Poetry Project Newsletter*, *Jacket2*, *Open Space/SFMOMA Blog*, *The Color of Vowels: New York School Collaborations* (ed. Mark Silverberg, Palgrave MacMillan, 2013), and in *Approaches to Teaching the Works of Gertrude Stein* (eds. L. Esdale and D. Mix, MLA , 2018). kaufman is the Director of the Bard College Institute for Writing & Thinking where she is also

Visiting Assistant Professor of Humanities. she also coordinates the Teacher Resource Center of ModPo, a Massive Online Open Course in Modern and Contemporary American Poetry hosted by the Kelly Writers House, University of Pennsylvania.

Susan Rudy is a Senior Research Fellow in the School of English and Drama at Queen Mary University of London. She has been writing, editing and publishing in the areas of contemporary experimental writing and feminist theory since the 1980s and taught at the University of Calgary in Canada for more than twenty years. The author or editor of many journal articles, book chapters and reviews, her book-length publications include *Poets Talk* (2005) and *Writing in Our Time* (2005), both co-authored with Pauline Butling. Recent academic articles on the work of Lisa Robertson and Erín Mouré appear (respectively) in the *British Journal of Canadian Studies* (2013) and *Canadian Literature* (2011). Recent book chapters on the work of Caroline Bergvall and Fred Wah appear (respectively) in *Generations: Canadian Women's Writing* (University of Alberta Press, 2014) and *Moving Archives* (Wilfrid Laurier University Press, forthcoming 2017). Susan regularly contributes articles on feminisms and the arts to *The New Statesman*.

Jennifer Scappettone is Associate Professor of English, Creative Writing and Romance Languages and Literatures, and Faculty Affiliate of the Center for the Study of Gender and Sexuality, at the University of Chicago. Jennifer works at the crossroads of writing, translation and scholarly research, on the page and off. She is the author of the scholarly monograph *Killing the Moonlight: Modernism in Venice* (Columbia University Press, 2014), which received Honorable Mention in the Modernist Studies Association's annual book prize competition, and of the hybrid-genre verse books *From Dame Quickly* (Litmus, 2009) and *The Republic of Exit 43: Outtakes & Scores from an Archaeology and Pop Up Opera of the Corporate Dump* (Atelos Press, late 2016). Her translations from the Italian of the polyglot poet and musicologist Amelia Rosselli were collected in *Locomotrix: Selected Poetry and Prose of Amelia Rosselli*, and won the Academy of American Poets' biennial Raiziss/De Palchi Book Prize. She is founder of PennSound Italiana, a new sector of the audiovisual archive devoted to experimental Italian poetry. In 2016, she shared a Mellon Fellowship for Arts and Scholarship with Caroline Bergvall and Judd Morrissey to work on a project called *The Data That We Breathe* at the Gray Center for Arts and Inquiry.

Sophie Seita is an Assistant Professor of English at Boston University and an artist and writer whose practice spans text- and archive-based work, translation, performance, lecture-performance and multimedia collaboration. She is the author of *Provisional Avant-Gardes: Little Magazine Communities from Dada to Digital* (Stanford University Press, 2019) and is currently working on a series of experimental essays tentatively called *Lessons of Decal*. Other critical writing includes articles on feminist hospitality in the *Journal of Modern Literature* and on contemporary digital publishing in the *Chicago Review*. She is the translator of Uljana Wolf's *i mean i dislike that fate that i was made to where* (Wonder, 2015) and *Subsisters: Selected Poems* (Belladonna*, 2017), for which she received a PEN Award, and the editor of *The Blind Man* (Ugly Duckling Presse, 2017), named one of the Best Art Books of 2017 by *The New York Times*. Her poetry, translations, interviews and performative texts have appeared in chapbooks, anthologies and magazines, most recently in the artist book *My Little Enlightenment* (Chicago: Other Forms, 2019). Recent readings and performances have taken place at Taller Bloc (Santiago, Chile), Kunsthalle (Darmstadt, Germany), the Royal Academy, the Serpentine, Bold Tendencies (all London), the Arnolfini (Bristol), La MaMa Galleria (NYC) and Cité Internationale des Arts (Paris). Her first solo show, *My Little Enlightenment Plays*, was exhibited at SPACE (London) in 2019.

Bibliography

Acker, Kathy, *Blood and Guts in High School*, annotated proofs. Box 4, Folder 2, Kathy Acker Papers, David M. Rubenstein Rare Book and Manuscript Library, Duke University.

Acker, Kathy, *Blood and Guts in High School*, annotated proofs. Box 4, Folder 2, Kathy Acker Papers, David M. Rubenstein Rare Book and Manuscript Library, Duke University.

Acker, Kathy, *Bodies of Work* (London: Serpent's Tail, 1997).

Acker, Kathy, *Bodies of Work: Essays* (New York: Serpent's Tail, 2006).

Acker, Kathy, 'Critical Languages', in *Bodies of Work: Essays* (New York: Serpent's Tail, 2006), p. 83.

Acker, Kathy, 'Dream Maps', two notebooks and five hand-drawn maps. Box 13, Folder 7, Kathy Acker Papers, David M. Rubenstein Rare Book and Manuscript Library, Duke University.

Acker, Kathy, *Eurydice in the Underworld*, excerpts. Box 17, Folder 6, Kathy Acker Papers, David M. Rubenstein Rare Book and Manuscript Library, Duke University.

Acker, Kathy, 'Eurydice Speaks', notebook. Box 17, Folder 4, Kathy Acker Papers, David M. Rubenstein Rare Book and Manuscript Library, Duke University.

Acker, Kathy, 'Rejects from *Don Quixote*', annotated typescripts, undated. Box 6, Folder 1, Kathy Acker Papers, David M. Rubenstein Rare Book and Manuscript Library, Duke University.

Acker, Kathy, 'Seeing Gender', in *Bodies of Work: Essays* (New York: Serpent's Tail, 2006).

Acker, Kathy, 'William Burroughs', typescript. Box 23, Folder 26, Kathy Acker Papers, David M. Rubenstein Rare Book and Manuscript Library, Duke University.

Acker, Kathy, and Greenaway, Peter, interview with Peter Greenaway by Kathy Acker, (1990), tape. Kathy Acker Reading Room, University of Cologne.

Adnan, Etel, 'Growing Up to Be a Woman Writer in Lebanon (1986)', in Margot Badran and Miriam Cooke (eds), *Opening the Gates: An Anthology of Arab Feminist Writing* (Bloomington: Indiana University Press, 2004).

Adnan, Etel, *Journey to Mount Tamalpais: An Essay* (Sausalito, CA: Post-Apollo Press, 1986).

Adnan, Etel, *Khams Hawas Li Mouten Wahed*, trans. Yusuf al-Khal (Beirut: Gallery One, 1973).

Adnan, Etel, 'Light: The Ultimate Material for Art' (1973), trans. Teresa Villa-Ignacio, in Anneka Lennsen, Sarah Rogers and Nada Shabout (eds), *Modern Art in the Arab World*, vol. 8, Primary Documents Publication Series (New York: Museum of Modern Art, 2018).

Adnan, Etel, 'On Small Magazines', *Bidoun*, 22 September 2015 <https://bidoun.org/news/etel-adnan-collection> (last accessed 23 June 2019).

Adnan, Etel, *Sea and Fog* (Callicoon, NY: Nightboat Books, 2012).

Adnan, Etel, *The Arab Apocalypse* (Sausalito, CA: Post-Apollo Press, 2006).

Adnan, Etel, 'The Enemy's Testament', in Walter Lowenfels (ed.), *Where is Vietnam? American Poets Respond: An Anthology of Contemporary Poems*, 1st edn (Garden City, NY: Anchor Books, 1967).

Adnan, Etel, 'The Unfolding of an Artist's Book', *Discourse: Journal for Theoretical Studies in Media and Culture* 20, no. 1 (March 2013).

Adnan, Etel, *To Look at the Sea Is to Become What One Is: An Etel Adnan Reader*, ed. Thom Donovan and Brandon Shimoda (Callicoon, NY: Nightboat Books, 2014).

Adnan, Etel, 'To Write in a Foreign Language', *Electronic Poetry Review* 1 (1996) <http://www.epoetry.org/issues/issue1/alltext/esadn.htm> (last accessed 23 June 2019).

Adnan, Etel, 'Writing Mountains', *Ab Print* 4 (Fall/Winter 2014).

Adnan, Etel, and al-Mayāssah Bint Ḥamad ibn Khalīfah Āl Thānī, *Etel Adnan in all her dimensions = Ītil ʻAdnān bi-kulli abʻādihā* (Qatar: Mathaf, 2014).

Ahmed, Sara, *The Promise of Happiness* (Durham, NC: Duke University Press, 2010).

Al-Musawi, Muhsin, 'The Republic of Letters: Arab Modernity?' *Cambridge Journal of Postcolonial Literary Inquiry* 1, no. 2 (September 2014): 265–80.

Al-Tayyib, Salih, *Bandarshah*, trans. Denys Johnson-Davies (New York and London: Kegan Paul, 1996).

Alcalay, Ammiel, and Cole Swenson, essays in Etel Adnan, *To Look at the Sea Is to Become What One Is: An Etel Adnan Reader*, ed. Thom Donovan and Brandon Shimoda (Callicoon, NY: Nightboat Books, 2014).

Ali, Wijdan, *Modern Islamic Art: Development and Continuity* (Gainesville: University Press of Florida, 1997), pp. 163–8.

Alighieri, Dante, *De vulgari eloquentia*, trans. Steven Botterill (Cambridge: Cambridge University Press, 1996).

Allen, Douglas, and Fedwa Malti-Douglas, 'Woman between Cultures: Interview with Etel Adnan, 8 January 1987'. Cited in Lisa Suhair Majaj and Amal Amireh (eds), *Etel Adnan: Critical Essays on the Arab-American Writer and Artist* (Jefferson, NC: McFarland & Co., 2002).

Altieri, Charles, and Nicholas D. Nace, *The Fate of Difficulty in the Poetry of Our Time* (Evanston, IL: Northwestern University Press, 2018).
Anderson, Benedict, *Imagined Communities: Reflections on the Origin and Spread of Nationalism* (London: Verso, 1983).
Antena, 'About Us' <http://antenaantena.org/about-us-2/> (last accessed 23 June 2019).
Antena, 'A Manifesto for Ultratranslation' (Antena Books/Libros Antena, 2013) <http://antenaantena.org/wp-content/uploads/2012/06/ultratranslation_eng.pdf> (last accessed 23 June 2019).
Appadurai, Arjun, *The Social Life of Things: Commodities in Cultural Perspective* (Cambridge: Cambridge University Press, 1988).
Apter, Emily, *Against World Literature: On the Politics of Untranslatability* (New York: Verso, 2013).
Arruzza, Cinzia, 'A Queer Union between Marxism and Feminism?' in *Dangerous Liaisons: The Marriages and Divorces of Marxism and Feminism* (Pontypool: Merlin Press, 2013), pp. 115–28.
Attridge, Derek, *The Work of Literature* (Oxford: Oxford University Press, 2015).
Baldwin, Kate A., *The Racial Imaginary of the Cold War Kitchen: From Sokol'niki Park to Chicago's South Side* (Lebanon, NH: Dartmouth College Press, 2016).
Bataille, Georges, *Visions of Excess: Selected Writings, 1927–1939*, edited with an introduction by Allan Stoekl (Minneapolis: University of Minnesota Press, 1985).
Baxter, Charles (ed.), *The Business of Memory: The Art of Remembering in an Age of Forgetting* (St Paul, MN: Graywolf, 1999).
Beale, Frances, 'Double Jeopardy: To Be Black and Female', in Beverly Guy-Sheftall (ed.), *Words of Fire: An Anthology of African-American Feminist Thought* (New York: The New Press, 1995), pp. 145–56.
Beasley, Rebecca, 'Migration, circulation, drift: Translation and visuality in modernist and contemporary poetry', in Stefan Kjerkegaard and Dan Ringgaard (eds), *Dialogues on Poetry: Mediatization and New Sensibilities* (Aalborg: Aalborg University Press, 2017), pp. 63–88.
Bellamin-Noël, Jean, 'Psychoanalytic Reading and the Avant-texte', in Jed Deppman, Daniel Ferrer and Michael Groden (eds), *Genetic Criticism: Texts and Avant-textes* (Philadelphia: University of Pennsylvania Press, 2004), p. 31.
Benjamin, Jessica, *Beyond Doer and Done To: Recognition Theory, Intersubjectivity and the Third* (Abingdon: Routledge, 2018).
Benjamin, Jessica, *The Bonds of Love: Psychoanalysis, Feminism, and the Problem of Domination* (New York: Pantheon Books, 1988).
Benjamin, Walter, *Charles Baudelaire: A Lyric Poet in the Era of High Capitalism*, trans. Harry Zohn (London: Verso, 1983).
Benjamin, Walter, 'Doctrine of the Simmilar', in *New German Critique* 17 (1979), Special Walter Benjamin Issue.

Benjamin, Walter, *Illuminations*, ed. Hannah Arendt (London: Jonathan Cape, 1970).
Benjamin, Walter, *On Hashish*, ed. Howard Eiland (Cambridge, MA: Harvard University Press, 2006).
Benjamin, Walter, *Selected Writings 1: 1913–1926*, trans. Marcus Bullock and Michael W. Jennings (Cambridge, MA: The Belknap Press of Harvard University, 2004).
Benjamin, Walter, *Selected Writings 4: 1938–1940*, trans. Howard Eiland and Michael W. Jennings (Cambridge, MA: The Belknap Press of Harvard University, 2006).
Benjamin, Walter, *The Arcades Project*, trans. Howard Eiland and Kevin McLaughlin (Cambridge, MA: The Belknap Press of Harvard University, 1999).
Benjamin, Walter, *Understanding Brecht*, trans. Anna Bostock (London: Verso, 1998).
Bennett, Tony, 'Texts in history: the determinations of reading and their texts', *Journal of the Midwest Modern Language Association* 18 (1985).
Bentley, Daniel, 'First annual results of David Cameron's happiness index published', *The Independent*, 24 July 2012 <http://www.independent.co.uk/news/uk/politics/first-annual-results-of-david-camerons-happiness-index-published-7972861.html> (last accessed 23 February 2017).
Bergvall, Caroline, *Alyson Singes* (Brooklyn, New York: Belladonna Books, 2008).
Bergvall, Caroline, *Cropper* (Southampton: Torque Press, 2008).
Bergvall, Caroline, *Drift* (Brooklyn and Callicoon, New York: Nightboat Books, 2014).
Bergvall, Caroline, *Drift* <http://carolinebergvall.com/work/drift-performance/> (last accessed 23 June 2019).
Bergvall, Caroline, 'Infra-materiality and Opaque Drifting', in Nicola Gardini, Adriana X. Jacobs, Ben Moran, Mohamed-Salah Omri, Matthew Reynolds (eds), *Minding Borders: Resilient Divisions in Literature, the Body, and the Academy* (Oxford: Legenda, 2016), pp. 89–96.
Bergvall, Caroline, *Éclat: sites 1–10* (London: Sound & Language, 1996).
Bergvall, Caroline, *Fig* (Cambridge: Salt, 2005).
Bergvall, Caroline, *Flèsh Acoeur* (London: Gefn Press, 2000).
Bergvall, Caroline, *Goan Atom 1: Doll* (San Francisco: Krupskaya, 2001).
Bergvall, Caroline, 'Methods of Engagement', keynote address, Words on the Move: A Day of Talks and Performances across Languages, Birkbeck, University of London, 1 November 2016.
Bergvall, Caroline, *Oh My Oh My*, performed at Kings College London, 17 October 2017. Included rendition of Documenta 14 audio commission *OH MY OH MY*. *(Pinktrombone, 21 January 2017)* <http://www.documenta14.de/en/public-radio/14720/oh-my-oh-my-pinktrombone-21-january-2017-> (last accessed 23 June 2019).

Bergvall, Caroline, *Processing Writing: From Text to Textual Interventions*, PhD thesis (University of Plymouth, 2000).
Bergvall, Caroline, *Ragadawn*, unpublished typescript (2016) <http://carolinebergvall.com/work/ragadawn/> (last accessed 23 June 2019).
Bergvall, Caroline, *Strange Passage: A Choral Poem* (Cambridge: Equipage, 1993).
Bergvall, Caroline, 'Via: 48 Dante variations', in *Fig [Goan Atom 2]* (Cambridge: Salt, 2005), pp. 63–71.
Bergvall, Caroline, 'Writing at the Crossroads of Languages', in Steven Marks and Mark Wallace (eds), *Telling it Slant: Avant-Garde Poetics of the 1990s* (Tuscaloosa and London: University of Alabama Press, 2002).
Bergvall, Caroline, and Ciran Maher, *Say Parsley*, installation at the Arnolfini Gallery, Bristol, 7 May – 3 July 2010 <https://www.arnolfini.org.uk/whatson/caroline-bergvall-ciran-maher-say-parsley> (last accessed 24 January 2018).
Bergvall, Caroline, and Erín Mouré, 'O YES', in Nate Dorwood (ed.), *Antiphonies: Essays on Women's Experimental Poetries in Canada* (Toronto: The Gig, 2008), pp. 167–76.
Bernstein, Charles, 'Charles Bernstein Interview' with Eric Denut, *The Argotist Online* (2006) <http://www.argotistonline.co.uk/Bernstein%20interview.htm> (last accessed 23 June 2019).
Bernstein, Charles, *Content's Dream: Essays 1975–84* (Evanston, IL: Northwestern University Press, 1986).
Bernstein, Charles, *Dark City* (Los Angeles: Sun and Moon Press, 1994).
Bernstein, Charles, 'Forefright' [1983], in *Republics of Reality 1975–1995* (Los Angeles: Sun and Moon Press, 2000).
Bernstein, Charles, 'Introduction', in Johanna Drucker, *Figuring the Word: Essays on Books, Writing, and Visual Poetics* (New York: Granary Books, 1998).
Bernstein, Charles, *My Way: Speeches and Poems* (Chicago: University of Chicago Press, 1999).
Bernstein, Charles, *Shadowtime* (Los Angeles: Green Integer, 2005).
Bernstein, Charles, 'The Klupzy Girl', in *Islets/Irritations* (New York: Roof Books, 1983).
Bernstein, Charles, *Veil* (La Farge: Xexoxial Editions, 1987).
Bernstein, Charles, *With Strings* (Chicago: University of Chicago Press, 2001).
Berry, Ellen, *Women's Experimental Writing: Negative Aesthetics and Feminist Critique* (London: Bloomsbury Academic, 2016).
Bertsch, C., 'Language in the Dark: The Legacy of Walter Benjamin in the Opera *Shadowtime*', in Stephen Paul Miller (ed.), *Radical Poetics and Secular Jewish Culture* (Tuscaloosa: University of Alabama Press, 2009).
Berwick, Robert C., and Noam Chomsky, *Why Only Us: Language and Evolution* (Cambridge, MA: MIT Press, 2016).

Bialosky, Jill, 'An Essay on Poetry and Memoir', *The Kenyon Review*, Spring 2013 <https://www.kenyonreview.org/kr-online-issue/2013-spring/selections/jill-bialosky-656342/> (last accessed 2 June 2018).

Blue, Ethan, 'Strange passages: Carceral Mobility of the Liminal in the Catastrophic History of American Deportation', *National Identities* 17 (2015): 175–94.

Bollobás, Enikö, 'In Imploded Sentences', *ARCADE: Literature, Humanities, and the World* (2015) <https://arcade.stanford.edu/content/imploded-sentences-charles-bernsteins-poetic-attentions> (last accessed 23 June 2019).

Braidotti, Rosi, *Nomadic Subjects: Embodiment and Sexual Difference in Contemporary Feminist Theory* (New York: Columbia University Press, 2011).

Bray, Joe, Alison Gibbons and Brian McHale (eds), *The Routledge Companion to Experimental Literature* (London: Routledge, 2012).

Briggs, Kate, *This Little Art* (London: Fitzcarraldo, 2017).

Broqua, Vincent, 'Caroline Bergvall's Poetics of the Infrathin', in Abigail Lang and David Nowell Smith (eds), *Modernist Legacies: Trends and Faultlines in British Poetry Today* (London: Palgrave Macmillan, 2015).

Brossard, Nicole, *Typhon Dru*, trans. Caroline Bergvall (London: Reality Street Editions, 1997).

Buck-Morss, Susan, *The Dialectics of Seeing: Walter Benjamin and the Arcades Project* (Cambridge, MA: MIT Press, 1989).

Burroughs, William, and Brion Gysin, *The Third Mind* (New York: The Viking Press, 1978).

Butler, Judith, *Notes Toward a Performative Theory of Assembly* (Cambridge, MA: Harvard University Press, 2015).

Cage, John, *I–VI* (Cambridge, MA: Harvard University Press, 1990).

Cage, John, *A Year from Monday: New Lectures and Writings by John Cage* (New York: Marion Boyars, 1968).

Cage, John, *A Year from Monday: New Lectures and Writings* (Middletown, CT: Wesleyan University Press, 1995).

Cage, John, 'Composition as Process', in *Silence* (Middletown, CT: Wesleyan University Press, [1961] 1973), pp. 18–56.

Cage, John, 'Diary: How to Improve the World (You Will Only Make Matters Worse) 1965', in *A Year from Monday: New Lectures and Writings* (Middletown, CT: Wesleyan University Press, 1995), pp. 3–20.

Cage, John, 'Diary: How to Improve the World (You Will Only Make Matters Worse) Continued 1969', in *M: Writings '67–'72* (London: Calder and Boyars, 1973), pp. 96–116.

Cage, John, 'Diary: How to Improve the World (You Will Only Make Matters Worse) Continued 1973–1982', in *X: Writings '79–'82* (London: Marion Boyars, 1983), pp. 155–69.

Cage, John, 'Foreword', in *A Year from Monday: New Lectures and Writings* (Middletown, CT: Wesleyan University Press, 1995), pp. ix–x.

Cage, John, 'Foreword', in *M: Writings '67–'72* (London: Calder and Boyars, 1973), pp. ix–xvi.
Cage, John, 'Juilliard Lecture', in *A Year from Monday: New Lectures and Writings* (Middletown, CT: Wesleyan University Press, 1995), pp. 95–111.
Cage, John, *M: Writings '67–'72* (London: Calder and Boyars, 1973).
Cage, John, *Silence* (Middletown, CT: Wesleyan University Press, [1961] 1973).
Cage, John, 'Themes and Variations', in *Composition in Retrospect* (Cambridge, MA: Exact Change, 1993), pp. 55–171.
Cage, John, 'Writing for the Fourth Time through *Finnegans Wake*', in *X: Writings '79–'82* (London: Marion Boyars, 1983), pp. 1–49.
Cage, John, *X: Writings '79–'82* (London: Marion Boyars, 1983).
Carlos Williams, William, *Paterson: Revised Edition*, ed. Christopher MacGowan (New York: New Directions, 1992), p. 50.
Carr, Nicholas G., 'Is Google Making Us Stupid? What the Internet Is Doing to Our Brains', *The Atlantic*, July/August 2008 <https://www.theatlantic.com/magazine/archive/2008/07/is-google-making-us-stupid/306868/> (last accessed 11 July 2019).
Carr, Nicholas G., *The Shallows: What the Internet Is Doing to Our Brains* (New York: W.W. Norton, 2010).
Carson, Anne, *Nay Rather* (Paris: Sylph Editions/Cahiers 21, 2013).
Catullus, Gaius Valerius, *Catulli Veronensis liber* (London: Cape Goliard Press, 1969).
Catullus, Gaius Valerius, et al., *Catullus: the complete poems for American readers* (New York: Dutton, 1970).
Catullus, Gaius Valerius, et al., *Catullus, Tibullus, and Pervigilium Veneris* (London and Cambridge: W. Heinemann, 1976).
Cayley, John, 'The Advent of Aurature and the End of (Electronic) Literature', in Joseph Tabbi (ed.), *The Bloomsbury Handbook of Electronic Literature* (New York and London: Bloomsbury Academic, 2018).
Cayley, John, '*The Listeners*: An Instance of Aurature', *Cream City Review* 40, no. 2 (2016): 173–87.
Cha, Theresa Hak Kyung, *Dictee* (Berkeley: University of California Press, 2001).
Chakrabarty, Dipesh, *Provincializing Europe* (Princeton: Princeton University Press, 2007).
Choi, Don Mee, and Christian Hawkey, untitled conversation, *Bomb* 142 (Winter 2018) <https://bombmagazine.org/articles/don-mee-choi-and-christian-hawkey/> (last accessed 12 January 2018).
Citton, Yves, *The Ecology of Attention [Pour une écologie de l'attention]* (Cambridge: Polity Press, 2017).
Cixous, Hélène, *Mother Homer is Dead*, trans. Peggy Kamuf (Edinburgh: Edinburgh University Press, 2018).
Clark-Oates, Angela et al., 'Understanding the Life Narratives of Immigrants through Naming Practices', in Star Medzerian Vanguri (ed.),

Rhetorics of Names and Naming (New York: Taylor and Francis, 2016).

Cohen, Lizabeth, 'A Consumers' Republic: The Politics of Mass Consumption in Postwar America', *Journal of Consumer Research* 31.1 (2004): 236–92.

Colby, Georgina, *Kathy Acker: Writing the Impossible* (Edinburgh: Edinburgh University Press, 2016).

Colebrook, Claire, 'The Once and Future Humans: Between Happiness and Extinction', in Alastair Hunt and Stephanie Youngblood (eds), *Against Life* (Evanston, IL: Northwestern University Press, 2016), pp. 63–85.

Colla, Elliott, 'Badr Shakir Al-Sayyab, Cold War Poet', *Middle Eastern Literatures* 18, no. 3 (2015).

Collins, Sophie, 'Three Kinds of Translation', *Currently & Emotion: Translations* (London: Test Centre, 2016).

Combahee River Collective, 'The Combahee River Collective Statement', in Keeanga-Yamahtta Taylor (ed.), *How We Get Free: Black Feminism and the Combahee River Collective* (Chicago: Haymarket Books, 2017), pp. 15–28.

Conard, Mark T., 'Introduction', in *The Philosophy of Film Noir* (Lexington: University Press of Kentucky, 2006), pp. 1–4.

Cooper, Esther V., 'The Negro Woman Domestics in Relation to Trade Unionism', Fisk University, 1940.

Crawley, Ashon T., *Blackpentecostal Breath: The Aesthetics of Possibility* (New York: Fordham University Press, 2017).

Dadi, Iftikhar, 'Rethinking Calligraphic Modernism', in Kobena Mercer (ed.), *Discrepant Abstraction* (Cambridge, MA and London: MIT Press, 2006).

Davies, Clare, *Decolonizing Culture: Third World, Moroccan, and Arab Art in Souffles/Anfas, 1966–1972*, Essays of the Forum Transregionale Studien 2 (Berlin: Forum Transregionale Studien e. V., 2015).

Davis, Angela, 'The Approaching Obsolescence of Housework: A Working-Class Perspective', in Angela Davis, *Women, Race, & Class* (New York: Vintage, 1983), pp. 222–44.

De Biasi, Pierre-Marc, 'Toward a Science of Literature: Manuscript Analysis', in Jed Deppman, Daniel Ferrer and Michael Groden (eds), *Genetic Criticism: Texts and Avant-textes* (Philadelphia: University of Pennsylvania Press, 2004), p. 38.

De Lauretis, Teresa, *Alice Doesn't: Feminism, Semiotics, Cinema* (Indianapolis: Indiana University Press, 1984).

DeKoven, Marianne, *A Different Language: Gertrude Stein's Experimental Writing* (Madison: University of Wisconsin Press, 1983).

Delabastita, Dirk, 'Focus on the Pun: Wordplay as a Special Problem in Translation Studies', *Target* 6.2 (1994).

Deleuze, Gilles, and Félix Guattari, *Kafka: Toward a Minor Literature*, trans. Dana Polan (Minneapolis: University of Minnesota Press, 1986).

Deming, R. (2010), 'Poetry Called Into Being', *Boston Review: A Political and Literary Forum* <http://bostonreview.net/deming-called-into-being> (last accessed 12 February 2018).

Deppman, Jed, Daniel Ferrer and Michael Groden (eds), *Genetic Criticism: Texts and Avant-textes* (Philadelphia: University of Pennsylvania Press, 2004).

Derrida, Jacques, *Monolingualism of the Other; or, The Prothesis of Origin*, trans. Patrick Mensah (Stanford: Stanford University Press, 1998).

Derrida, Jacques, 'Hospitality', trans. Barry Stocker and Forbes Morlock, *Angelaki*, 5.3 (2000), pp. 3–18.

Dewey, John, *Art as Experience* (New York: Perigee Books, 2005).

Dorwood, Nate (ed.), *Antiphonies: Essays on Women's Experimental Poetries in Canada* (Willowdale: The Gig Press, 2008).

Drucker, Johanna, 'Diagrammatic Writing and Performative Materiality', *Disrupting the Humanities: Towards Posthumanities*, vol. 19, issue 2 (Fall 2016), n.p.

Drucker, Johanna, 'Diagrammatic Writing and Stochastic Writing and Poetics', *The Iowa Review*, vol. 44, issue 3 (Winter 2014/15), pp. 122–32.

Drucker, Johanna, *Figuring the Word: Essays on Books, Writing, and Visual Poetics* (New York: Granary Books, 1998).

Drucker, Johanna, *General Theory of Social Relativity* (Singapore: Elephants, 2018).

Dworkin, Craig, *Reading the Illegible* (Evanston: Northwestern University Press, 2003).

El Amrani, Issandr, 'In the Beginning There Was *Souffles*: Reconsidering Morocco's Most Radical Literary Quarterly', *Bidoun* 13: *Glory* (Winter 2008) <https://bidoun.org/articles/in-the-beginning-there-was-souffles> (last accessed 23 June 2019).

Elwell-Sutton, L. P., *Elementary Persian Grammar* (Cambridge: Cambridge University Press, 1963).

Fanon, Frantz, *Black Skin, White Masks*, forewords by Ziauddin Sardar and Homi K. Bhabha, trans. Charles Lamb Markmann (London: Pluto, 2008).

Fattal, Simone, 'A Few Years in Journalism', *Etel Adnan* <http://www.eteladnan.com/journalism/> (last accessed 23 June 2019).

Fattal, Simone, 'On Perception: Etel Adnan's Visual Art', in *Etel Adnan: Critical Essays on the Arab-American Writer and Artist*, ed. Lisa Suhair Majaj and Amal Amireh (Jefferson, NC: McFarland & Co., 2002).

Federici, Silvia, *Revolution at Point Zero* (Los Angeles: PM Press, 2012).

Fink, Thomas, and Judith Halden-Sullivan, *Reading the Difficulties: Dialogues with Contemporary American Innovative Poetry* (Tuscaloosa: University of Alabama Press, 2014).

Fitterman, Robert, *Rob the Plagiarist* (New York: Roof Books, 2009).

Fitzgerald, Adam, 'An Interview with Fred Moten, Part 1', *Literary Hub*, 5 August 2015 <https://lithub.com/an-interview-with-fred-moten-pt-i/> (last accessed 23 June 2019).

Fox, Cybelle, *Three Worlds of Relief: Race, Immigration, and the American Welfare State from the Progressive Era to the New Deal* (Princeton: Princeton University Press, 2012).

Fraser, Kathleen, 'editor's notes &', *The HOW(ever) Archive*, n.d. <https://www.asu.edu/pipercwcenter/how2journal/archive/online_archive/v1_1_1999/ednote.html> (last accessed 30 January 2018).

Friedan, Betty, *The Feminine Mystique* (New York: Dell Books, 1964).

Funkhouser, Christopher T., 'Le(s) Mange Texte(s): Creative Cannibalism and Digital Poetry', in *E-Poetry 2007* (Paris: Université Paris, 2007).

Gardiner, Alan H., *Egyptian Grammar: Being an Introduction to the Study of Hieroglyphs* (Oxford: Griffith Institute Publications, 1957), p. 438.

Geary, Daniel, *Beyond Civil Rights: The Moynihan Report and Its Legacy* (Philadelphia: University of Pennsylvania Press, 2015).

Gibb, H. A. R, *The Encyclopaedia of Islam*, new edn (Leiden: Brill, 1960).

Gibbons, Alison, *Multimodality, Cognition and Experimental Literature* (London: Routledge, 2012).

Gimenez, Martha, 'The Dialectics of Waged and Unwaged Work: Waged Work, Domestic Labor, and Household Survival in the United States', in Jane L. Collins and Martha Gimenez (eds), *Work Without Wages: Comparative Studies of Domestic Labor and Self-Employment* (New York: SUNY Press, 1990), pp. 25–46.

Glazier, L. P., 'Charles Bernstein' (1996), Electronic Poetry Centre <http://epc.buffalo.edu/authors/bernstein/reviews/glazier.html#MainEssaySection> (last accessed 9 January 2018).

Glenn, Evelyn Nakano. *Forced To Care: Coercion and Caregiving in America* (Cambridge: Harvard University Press, 2012).

Glissant, Édouard, *Caribbean Discourse: Selected Essays*, trans. with an introduction by J. Michael Dash (Charlottesville: University of Virginia Press, 1989).

Glissant, Édouard, *Le Discours antillais* (Paris: Éditions du Seuil, 1981).

Glissant, Édouard, *Poetic Intention*, trans. Nathanaël, with Anne Malena (Callicoon, NY and Lebanon, NH: Nightboat Books, 2010).

Golding, John, 'Visions of the Modern' (Oakland: University of California Press, 1994).

Goldsmith, Kenneth, in João Bandeira and Lenora de Barros (eds), *Poesia concreta: o projeto verbivocovisual* (São Paulo: Artemeios, 2008).

Gorman, Samantha, and Daniel Cannizzaro, *Pry* (Tender Claws, 2014), app for iOS.

Goyal, Yogita, 'We Need New Diasporas', *American Literary History* 29, no. 4 (December 2017): 640–63 <https://doi.org/10.1093/alh/ajx030> (last accessed 23 June 2019).

Greene, Roland (ed.), *The Princeton Encyclopedia of Poetry and Poetics*, 4th edn (Princeton: Princeton University Press, 2012).

Guy-Bray, Stephen, 'Coming Out In/To Poetry', Queer London Research Forum, University of Westminster, 17 November 2017 <https://www.

westminster.ac.uk/news-and-events/news/2017/westminster-queer-london-research-forum-hosts-successful-coming-out-in-to-poetry-event> (last accessed 7 December 2017).

Haifa Saud, Alfaisal, 'World Reading Strategies: Border Reading Bandarshah/ «استراتيجيات» العالمية: القراءة حدودية ل «بندرشاه»', *Alif: Journal of Comparative Poetics* no. 34 (2014).

Halberstam, Judith, *In a Queer Time and Place: Transgendered Bodies, Subcultural Lives* (New York and London: New York University Press, 2005).

Halden-Sullivan, Judith, *Reading the Difficulties: Dialogues with Contemporary American Innovative Poetry* (Tuscaloosa: University of Alabama Press, 2014).

Harrison, Olivia C., 'Cross-Colonial Poetics: *Souffles-Anfas* and the Figure of Palestine', *PMLA* 128, no. 2 (March 2013).

Harrison, Olivia C., and Teresa Villa-Ignacio, *Souffles-Anfas: A Critical Anthology from the Moroccan Journal of Culture and Politics* (Stanford: Stanford University Press, 2015).

Hawkey, Christian, *Ventrakl* (New York: Ugly Duckling Presse, 2010).

Hay, Louis, 'Genetic Criticism: Origins and Perspectives', in Jed Deppman, Daniel Ferrer and Michael Groden (eds), *Genetic Criticism: Texts and Avant-textes* (Philadelphia: University of Pennsylvania Press, 2004), pp. 17–27; 18.

Hayles, Katherine, *How We Think: Digital Media and Contemporary Technogenesis* (Chicago: The University of Chicago Press, 2012).

Hayles, N. Katherine, 'Hyper and Deep Attention: The Generational Divide in Cognitive Modes', *Profession* 2007, no. 1.

Hayles, N. Katherine, *Writing Machines* (New York: MIT Press, 2002).

Heisler, Eva, 'Caroline Bergvall, Propelled to the Edges of a Language's Freedom, and to the Depths of Its Collective Traumas', *Asymptote* (2018) <https://www.asymptotejournal.com/visual/eva-heisler-caroline-bergvall-propelled-to-the-edges-of-a-languages-freedom/> (last accessed 23 June 2019).

Hejinian, Lyn, 'Background Notes for *Happily*' (1998). Box 110, Folder 11, Hejinian Archive, Mandeville Special Collections Library, University of California San Diego.

Hejinian, Lyn, *Happily* (Sausalito: The Post Apollo Press, 2000).

Hejinian, Lyn, 'Letter to Susan Howe' (23 December 1994). Box 22, Folder 13 Hejinian Archive, Mandeville Special Collections Library, University of California San Diego.

Hejinian, Lyn, *My Life* (Los Angeles: Green Integer, [1987] 2002).

Hejinian, Lyn, 'The Person and Description', in *The Language of Inquiry* (Berkeley: University of California Press, 2000), pp. 199–208.

Hickman, Ben, *Crisis and the US Avant-Garde: Poetry and Real Politics* (Edinburgh: Edinburgh University Press, 2015), p. 3.

Hochschild, Arlie, *The Second Shift: Working Families and the Revolution at Home* (Harmondsworth: Penguin Books, 2012).

Hofer, Jen, and Sawako Nakayasu, 'Can Can', ON: *Contemporary Practice*, 1 (2008).

HoSang, Daniel Martinez, and Joseph E. Lowndes, *Producers, Parasites, Patriots: Race and the New Right-Wing Politics of Precarity* (Minneapolis: University of Minnesota Press, 2019).

Houen, Alex, *Powers of Possibility: Experimental American Writing since the 1960s* (Oxford University Press, 2011).

Houen, Alex, and Geoff Gilbert, 'Sun-Dog Express', *Glasgow Review of Books*, 31 March 2017 <https://glasgowreviewofbooks.com/2017/03/31/new-poetry-by-alex-houen-and-geoff-gilbert/> (last accessed 23 February 2017).

Howe, Susan, 'The Art of Poetry No. 97', interview by Maureen N. McLane, *Paris Review* issue 203 (Winter 2012), n.p. <https://www.theparisreview.org/interviews/6189/susan-howe-the-art-of-poetry-no-97-susan-howe> (last accessed 23 June 2019).

Howe, Susan, *My Emily Dickinson* (London: New Directions, 2007).

Howe, Susan, *Spontaneous Particulars: The Telepathy of the Archive* (New York: New Directions, 2014).

Hunt, Erica, 'Notes for an Oppositional Poetics', in Charles Bernstein (ed.), *The Politics of Poetic Form* (New York: Roof Books, 1990).

Hunt, Erica, *Piece Logic* (Durham, NC: Carolina Wren Press, 2002).

Hunter, Tera, *To 'Joy My Freedom: Southern Black Women's Lives and Labors after the Civil War* (Cambridge, MA: Harvard University Press, 1998).

Hutchinson, John, and Anthony D. Smith, *Nationalism* (New York: Oxford University Press, 1994).

Iijima, Brenda, and Joan Retallack, 'Brenda Iijima & Joan Retallack', in Jennifer Firestone and Dana Teen Lomax (eds), *Letters to Poets: Conversations about Poetics, Politics and Community* (Philadelphia: Saturnalia Books, 2009), pp. 255–77.

'International Wages for Housework flier'. Freedom Archives, accessed 8 September 2019. https://freedomarchives.org/Documents/Finder/DOC50_scans/500.020.Wages.for.Housework.pdf

'J301 – M*A*S*H – the Pilot' (1972), *Springfield TV Episode Scripts* <https://www.springfieldspringfield.co.uk/view_episode_scripts.php?tv-show=mash&episode=s01e01> (last accessed 23 June 2019).

Jacobson, Matthew Frye, *Whiteness of a Different Color* (Cambridge, MA: Harvard University Press, 1999).

Jameson, Fredric, *Postmodernism, or, The Cultural Logic of Late Capitalism* (New York: Verso, 1991).

Jenkins, Grant Matthew, *Poetic Obligation: Ethics in Experimental American Poetry after 1945* (Iowa City: University of Iowa, 2008).

Jones, Claudia, 'An End to the Neglect of the Problems of Negro Women', in Carole Boyce Davies (ed.), *Claudia Jones: Beyond Containment* (Banbury: Ayebia Clarke Publishing Limited, 2011), pp. 74–86.

Jones, Jacqueline, *Labor of Love, Labor of Sorrow* (New York: Basic Books, 2010).
Judy, Ronald A. T., *(Dis)Forming the American Canon: African-Arabic Slave Narratives and the Vernacular* (Minneapolis: University of Minnesota Press, 1993).
Kant, Immanuel, 'Analytic of the Beautiful', in *Critique of the Power of Judgement* [1790] (Cambridge University Press, 2000), pp. 89–127.
Kaplan, Genevieve, 'How we read Caroline Bergvall's "Via" and why we should care', *Jacket* 38 (2009) <http://jacketmagazine.com/38/bergvall-by-kaplan.html> (last accessed 22 November 2017).
Karasick, A., 'In the Shadow of Desire: Charles Bernstein's *Shadowtime* and Its Kabbalistic Trajectories', in Stephen Paul Miller (ed.), *Radical Poetics and Secular Jewish Culture* (Tuscaloosa: University of Alabama Press, 2014).
Kaufmann, David, 'David Kaufmann reviews Caroline Bergvall's *Drift*', *Asymptote*, 2017 <https://www.asymptotejournal.com/criticism/caroline-bergvall-drift/> (last accessed 7 December 2017).
Keene, John, 'Translating Poetry, Translating Blackness', *Harriet*, 28 April 2016 <https://www.poetryfoundation.org/harriet/2016/04/translating-poetry-translating-blackness> (last accessed 30 January 2018).
Kennedy, David, and Christine Kennedy, 'Caroline Bergvall, Elizabeth James/Frances Presley and Redell Olsen: Virtual Spaces', in *Women's Experimental Poetry in Britain 1970–2010: Body, Time and Locale* (Liverpool: Liverpool University Press, 2013), pp. 126–44.
Khatibi, Abdelkebir, 'A Note on the Calligraphic Sign', originally published in *Intégral* 2 3/4 (January 1973), trans. Teresa Villa-Ignacio, in Anneka Lennsen, Sarah Rogers and Nada Shabout (eds), *Modern Art in the Arab World*, vol. 8, Primary Documents Publication Series (New York: Museum of Modern Art, 2018).
Khatibi, Abdelkebir, *La Blessure du nom propre* (Paris: Les Lettres nouvelles, 1974).
King, Deborah K., 'Multiple Jeopardy, Multiple Consciousness: The Context of a Black Feminist Ideology', *Signs* 14, no. 1 (1988): 42–72.
Kinnahan, Linda, 'An interview with Caroline Bergvall', *Contemporary Women's Writing* 5:3 (2011), pp. 232–50.
Kirby, Michael, 'Happenings: An Introduction', in Mariellen R. Sandford (ed.), *Happenings and Other Acts* (London: Routledge, 1995), pp. 1–28.
Kostelanetz, Richard, *Conversing with John Cage* (London: Routledge, 2003).
Kunin, Aaron, *Love Three: A Study of a Poem by George Herbert* (Seattle: Wave Books, 2019).
Kraus, Chris, *After Kathy Acker* (London: Penguin, 2017).
Kurjaković, Daniel, and Etel Adnan, 'Etel Adnan: Every One of Us Is a Radio Transmitter', trans. Patrick Gillot, *ArtAsiaPacific* no. 101 (December 2016).

Laâbi, Abdellatif, 'La culture nationale, donée et exigence historique', *Souffles* 4 (1966).

Lewis, Oscar, 'The Culture of Poverty', *Scientific American* 215, no. 4 (1966): 19–25.

Lowenfels, Walter (ed.), *Where is Vietnam? American Poets Respond: An Anthology of Contemporary Poems*, 1st edn (Garden City, NY: Anchor Books, 1967).

Machado, Aditi, 'On Etel Adnan's "The Arab Apocalypse"', *Jacket2*, 30 November 2016 <https://jacket2.org/article/etel-adnans-arab-apocalypse> (last accessed 23 June 2019).

Marx, Karl, *Capital: A Critique of Political Economy: Vol. 1* (Moscow: Progress Publishers, 1978).

Mason, Jennifer, *Affinities: Potent Connections in Personal Life* (Cambridge: Polity, 2018).

Mayer, Sophie, 'All at sea', *The F word: Contemporary UK Feminism*, 2014 <https://www.thefword.org.uk/2014/08/all_at_sea/> (last accessed 23 June 2019).

McCormick, Kathleen, and Gary F. Waller (1987), 'Text, Reader, Ideology: The Interactive Nature of the Reading Situation', *Poetics* vol. 16.1.

McGovern, Charles F., *Sold American: Consumption and Citizenship, 1890–1945* (Durham: University of North Carolina Press, 2006).

McKenzie, D. F, 'The book as an expressive form', in *Bibliography and the Sociology of Texts* (Cambridge: Cambridge University Press, 1999).

Mejcher-Atassi, Sonja, 'Breaking the Silence: Etel Adnan's *Sitt Marie-Rose* and *The Arab Apocalypse*', in Andreas Pflitsch and Barbara Winckler (eds), *Poetry's Voice – Society's Norms: Forms of Interaction between Middle Eastern Writers and their Societies* (Wiesbaden: Reichert, 2006).

Melehi, Mohammed, 'Questionnaire', *Souffles*, special issue on 'Situation arts plastiques Maroc': 7–8 (1967): 56–68 <http://www.lehman.edu/deanhum/langlit/french/souffles/S0708EMP/13m_7.HTM> (last accessed 23 June 2019).

Mignolo, Walter, *Local Histories/Global Designs: Coloniality, Subaltern Knowledges, and Border Thinking*, Princeton Studies in Culture/Power/History (Princeton: Princeton University Press, 2012).

Miller, Nancy K., *Subject to Change: Reading Feminist Writing* (New York: Columbia University Press, 1988).

Milne, Drew, 'A veritable Dollmine: Caroline Bergvall, *Goan Atom*, 1', *Jacket* 12 (2000) <http://jacketmagazine.com/12/milne-bergvall.html> (last accessed 7 December 2017).

Mitropoulos, Angela, *Contract & Contagion: From Biopolitics to Oikonomia* (New York: Minor Compositions, 2012).

Moulthrop, Stuart, and Dene Grigar, *Traversals: The Use of Preservation for Early Electronic Writing* (Cambridge, MA: The MIT Press, 2017).

Mouré, Erín, 'But do we need a second language to translate?', in Sophie Collins (ed.), *Currently and Emotion; Translations* (London: Test Centre, 2016), pp. 29–30.

Murray, Charles, *Coming Apart: The State of White America, 1960–2010* (New York: Crown Forum, 2013).
Naples, Nancy A., 'The "New Consensus" on the Gendered "Social Contract": The 1987–1988 US Congressional Hearings on Welfare Reform', *Signs* vol. 22, no. 4: 907–45.
Nashashibi, Salwa Mikdadi, *Forces of Change: Artists of the Arab World* (Lafayette, CA and Washington, DC: International Council for Women in the Arts; National Museum of Women in the Arts, 1994).
Nealon, Christopher, *The Matter of Capital: Poetry and Crisis in the American Century* (Cambridge, MA: Harvard University Press, 2011).
Noel-Tod, Jeremy, 'Bergvall, Caroline', in Jeremy Noel-Tod and Ian Hamilton (eds), *The Oxford Companion to Modern Poetry in English*, 2nd edn (Oxford: Oxford University Press, 2013).
NourbeSe Philip, M., 'Über ein Gedicht von NourbeSe Philip', *Akzente* 64.2 (June 2017).
NourbeSe Philip, M., *Zong!* (Middletown: Wesleyan University Press, 2011).
O'Sullivan, Maggie, *Out of Everywhere: Linguistically Innovative Poetry by Women in North America and the UK* (London: Reality Street, 1996).
Obrist, Hans-Ulrich (ed.), *Mapping It Out: An Alternative Atlas of Contemporary Cartographies* (London: Thames & Hudson, 2014), p. 182.
Olsen, Redell, 'Review of Memnoir', *The Poetry Project Newsletter* 201 (December/January 2004–2005): 24.
Orgera, Alexis, '(Eggs and Bacon): The Poem as Memoir?' *HTMLGIANT* <http://htmlgiant.com/craft-notes/eggs-and-bacon-the-poem-as-memoir/> (last accessed 23 June 2019).
Ovid, and Rolfe Humphries, *Ovid: Metamorphoses* (Bloomington: Indiana University Press, 1971).
Pedwell, Carolyn, 'Cultural Theory as Mood Work', *New Formations* 82 (2014): 47–63.
Pequeño Glazier, Loss, email dated 3 September 1996 to Electronic Poetry List regarding Assembling Alternatives: An international poetry conference/festival held at the University of New Hampshire, Durham, 29 August – 2 September 1996 <http://epc.buffalo.edu/documents/assembling/contents.html#glazier> (last accessed 2 January 2018).
Perloff, Marjorie, 'ex/Creme/ental/eaT/ing': An Interview with Caroline Bergvall', *Sources*, 2002 <http://epc.buffalo.edu/authors/bergvall/Perloff-Bergvall-Interview-2000.pdf> (last accessed 7 December 2017).
Perloff, Marjorie, *Unoriginal Genius: Poetry by Other Means in the New Century* (Chicago: University of Chicago Press, 2000).
Portela, Manuel, *Scripting Reading Motions: The Codex and the Computer as Self-Reflexive Machines* (Cambridge, MA: MIT Press, 2013).
Prince, Gerald, 'Recipes', *Studies in Twentieth-Century Literature* vol. 9, issue 2 (1985), pp. 207–12.
Progler, Yusef, 'Ben Ali and His Arabic Diary: Encountering an African Muslim in Antebellum America', *Muslim and Arab Perspectives* no. 5–11 (2004).

Rabaté, Jean Michel, *James Joyce and the Politics of Egoism* (Cambridge: Cambridge University Press, 2001).
Reed, Anthony, *Freedom Time: The Poetics and Politics of Black Experimental Writing* (Baltimore: Johns Hopkins University Press, 2014).
Retallack, Joan, 'Alterity, Misogyny & the Agonistic Feminine', *Jacket2* (February 2018) <https://jacket2.org/article/alterity-misogyny-and-agonistic-feminine> (last accessed 23 June 2019).
Retallack, Joan, *Memnoir* (Sausalito, CA: Post-Apollo, 2004).
Retallack, Joan, 'Poethics of a Complex Realism', in Marjorie Perloff and Charles Junkerman (eds), *John Cage: Composed in America* (Chicago: The University of Chicago Press, 1994), pp. 242–73.
Retallack, Joan, *The Poethical Wager* (Berkeley: University of California, 2003).
Retallack, Joan, 'What Is Experimental Poetry and Why Do We Need It?', *Jacket* 32 (April 2007) <http://jacketmagazine.com/32/p-retallack.shtml> (last accessed 23 June 2019).
Revill, David, *The Roaring Silence. John Cage: A Life* (London: Bloomsbury, 1992).
Richet, Charles, 'Xenoglossie ou l'écriture automatique en langues étrangères', *Proceedings of the Society for Psychical Research* no. 19 (July 1905): 162–266.
Robertson, Lisa, 'Etel Adnan by Lisa Robertson', *BOMB Magazine* no. 127 (1 April 2014) <https://bombmagazine.org/articles/etel-adnan/> (last accessed 23 June 2019).
Robinson, Sophie, 'Caroline Bergvall in conversation with Sophie Robinson', in *Strictly Speaking on Caroline Bergvall*, *How2* 3.3 (2009) <https://www.asu.edu/piper/how2journal/vol_3_no_3/bergvall/bergvall-robinson-interview.html> (last accessed 7 December 2017).
Robinson, Sophie, '"Now that's what I'd call morphing": Building a Queer Architecture in Caroline Bergvall's *Éclat*', in *Strictly Speaking on Caroline Bergvall*, *How2* 3.3 (2009) <http://www.asu.edu/pipercwcenter/how2journal/vol_3_no_3/bergvall/robinson-bergvall.html (last accessed 7 December 2017).
Robinson, Sophie, *Queer Time and Space in Contemporary Experimental Writing*, PhD (Royal Holloway, University of London, 2012).
Ruddick, Lisa, 'When Nothing is Cool', in Angelika Bammer and Ruth-Ellen Beortcher Joeres (eds), *The Future of Scholarly Writing: Critical Interventions* (New York: Palgrave MacMillan, 2015).
Rudy, Susan, unpublished transcript of interview with Caroline Bergvall in which we talk about *Ragadawn*, Islington, London, 2016.
Rudy, Susan, unpublished interview with Caroline Bergvall in which we talk about queer poetics and *OH MY OH MY*, Islington, London, 2017.
Rudy, Susan, '"& how else can I be here?": Reading Cross-Wise through Some Poetries of Canada', in Romana Huk (ed.), *Assembling Alternatives: Reading Postmodern Poetries Transnationally* (Middletown, CT: Wesleyan University Press, 2003), pp. 284–98.

Rudy, Susan, 'A Conversation with Caroline Bergvall', *Jacket2* (2011) <jacket2.org/interviews/conversation-caroline-bergvall> (last accessed 22 November 2017).

Rudy, Susan, 'Reading for Queer Openings: Moving. Archives of the Self. Fred Wah', in Linda M. Morra (ed.), *Moving Archives* (Waterloo, ON: Wilfrid Laurier University Press, forthcoming), 33 ts. pp.

Rudy, Susan, '"Say language keels over": Caroline Bergvall's Queer Writing Practice', unpublished public lecture, Gender Institute, London School of Economics, 15 February 2012.

Rudy, Susan, 'Women who invite collaboration: Caroline Bergvall, Erín Mouré et al', in Marie Carrière and Pat Demers (eds), *Generations: Canadian Women's Writing/Générations: écritures des femmes du Canada* (Edmonton: University of Alberta, 2014), pp. 21–38.

Rudy Dorscht, Susan, 'poems dressed in a(d)dress and naked: sweet lines from Phyllis', *West Coast Line* 25.3 (1992): 54–63.

Ryan, William, 'The New Genteel Racism', *The Crisis* no. 72 (1965).

Said, Edward W., *Culture and Imperialism*, 1st edn (New York: Knopf, 1993).

Saunders, George R., '"Critical Ethnocentrism" and the Ethnology of Ernesto De Martino', *American Anthropologist* 95, no. 4 (1993): 875–93.

Scappettone, Jennifer, 'Phrasebook Pentecosts and Daggering Lingua Francas in the Poetry of LaTasha N. Nevada-Diggs', in Charles Altieri and Nicholas Nace, *The Fate of Difficulty in the Poetry of Our Time* (Evanston, IL: Northwestern University Press, 2017).

Scappettone, Jennifer, '"Più mOndo i:/tUtti!": Traffics of Historicism in Jackson Mac Low's Contemporary Lyricism', *Modern Philology* 105, no. 1 (2007) <https://doi.org/10.1086/587207> (last accessed 23 June 2019).

Schnapp, Jeffrey T., 'Propeller Talk', *Modernism/Modernity* 1, no. 3 (September 1994).

Schreber, Daniel Paul, *Memoirs of My Nervous Illness* [1903], trans. Ida Macalpine and Richard A. Hunter (Cambridge, MA: Harvard University Press, 1988).

Sedgwick, Eve, *Tendencies* (London: Routledge, [1993] 1994).

Sedgwick, Eve Kosofsky, 'Paranoid Reading and Reparative Reading, or, You're so Paranoid, You Probably Think This Essay Is About You', in *Touching Feeling: Affect, Pedagogy, Performativity* (Durham, NC: Duke University Press, 2005).

Segi, Shinichi, *Yoshitoshi: The Splendid Decadent* (New York: Kondansha USA, 1985). Kathy Acker Reading Room, University of Cologne.

Seita, Sophie, and Uljana Wolf, 'How to Subsister: An Afterword', *Subsisters: Selected Poems* (Brooklyn: Belladonna*, 2017).

Sensei, Duncan, 'The Japanese Writing System', *DuncanSensei*, 19 February 2015 <http://duncansensei.com/2015/02/japanese-writing-system/>.

Seymour-Jorn, Caroline, '*The Arab Apocalypse* as a Critique of Colonialism and Imperialism', in Lisa Suhair Majaj and Amal Amireh (eds), *Etel*

Adnan: Critical Essays on the Arab-American Writer and Artist (Jefferson, NC: McFarland & Co., 2002).

Shockley, Evie, *Renegade Poetics: Black Aesthetics and Formal Innovation in African-American Poetry* (Iowa City: University of Iowa Press, 2011).

Silliman, R., 'Benjamin Obscura', in *L=A=N=G=U=A=G=E* 6 (1978).

Simanowski, Roberto, 'Death of the Author? Death of the Reader!', *dichtung-digital* (2001).

Simanowski, Roberto, 'Digital Anthropophagy: Refashioning Words as Image, Sound and Action', *Leonardo* 43, no. 2 (2010).

Smyth, Cherry, 'Queer Poetry by Definition', *Poetry Review* 102:4 (2012) <http://poetrysociety.org.uk/wp-content/uploads/2014/12/1024SmythQueerPoetry.pdf> (last accessed 22 November 2017).

Sollers, Philippe, *Writing and the Experience of Limits*, trans. Philip Barnard (New York: Columbia University Press, 1983).

Spahr, Juliana, and Jena Osman, 'Editors' Notes', *Chain* 10 (Summer 2003).

Spahr, Juliana, Jena Osman and Kerry Sherin (eds), *Chain 7: memoir/anti-memoir* (Summer 2000).

Spicer, Jack, *The House That Jack Built: The Collected Lectures of Jack Spicer*, ed. Peter Gizzi (Middletown, CT: Wesleyan University Press, 2010).

Spivak, Gayatri Chakravorty, *A Critique of Postcolonial Reason: Toward a History of the Vanishing Present* (Cambridge, MA: Harvard University Press, 1999).

Spivak, Gayatri Chakravorty, *Can the Subaltern Speak?: Reflections on the History of an Idea*, ed. Rosalind C. Morris (New York: Columbia University Press, 2010).

Spivak, Gayatri Chakravorty, *Outside in the Teaching Machine* (London and New York: Routledge, 1993).

Stein, Gertrude, *Gertrude Stein: Selections*, ed. Joan Retallack (Berkeley: University of California Press, 2008).

Stein, Gertrude, *Tender Buttons. Objects. Food. Rooms* [1914] (New York: Haskell House Publishers, 1970).

Stiegler, Bernard, *States of Shock: Stupidity and Knowledge in the Twenty-First Century [États de choc: Betise et savoir au XXIè siecle]*, trans. Daniel Ross (Cambridge: Polity, 2015).

Stiegler, Bernard, *What Makes Life Worth Living: On Pharmacology [Ce qui fait que la vie vaut la peine d'être vécu]*, trans. Daniel Ross (Cambridge: Polity, 2013).

Suhair Majaj, Lisa, and Amal Amireh (eds), *Etel Adnan: Critical Essays on the Arab-American Writer and Artist* (Jefferson, NC: McFarland & Co., 2002).

Tillman, Lynne, and Etel Adnan, 'Etel Adnan: Children of the Sun', *Bidoun* no. 18: Interviews (Summer 2009).

Tomasula, Steve, et al., *TOC, FC2* (Tuscaloosa: University of Alabama Press, 2009), DVD.

Toufic, Jalal, foreword to *The Withdrawal of Tradition Past a Surpassing Disaster* (Forthcoming Books, 2009) <http://www.jalaltoufic.com/

downloads/Jalal_Toufic,_The_Withdrawal_of_Tradition_Past_a_Surpassing_Disaster.pdf> (last accessed 23 June 2019).

Treichl, Christiane, *Art and Language: Explorations in (Post) Modern Thought and Visual Culture* (Kassel: Kassel University Press, 2017).

Tremblay-McGaw, Robin, 'Questions, Read-Thrus & Alterity in the Work of Joan Retallack: An Interview with Robin Tremblay-McGaw & Auto Fairy', *Aufgabe* 12 (2015): 309–23.

Trithemius, Johannes, *In Praise of Scribes: De Laude Scriptorum* (Lawrence, KS: Coronado Press, 1974).

Tronti, Mario, 'La Fabbrica e La Società', *Quaderni Rossi* no. 2 (1962).

Ulmer, Gregory L., *Applied Grammatology: Post(e)-Pedagogy from Jacques Derrida to Joseph Beuys* (Baltimore: Johns Hopkins University Press, 1985).

Veenhoven, Ruut (director), *World Database of Happiness* <https://www.worlddatabaseofhappiness.eur.nl/index.html> (last accessed 23 February 2017).

Venuti, Lawrence, *The Translator's Invisibility: A History of Translation*, 2nd edn (London and New York: Routledge, 2008).

Villa, Emilio, 'Cy Twombly: Talento bianco', *Appia Antica* 1 (July 1959).

Villa-Ignacio, Teresa, 'Apocalypse and Poethical Daring in Etel Adnan's There: In the Light and the Darkness of the Self and of the Other', *Contemporary Literature* 55, no. 2 (2014).

Virno, Paolo, *Multitude: Between Innovation and Negation*, trans. Isabella Bertoletti, James Cascaito and Andrea Casson (Los Angeles: Semiotext(e), 2008).

Waldrop, Rosmarie, 'Between Tongues: An Interview', by Matthew Cooperman, *Conjunctions*, 17 December 2005 <http://www.conjunctions.com/online/article/matthew-cooperman-12-17-2005> (last accessed 30 April 2018).

Waldrop, Rosmarie, *Lavish Absence: Recalling and Rereading Edmond Jabès* (Middletown, CT: Wesleyan University Press, 2002).

Waldrop, Rosmarie, 'Mallarmé as Philologist, Dying', in *Blindsight* (New York: New Directions, 2003).

Waldrop, Rosmarie, 'The Joy of the Demiurge', *OmniVerse*, 2017 <http://omniverse.us/rosmarie-waldrop-on-translation-joy-of-the-demiurge/> (last accessed 27 February 2018).

Walkowitz, Rebecca, *Born Translated: The Contemporary Novel in an Age of World Literature* (New York: Columbia University Press, 2015).

Watten, Barrett, 'Poetics in the Expanded Field: Textual, Visual, Digital . . .', in Adalaide Morris and Thomas Swiss (eds), *New Media Poetics: contexts, technotexts, and theories* (Cambridge, MA: MIT Press, 2006), pp. 335–70.

Weeks, Jeffrey, *Coming Out: Homosexual Politics in Britain, from the Nineteenth Century to the Present* (London: Quartet Books, 1977).

Wilson-Goldie, Kaelen, *Etel Adnan*, Contemporary Painters Series (London: Lund Humphries, 2018).

Wittgenstein, Ludwig, *Philosophical Investigations*, 3rd edn, trans. G. E. M. Anscombe (London: Macmillan, 1968).
Wittig, Monique, 'The Straight Mind', *Feminist Issues* 1.1 (1980).
Wolf, Christa, *Medea: A Modern Retelling* (London: Virago, 1998).
Wolf, Uljana, 'dancing double speech', in *Subsisters: Selected Poems*, trans. Sophie Seita (Brooklyn: Belladonna*, 2017).
Wolf, Uljana, 'Messages from a Beehive: On Translating from Belarusian', in *Subsisters: Selected Poems*, trans. Sophie Seita (Brooklyn: Belladonna*, 2017), pp. 164–7.
Wolf, Uljana, 'Schreiben und Übersetzen heißt, sich Meta-artiges Desaster einzuladen', interview with Anna Burck, *Daktylos Media* (April 2014), online.
Wolf, Uljana. *Wandernde Errands: Theresa Hak Kyung Chas translinguale Sendungen* (Heidelberg: Wunderhorn, 2016).
Wolf, Uljana, and M. NourbeSe Philip, 'Poesiegespräch: M. NourbeSe Philip "exaqua"', *Haus für Poesie*, 4 September 2017 <https://www.haus-fuer-poesie.org/de/literaturwerkstatt-berlin/gespraech-des-monats/2017> (last accessed 1 February 2018).
Yildiz, Yasemin, *Beyond the Mother Tongue: The Postmonolingual Condition* (New York: Fordham University Press, 2012).
Young, Iris Marion, 'Beyond the Unhappy Marriage: A Critique of the Dual Systems Theory', in Lydia Sargent (ed.), *Women and Revolution: A Discussion of the Unhappy Marriage of Marxism and Feminism* (Boston: South End Press, 1981), pp. 43–70.

Index

Abdel-Amir, Chawqi, 36
abstraction, 2, 33, 34, 35, 77, 89, 90, 92, 186, 198, 200, 204n33
  abstract art, 19, 23, 27, 29, 79
  economic, 101, 103, 106, 107, 108, 109, 110, 117
Acker, Kathy
  Acker, *Don Quixote*, 76
  'Against Ordinary Language: The Language of the Body', 76
  Blood and Guts in High School original proofs, 74–98
  'Critical Languages', 83
  Empire of the Senseless, 85
  Eurydice in the Underworld (notebooks, 77), 76
  Kathy Acker Papers, 82
  original artwork for *Blood and Guts in High School*, 86–95
  original notebooks for *Pussy, King of the Pirates*, 82, 83
  'Seeing Gender', 80
Adnan, Etel, 9–10, 15–42
  Al-Sayyab, Mother and Lost Daughter, 27–34
  L'apocalypse arabe, 6, 20, 34–42

Le Livre de la mer, 23
Rihla ila Jabal Tamalpais, 16–18
Sea and Fog (2012), 42
Ahmed, Sara, 10, 51, 52, 53, 55, 56, 68, 70
Aichinger, Ilse, 135, 140
Ajens, Andrés, 131
al-Khal, Yusuf , 25
al-Sayyab, Badr Shakir, 27, 28, 34, 46n45
al Saïd, Shaker Hassan, 27
Alcalay, Ammiel, 45n17, 49n49
Algerian War of Independence, 6, 9, 15, 21, 26
Ali, Wijdan, 27
Altieri, Charles, 2, 4, 5
Amireh, Amal, 25, 42n1
Anderson, Benedict, 11, 43n7, 105
Anna O., 140
Antena, 124, 142n3
antimemoir, 147
Apter, Emily, 125
archives, 10, 42n2, 74–95, 190, 197; *see also* avant-texte
Aristotle, 52, 79
Artaud, Antonin, 36
Artificial Intelligence (AI), 199–200
Ashbery, John, 141n2

attention, 12, 82, 153, 160, 173, 192, 193, 195, 196, 199
authorship, 2, 3, 32, 78, 82, 125
  and mastery, 2, 3, 146
avant-texte, 10, 77, 78, 80, 81, 80–2, 84, 87, 89, 95; *see also* archives

Bachelard, Gaston, 21
Baldwin, Kate, 111
Balla, Giacomo, 79
Barthes, Roland, 190
Bartleby, 31
Barton, Rick, 26
Bataille, George, 75
Baudelaire, Charles, 21, 39, 83
Baxter, Charles, 147, 148, 149
Beale, 122n60
Beasley, Rebecca, 169
Beckett, Samuel, 137
Bellamin-Noël, Jean, 78, 81
Bellamy, Dodie, 7
Benjamin, Jessica, 12, 163, 166
Benjamin, Walter, 13, 39, 135
  The Arcades Project, 205–24
Bergvall, Caroline, 6, 8, 12, 32, 95, 131, 163–81
  'Croup', 171
  Drift, 163–81
  Éclat, 167
  Flèsh Acoeur, 170
  hyphenated practice, 163–81
  Oh My, Oh My, 173, *175*
  Ragadawn, 164–6, 169, 176–8
  'Say Parsley', 178–81
  'Via', 169
Berlant, Lauren, 178

Bernstein, Charles, 1, 80, 205–24
  'Forefright' (1983), 213
  Shadowtime, 220
  'The Klupzy Girl' (1983), 214, 215
  'The Lives of the Toll Takes', 218
  Veil (1987), 217
Berry, Ellen E., 14n1
Bervin, Jen, 173
Bialosky, Jill, 145, 146
bibliography, 77, 84
Black Mountain College, 58
Black Women for Wages for Housework, 118–19
book art, 75, 185, 186, 193, 200
Boone, Bruce, 7
border politics, 6, 8–9, 12, 126, 171, 180
  critique of in poetry, 6, 126, 131, 165, 179
  linguistic borders, 123, 142n13, 174
  and linguistic porosity, 9, 136
Boulus, Sargon, 25
Bounoure, Gabriel, 21, 25
Braidotti, Rosi, 43n7
Brancusi, Constantin, 79
Brathwaite, Kamau, 95
Bray, Joe, 14n1
Brecht, Bertolt, 137
Briggs, Kate, 125, 137, 139
Brossard, Nicole, 168, 170
Brown, Wilmette, 118
Burroughs, William, 64, 87, 89
Butler, Judith, 178

Cage, John, 5, 10, 84, 152
  A Year From Monday (1968), 61
  Anarchy, 63

'chance determinations', 57–9
Diary: How to Improve the World (You Will Only Make Matters Worse (1965–1982), 61
'Indeterminacy', 60, 62
'Juilliard Lecture' (1952), 59
mesostics, 64–9
'Themes and Variations' (1982), 65
'Writing for the Fourth Time Through *Finnegans Wake*' (1983), 64
calligraphy, 26, 27, 28, 33, 37
 calligraphic modernism, 34
 calligraphic writing, 27
Cameron, David, 51
Cameron, James, 52
Canetti, Elias, 85
Cannizzaro, Danny, 13
 Pry, 195
canonisation, xii, 7, 25, 34, 42, 124, 194
capitalism, 4, 5, 11, 19, 89, 100–19, 121n39
care work, 122n67
Carson, Anne, 9, 137, 138
Cassar, Anja, 74
Catullus, 92, 98n55
Cavell, Stanley, 21
Cha, Theresa Hak Kyung, *Dictee*, 27, 123, 131, 139, 140
Chakrabarty, Dipesh, 34
Chen, Peyee, 177
Choi, Don Mee, 137
Chomsky, Noam, 197, 204n33
Cicero, Marcus Tullius, 154
citizenship, 9, 10, 15–42, 103, 104, 105, 106, 110, 111, 180
 queer citizenship, 167
Cixous, Hélène, 81, 140

climate change, 4, 47n56, 52, 61–3, 66, 149
Cohen, Lizabeth, 116, 117
Cold War
 imaginary, 101
 kitchen, 110–19
Colebrook, Claire, 10, 52, 56, 62
collage, 59, 83, 85, 92, 95, 214, 215
Collins, Sophie, 9, 124, 125
colonialism, 24, 48n77, 137
 neo-colonialism, 119
commodity fetishism, 102, 106–19, 120n31
Conard, Mark T., 156
Concrete poetry, 75, 195
Cramer, Florian, 203n29
cut-ups, 89–91, 95

Dadi, Iftikhar, 33, 34
Dalla Costa, Mariarosa, 114, 115
Dante, 32, 43n7, 170, 175, 176
Davis, Angela, 114, 122n60
de Andrade, Oswald, 191
de Biasi, Pierre-Marc, 81
de Brosses, Charles, 108
de Lauretis, Teresa, 76
decolonisation, 19, 20, 25, 33, 34, 40, 137, 139
 decolonising languages, 22
 decolonising writing, 33
 and habits of reading, 124
DeKoven, Marianne, 3
Delabastita, Dirk, 135
Deleuze, Gilles, 44n13, 139
Deppman, Jed, 78, 84
Derrida, Jacques, 124, 140, 141n1, 187, 188, 197, 201n3, 202n5
 archi-writing, 187

Dewey, John, 12, 150
diagrammatic writing 10, 11,
    75, 78, 79, 80, 81, 92, 95
  and modernism, 79
diaspora, 8, 20, 33, 43n9
Dickinson, Emily, 74, 173
difficulty, 1, 2, 3, 4, 11, 78,
    123, 125, 158, 167
digital cultures, 6, 7
digital language art, 13,
    185–201, 203n29
Documenta, 13, 27
Drucker, Johanna, 10, 13, 75,
    78, 79, 80, 81, 87, 92, 95
  *General Theory of Social
    Relativity* (2018), 13,
    185–201
Duchamp, Marcel, 61, 65

Edelman, Lee, 178
El Amrani, Issandr, 46n39
Eliot, T. S., 46n45
Enikö Bollobás, 219
Eurydice, 76, 77, 151, 155,
    156, 158
Evens, Aden, 203n29
experience, 2, 4, 8, 9, 12, 29,
    33, 34, 36, 38, 41, 42,
    49n94, 54, 56, 67, 68, 71,
    87, 102, 105, 110, 132, 135,
    148–60, 163, 164, 165, 166,
    167, 168, 173, 174, 176,
    178, 179, 183n68, 186, 187,
    189, 190, 195, 196, 206,
    207, 210, 216, 222
experimental writing, 1–13,
    14n1, 53, 57, 78, 95, 99,
    119n3, 183n77, 185, 186,
    188, 189, 190, 191, 192,
    193, 196, 198

Fanon, Frantz, 22, 43n3, 45n25
Fattal, Simone, 26, 35, 42n1

Federici, Silvia, 114, 115
feminism
  and the archive, 78
  colonisation of the household,
    117
  International Wages for
    Housework Campaign,
    114, 119
  and kitchen debate, July
    1959, 111
  and labour, 114–19
  Marxist-Socialist feminist
    debates, 122n60
  and materiality, 85
  and *Memnoir*, 158
Ferneyhough, Brian, 220
Ferrer, Daniel, 78
Feuerbach, Ludwig, 120n31
film noir, 147–56, 158
Fink, Thomas, 1, 2
Fitterman, Rob, 215
forced migration, 8, 9, 15,
    19, 20, 22, 34, 40, 41,
    43n8, 104, 126, 140, 165,
    167, 168
Fraser, Kathleen, 183n59
Freidan, Betty, 116
Freud, Sigmund, 139, 140
Fuller, Buckminster, 10, 61,
    62, 65
Futurist Manifesto, 18, 38, 39

Galistell, Charles R., 204n33
Gardiner, Allan H., 87
Genet, Jean, 75
genetic criticism, 10, 78, 81,
    82, 83
Gibbons, Alison, 14n1
Gimenez, Martha, 114
Ginsberg, Allen, 64
Glissant, Édouard, 21, 41,
    137, 139
glossolalia, 20, 40

Glück, Robert, 7
Golding, John, 79
Goldsmith, Kenneth, 32, 48n64, 215
Gorman, Samantha, 5, 13, 195
Goyal, Yogita, 43n9
grammalepsy, 13, 187–201
Greenaway, Peter, 82
Groden, Michael, 78
Guattari, Felix, 44n13, 139
Gysin, Brion, 87

Halden-Sullivan, Judith, 1
handwriting, 26, 27, 81–2, 85, 87, 180
happiness, 10, 38, 51, 52, 53, 54, 55, 56, 58, 62, 68, 69, 70, 71, 150
Hawkey, Christian, 137, 141
Hay, Louis, 78
Hayles, N. Katherine, 75, 193
H.D., 180
Heisler, Eva, 173
Hejinian, Lyn, 4, 65, 68, 70
  Happily (2000), 10, 53–4, 57
  My Life (1980, 1987), 54–5
  'The Person and The Description', 55
Herd, David, 8, 9
Hickman, Ben, 5
hieroglyphs, 35, 83, 87, 88, 89
Hofer, Jen, 124
HoSang, Daniel Martinez, 121n50
Houen, Alex, 14n1
Howe, Susan, 74
Hunt, Erica, *Piece Logic*, 5, 11, 99–119
Hurufiyya movement, 27, 33

illegibility, 158, 164, 167, 180, 199; *see also* indecipherability

immigration policy
  UK, 9
  US, 103
improvisation, bop, 99
indecipherability, 87, 165, 211; *see also* opacity
indeterminacy, 2, 3, 60, 61, 62, 80, 82, 84, 85
Intégral (journal), 19, 38
Irvine, Martin, 5

Jackson, Shelley, 203n29
Jakobson, Roman, 125, 140
James, Selma, 114, 115
James, William, 161n36
Jameson, Frederic, 57
Jandl, Ernst, 222, 223
Jenkins, Grant Matthew, 152
Jhave Johnston, David, *ReRites*, 200–1, 204n34
Jones, Jacqueline, 116, 122n61
Joyce, James
  Finnegans Wake (1939), 64
  Tales Told of Shem and Shaum, 79

Kant, Immanuel, 60
Kaplan, Genevieve, 176
Kaufmann, David, 171, 172, 180
Keene, John, 124
Khatibi, Abdelkebir, 27
Killian, Kevin, 7
King, Deborah K., 122n60
Kinnahan, Linda, 95
Kosofsky Sedgwick, Eve, 10, 56, 57, 61, 70
Kunin, Aaron 32

$L=A=N=G=U=A=G=E$ (magazine), 210–11
Laâbi, Abdellatif, 25
Lacan, 43n7, 179

Index

Language Poets, 5, 185
Leahsdottir, Alain, 151
Lebanese Civil War, 15, 26, 34
Lee, Mike, 53
leporello, 23, 26, 27, 29, 31, 33, 34, 39, 47n56
Lewis, Oscar, 113
listening, 8, 67, 84, 139, 168, 170, 175, 179, 187, 190, 199, 202n12, 219, 220; *see also* sonic art
Lowndes, Joseph E., 121n50

M*A*S*H, 201–11, 212
Machado, Aditi, 36
Majaj, Lisa Suhair, 25, 42n1
Mallarmé, Stéphane, 78, 79, 80, 83, 84, 89, 133
manuscript practice, 6, 40, 49n94, 74–98, 106, 173, 205, 206, 208; *see also* archives
Marchand, Heinrik, 145
Marinetti, Filippo Tommaso, 38, 39
Marx, Groucho, 221
Marx, Karl, 100, 102, 107, 108, 109, 115, 120n31, 221
materiality, 10, 18, 22, 75, 78, 80, 83, 84, 85, 175, 198
  atomic, 107
  performative, 10, 80, 95
  of voice, 187
May, Theresa, 9
McCormick, Kathleen, 166
McGovern, Charles, 101
McKenzie, D. F., 77–8, 84
McLuhan, Marshall, 61, 65
Mejcher-Atassi, Sonja, 35
Melehi, Mohammed, 19, 29, 30, 44n16
memoir, 12
  non-linear memoir, 146–60

memory, 12, 133, 145–60, 195, 205
  collective, 168
  historical, 117
  hypostatic, 190
  involuntary, 220
Mignolo, Walter, 44n13
migration, 6, 8, 30, 103, 104, 142n13, 167, 168, 173
Miller, Nancy, 174
Milne, Drew, 14n15
Mitropoulos, 121n39
monolingualism, 12, 20, 45n19, 105, 124, 131, 140, 141
Montfort, Nick, 199, 200, 203n31
Moretti, Franco, 193
Moten, Fred, 49n94, 137
Mouré, Erín, 9, 125, 136, 142n2, 174
Moynihan, Daniel Patrick, 100, 112, 113, 119
Moynihan Report, 100, 101, 112, 113, 119
multilingual writing, 6, 11, 47n50, 95, 123–41, 163–81
multilingualism, 8, 9, 12, 13, 15, 16, 17, 19, 22, 29, 40, 45n19
multimedia writing, 8, 32, 163–81, 191, 195, 196, 198
Murray, Charles, 121n50

Nace, Nicholas D., 2, 4, 5
Nakayasu, Sawako, 124
Naples, Nancy A., 119
nationalism, 18, 20, 25
  material, 101
  national belonging, 103
  neonationalism, 37
Nealon, Christopher, 4, 5
New Narrative, 7
Nielsen, Aldon Lynn, 99, 119n3

Nietzsche, Friedrich, 21, 36
Nussbaum, Martha, 52

Obrist, Hans Ulrich, 26, 46n42
O'Hanlon, Ann, 23
Olsen, Redell, 150–1, 153, 154
Olson, Charles, 5, 58
Ong, Walter, 203n28
Ono, Yoko, 141n2
opacity, 2, 21, 27, 34, 41, 42, 83, 137, 165
oppositional poetics, 11, 24, 99
Orgera, Alexis, 151
Osman, Jena, 131
O'Sullivan, Maggie, 173, 183n77
Oulipo, 99
Ovid, 156, 159

painting, 10, 19, 20, 21, 22, 23, 25, 26, 29, 31, 32, 35, 38, 42
Pedwell, Carolyn, 138
perception, 3, 8, 77, 89, 222
performativity, 10, 26, 31, 37, 40, 41, 69, 78, 80, 83, 95, 178
Perloff, Marjorie, 164
Philip, M. NourbeSe, *Zong!*, 12, 123, 126, 138, 140
Plath, Sylvia, 12, 146
Plato, 18, 186
Pleuker, John, 124
porosity, 9, 136
possibility, 10, 40, 51, 52, 53, 55, 56, 57, 63, 65, 67, 70, 84, 118, 137, 150, 189, 191, 207
potentiality, 10, 52–6, 67
of language, 149
Prescod, Margaret, 118
Prince, Gerald, 4
procedural writing, 32, 103, 106
Oulipian, 99

process, 82, 148, 187
and translation, 168
Proust, Marcel, 219

Quant, S. M., 158
queer writing, 163–81

Rabaté, Jean-Michel, 78
race, 11, 16, 37, 99–119
and commodity fetishism, 100
Ramey, Laura, 99
reading practices
'ardent reading', 166, 176
and decolonisation, 124
experimental, 1, 3, 4, 5, 9, 10, 13, 17, 27, 28, 59, 63, 67, 71, 80, 105
hermeneutic reading, 192
'interdependent reading', 168
prejudicial reading, 191
problems of reading, 196
'reading formations', 166
relation between reader and writer, 163
'reparative reading', 57, 61, 70, 139
and translation, 124, 125
and voice, 187
Reed, Anthony, 7, 14n1, 99
Renan, Ernest, 105, 120n18
resistance
aesthetic, 3, 5, 11, 12, 18, 20, 34
to meaning, 85, 95
political, 99, 101
Retallack, Joan
Memnoir, 4, 6, 12, 70, 145–60
'process note', 148
'The Difficulties of Gertrude Stein I & II', 158
'What is Experimental Poetry and Why Do We Need It?', 14n15, 149

revolution, 18, 20, 27, 29, 33, 61, 63, 69, 70, 80
rewriting, 65, 79, 83, 89, 169, 176
Rimbaud, Arthur, 21, 83
Robertson, Lisa, 34
Robinson, Elizabeth, 3
Robinson, Sophie, 167
Ruddick, Lisa, 13, 166
Ryan, William, 113

Sachs, Nelly, 140
Said, Edward, 44n13
Salih, al-Tayyeb, 30, 31, 36
Sang, Yi, 137
Sedgwick, Eve Kosofsky, 56, 139, 166, 170
Segi, Sinichi, 75
Sexton, Anne, 12, 146
Seymour-Jorn, Caroline, 35
Sherrin, Kerry, 145
Shi'r (magazine), 25
Shockley, Evie, 99
silence, 59, 60, 64, 67, 87, 126, 139, 189, 190; *see also* listening
Silliman, Ron, 99, 209
Skoulding, Zoë, 125
Smyth, Cherry, 171
social reproduction, 102, 111, 112, 114, 116
Social Security Act, 1935, 118
Socratic dialogue, 147
solidarity, 21, 24, 26, 42
Sollers, Phillippe, 76
sonic art, 176–8
Sontag, Susan, 140
Souriau, Étienne, 21
Spahr, Juliana, 131
Spicer, Jack, 4, 39
Spivak, Gayatri Chakravorty, 44n13, 139

Stefans, Brian Kim, 203n29
Stein, Gertrude, 31, 40, 180
  Blood on the Dining Room Floor, 158
  and composition, 153
  'continuous present', 15
  Everybody's Autobiography, 75
  Sentences, 81
  Tender Buttons, 171
Stein, Kurt, 126
Stiegler, Bernard, 192, 202n8
Suzuki, Daisertz, 61, 65
Swensen, Cole, 45n17
Syrian civil war, 40

Tel Quel, 76
textuality, 5, 8, 10, 18, 22, 34, 41, 55, 56, 60, 62, 67, 74, 78, 81, 82, 84, 110, 119n3, 127, 170, 186, 195, 197, 215; *see also* materiality
Tillman, Lynne, 22, 42n1
Tomasula, Steve, 195, 203n29
Toufic, Jalal, 36, 37, 38, 48n79
transcription, 10, 18, 20, 21, 22, 27, 29, 31, 32, 38
translation, 25, 27, 28, 32, 33, 34, 36, 38, 92, 123–41, 175, 176, 194, 200, 222
  experimental translation, 6, 9, 11, 12
  as a reading practice, 124
  see also translingual writing
translingual writing, 11, 123–41, 142n2, 203n28
transnational turn, 6, 126, 142n13; *see also* transnationalism
transnationalism, 19, 25, 36, 38, 40, 124, 139, 167
Treichl, Christopher, 33

Trithemius, Johannes, 31
Tronti, Mario, 115
Twombly, Cy, 19
typography, 79, 83, 84, 85, 186, 190, 194, 197

Valéry, Paul, 84
Vallejo, César, 83
Vicuña, Cecilia, 131
Viegener, Matias, 74, 96
Villa, Emilio, 19
Villa-Ignacio, Teresa, 47n56, 49n96
visual epistemology, 84–95
voice, 8, 21, 32, 44, 75, 89, 125, 139, 140, 141, 147, 151, 157, 158, 168, 171, 172, 174, 176, 177, 178, 181n12, 186–201, 202n5

Waidner, Isabel, 7
Waldrop, Rosemarie, 123, 131, 133
Walkowitz, Rebecca, 42n1, 135
Waller, Gary F., 166

welfare state, US, 122n79
Wilson-Goldie , 25, 42n1
Wittgenstein, Ludwig, 76, 85, 158
Wittig, Monique, 169
Wolf, Christa, 172
Wolf, Uljana, 5, 6, 11, 12, 123, 124, 125, 126
   'Babeltrack', 127
   meine schönste lengevitch, 126
   Subsisters: Selected Poems, 128–38
   Wandering Errands, 139–41
Women's March, 2017 (London), 173
Woolf, Virginia, 180
writing systems, non-Latin, 17, 87

xenoglossia, 6, 10, 18, 20, 44n11, 49n93
xenophobia, 6, 104

Yildiz, Yasemin, 43n7, 45n19
Younge, C. D., 154

EU representative:
Easy Access System Europe
Mustamäe tee 50, 10621 Tallinn, Estonia
Gpsr.requests@easproject.com

www.ingramcontent.com/pod-product-compliance
Lightning Source LLC
Chambersburg PA
CBHW071830230426
43672CB00013B/2806